JERSEY JUSTICE

JERSEY JUSTICE

The Story of the Trenton Six

Cathy D. Knepper

RIVERGATE BOOKS

AN IMPRINT OF RUTGERS UNIVERSITY PRESS

NEW BRUNSWICK, NEW JERSEY, AND LONDON

Library of Congress Cataloging-in-Publication Data

Knepper, Cathy D.

Jersey justice : the story of the Trenton Six / Cathy D. Knepper.

p.   cm.

Includes bibliographical references and index.

ISBN 978–0–8135–5127–2 (hardcover : alk. paper)

1. Trenton Six Trial, Trenton, N.J., 1948–1951.   2. Trials (Murder)—New Jersey—Trenton.   I. Title.

KF224.T74K58 2011

345.749′6602523—dc22

2010048427

A British Cataloging-in-Publication record for this book is available from the British Library.

Visit our Web site: http://rutgerspress.rutgers.edu

Manufactured in the United States of America

Typesetting: Jack Donner, BookType

To Mark

CONTENTS

ACKNOWLEDGMENTS

As I was beginning my study of the Trenton Six, Ross Knepper and Jenae Lowe provided a much-needed boost. Ross also gave technical assistance above and beyond the call of duty. The staff of the Law Library of the New Jersey State Library always addressed my requests cheerfully and quickly throughout my six weeks of work there. Julie Herrada, curator of the Labadie Collection of Social Protest Material in the Special Collections Library of the University of Michigan, deserves my thanks. Wendy M. Nardi, curator of the wonderful and amazing Trentoniana Collection at the Trenton Public Library, generously contributed her time and knowledge. William A. Reuben, who died in 2004, began his career as an investigative journalist working for the *National Guardian*, writing a series of articles on the Trenton Six. His interviews and analysis from 1948 to 1951 provided much material that would otherwise have been impossible to recover at this date. Robert Shogan, journalist and author, told me the story of Irving Feiner, which he reported for the Syracuse University student newspaper. The historian Jack Washington furnished helpful pointers, while Rachel Friedman and Willa Speiser assisted with much-needed editing. Special thanks to my literary agent, Ron Goldfarb, who found a home for my book. And my gratitude goes most of all to Marlie Wasserman, who believed strongly that the story of the Trenton Six deserved to be told.

JERSEY JUSTICE

CHAPTER 1

THE CRIME AND
THE TRENTON SIX

On January 27, 1948, the front-page above-the-fold headline in the *Trenton Evening Times* trumpeted "Elderly Couple Beaten in Holdup by 3 Thugs at Second-Hand Store." A sidebar proclaimed "Man and Wife Brutally Attacked by Robbers." Elizabeth Horner told police that two men had asked to see a mattress in the back room of the shop, which Mr. Horner showed them; another man entered asking to see a stove in the front room. While assisting him, she heard a commotion in the rear of the store. A man then hit her over the head, and all three, whom she described as "young, light-skinned Negroes," left the shop.[1]

The closest these events came to having an outside eyewitness was in the form of a Trenton cigar salesman named Frank Eldracher. At about 10:30 that morning he was calling on customers in the 200 block of North Broad Street; he saw two men emerge from the Horner store but gave them no further thought. A short time later, when he was back at his car pulling more cigar boxes from the trunk, the door of the secondhand shop opened and a woman began screaming. Eldracher saw her slumped in the doorway with her face covered in blood. "I dropped bag, boxes, cigars, and everything and I ran to the corner in a hurry to get the officer."[2]

Patrolman Fred Sigafoos hurried down the street and into the store. The woman propped against the front door had two swollen and bruised eyes, a large, heavily bleeding gash on the back of her head, and skinned and bruised legs; she was holding her sides, moaning and complaining of pains in her chest. She mumbled something that sounded like "back room," so Sigafoos continued on to the rear of the store, following the narrow path slicing through the collection of battered furniture, ancient stoves, refrigerators, and assorted bric-a-brac climbing to the ceiling, until he came to a small room.

Here he found a gaunt, elderly man whose matted, scraggly gray hair revealed a lump already grown to the size of a golf ball on the top of his head. Sigafoos hurried to the nearest call box and rang for an ambulance. Two responded, as did a number of patrolmen. Four patrolmen carried Horner to the front of the store, as there was not room for a stretcher; an ambulance raced him to Mercer Hospital, where the seventy-five-year-old died at 4:00 P.M.[3] Another ambulance took Elizabeth Horner to McKinley Hospital, where she received treatment for her injuries, and survived.

By 11:00 A.M. half a dozen detectives and at least twenty patrolmen had swarmed to the scene of the crime, led by Andrew Delate, an acting city police captain. By 11:30 A.M. two hundred curious onlookers were getting in the way of policemen, detectives, and police and newspaper photographers all trying to do their job in the small space. Detective Lieutenant William Stanley and his white-haired, bespectacled partner, Detective Donald Toft, headed the investigation. They took a green soda bottle and a broken brown soda bottle found in the back room of the shop and dropped both items off with the police department's Identification Bureau.[4] Detectives discovered another witness, Mrs. Virginia Barclay, who lived about fifty yards north of the Horner store. She could not actually see the shop from her front window, but she had seen three men, young African Americans, one wearing metal-rim glasses, hurry into a car parked in front of her house. She noticed them because the car screeched off before the backseat passenger had even closed the rear door. Based on Barclay's description, police decided a fourth man had served as driver, and they notified five surrounding states to be on guard for the four in case they fled further afield. At the same time, other detectives searched for the source of the soda bottles. They soon came across the nearby New Life Restaurant, whose owner, Mrs. Argiros Kokenakes, told of selling soda pop, one green and one brown bottle, to two African American men at approximately 10:00 A.M. On January 29, 1948, police picked up Nelson Johnson, age twenty-two, who had been spotted running near the Horner store shortly after the crime. When detectives took him to Elizabeth Horner in her hospital bed she shook her head slowly, stating, "That's not the man." Police Court Judge Albert Cooper held him anyway, with bail of five hundred dollars, for action by the grand jury.[5]

The same day, in response to the Horner murder, the *Trenton Evening Times* published an editorial headlined "The Idle Death Chair," calling for more electrocutions to maintain public law and order.[6] New Jersey had become the fourth state to try the new method of execution in 1906. Electrocution promised to be "clean, progressive, and humane."[7] Thomas

Edison championed the invention of the electric chair, and the first one came from his laboratory in Menlo Park, New Jersey, after the electrocution of numerous dogs, calves, and two horses to determine the voltage and electrical power appropriate for use on a human being.[8] The most famous person electrocuted in New Jersey up to that time was Bruno Richard Hauptmann, the kidnapper and murderer of Charles Lindbergh's baby; Hauptmann was killed on April 3, 1936. The evidence against Hauptmann was largely circumstantial, and he went to his death proclaiming his innocence.[9]

Harry Camisa, a longtime prison guard in the Trenton State Prison, agreed to work executions because he needed the overtime pay. New Jersey killed its prisoners on Tuesdays at 10:00 P.M., and Camisa characterized the process as so "smoothly choreographed, it was over before I had chance to come to grips with the idea that a life was being snuffed out in front of me."[10] He witnessed thirteen executions and described in detail the first one, that of Theodore Walker in 1954, in *Inside Out*, his memoir. The four officers standing near the chair swiftly buckled three-inch-wide leather straps around Walker's arms and legs. One officer then placed a wide strap around the chest area and handed the executioner a leather mask with a hole cut out for the nose. The mask was placed over Walker's face, and a wet sponge and a metal cap were fitted snugly onto his head. "I remember thinking that this guy ought to look terrified, but his expression was more of an interested curiosity than fear. I think that was one of the reasons the process was carried out so fast—to keep the condemned man from thinking about what was happening to him."[11] The executioner, Joseph Francel from Cairo, New York, was a licensed electrician, as required by New Jersey law. Camisa described him as "about five feet-seven inches tall, balding, kind of meek-looking and dressed in a rumpled, dark business suit."[12] By the time Walker was executed, Francel had electrocuted more than 150 people at $150 per head and gained fame by including Julius and Ethel Rosenberg, sentenced to die for passing atom bomb secrets to the Soviets, in that number. When he spun the wheel, two thousand volts entered the condemned man and his chest lunged against the leather strap. Typically, after this process was repeated five times the prisoner was dead. However, Camisa described a unique feature of Walker's execution. Walker, like many in prison, "got religion," and on a hot night was wearing no shirt: "Because of the heavy humidity and the perspiration on Walker's chest, the metal crucifix he wore must have picked up the current and the cross started to glow; it looked like it was burning and embedding itself in Walker's chest—a grisly, but I have to admit, fascinating sight."[13] Walker entered the death chamber at 10:00 P.M. and was certified dead at 10:05 P.M.

At the time of the Horner murder, New Jersey had executed 136 men in the electric chair located inside the Trenton State Prison.[14]

On January 30, 1948, three days after the Horner murder, Trenton's director of public safety, and thus the head of the city's police officers and detectives, Andrew J. Duch, held a press conference. He announced that fifteen police officers would cruise nightly through the city's streets, detaining all blacks who were out after dark without good reason. Since the only thing known about Horner's murderers was their race, the fourteen thousand blacks in Trenton quickly realized they were being placed under curfew. The *Trenton Evening Times* editorial, "The Idle Death Chair," had a day earlier observed, "Trenton has recently been the scene of an increasing number of crimes of violence, including muggings, hold-ups, attacks upon women and finally the murder of William Horner." It concluded, "There are a number of reasons for the increasing boldness and viciousness of the criminal elements of Trenton and of New Jersey. One of them is inadequate punishment, as reflected in the fact that although murders are fairly common occurrences in the State there has been no execution since December 14, 1945."[15]

"Well-meaning people may accuse us of acting like a Gestapo," Duch acknowledged privately as he handed a Thompson submachine gun to each of the fifteen policemen he had just organized into a special Negro-hunting squad, as the defense lawyers would later refer to it. "But if we can bring in the Horner killers, I'm willing to take all their criticism." He ordered the police to shoot to kill.[16] Called the Crime Crushers and the Trenton Gestapo, this group created a reign of terror in the black community. By February 2 it had begun began its work as "mobile personnel covering the entire city in an effort to break up a serious condition which has caused city officials considerable anxiety." Duch urged them to do everything possible to "break up the crime wave."[17] Police with tommy guns rounded up random black men whom they questioned, bludgeoned, and then released without charge.[18] Trenton's police force, since the end of World War II, had shot at least six blacks for "resisting arrest." The National Association for the Advancement of Colored People (NAACP) had documented more than thirty instances of police officers using violence against city blacks since 1945.[19]

This appears, on the surface, to be an excessive reaction to the murder of one elderly junk shop owner. But it revealed the deep unease of city officials, as well as the entire white population, at Trenton's rapidly growing numbers of African Americans. In 1920 Trenton had 5,315 blacks, who made up just 4 percent of the city's population. Small numbers of Southern blacks came north during World War I and continued steadily throughout the Great

Depression. This trickle became a flood after World War II, in spite of the fact that Jim Crow laws, regarded as a southern institution, flourished in Trenton. In the South, blacks had to use "colored" waiting rooms, train cars, and water fountains. To see a movie they had to perch in the balcony. If a white passed on the sidewalk, they had to step into the street. They could not vote without paying a prohibitively high poll tax. These rules were demeaning and meant to be so.

In Trenton, blacks would not receive service in a downtown restaurant or bar, could not sit in the main section of a movie theater, and were hired only for low-paying, menial jobs; they were ineligible for union membership.[20] The men ultimately tried for Horner's murder held jobs typical for blacks as janitors, chicken flickers, potato pickers, and unskilled day laborers.[21]

The new southern immigrants jammed into the neighborhoods of Five Points and Coalport where four Baptist churches and two African Methodist Episcopal churches served as social centers and the ministers acted as leaders in the African American community. In black residential areas there were overcrowded, dilapidated hovels, garbage-strewn streets, endemic health problems, and petty crime, all of which worried white city officials.[22] As the black population increased, it spread from central Trenton into largely Sicilian-populated north Trenton, causing conflict between the two groups. Black women increasingly found work in homes of the white elite, replacing Irish and Polish women, while black men struggled to find jobs as field hands and janitors.

Between 1940 and 1950, Trenton's total population grew only by 2.7 percent, while the black population increased from 7.5 percent to 11.4 percent. Without the nonwhite increase, Trenton would have been one of the few cities in the nation to experience a population decline.[23] At the same time, postwar Trenton's manufacturing plants, which made ceramics, wire and steel cables, steam turbines, and rubber goods, slowly began to lose jobs, creating much tension among blue-collar workers. Trenton's whites blamed their job difficulties, decreasing wages, and increased crime on the blacks moving into their town.[24] New Jersey had been one of the last states of the North to abolish slavery. Nearby Princeton University long attracted white men from the South and provided housing for their slaves. During the first half of the twentieth century the Ku Klux Klan and the American Nazi German American Bund found New Jersey an appealing place for their activities.[25] Racial violence, once mainly a southern phenomenon, followed the blacks as they came north. All of this set the stage for what followed.

On the morning of Saturday, January 31, 1948, the Reverend Clifford G. Pollock officiated at the funeral of William Horner, who was laid to rest in Wall Cemetery in Belmar, New Jersey.[26] A few days after the funeral, on February 4, the *Trenton Evening Times* carried the headline: "Bordentown Woman Claims She Was Wife of Murdered Storeman Here, Seeks Estate." A lawyer for a Mrs. Ellen A. Horner of 415 Oliver Street in Bordentown filed a claim to the estate of William Horner, saying she was his legal widow and mother of his six children.[27] It seemed that Horner left his wife and children, moved to Trenton, and began life with Elizabeth McGuire, who was known as Elizabeth Horner, but he never received a divorce from his wife, Ellen.

By then, police had detained more than twenty suspects for questioning. They released the teletype description of the suspects that had been sent to neighboring states the day of the murder, stating that the men were black. They described the first as twenty years old, 135 pounds, 5 feet 3 inches tall, wearing a tan slouch hat, tan overcoat, and silver-rimmed glasses. The second weighed 165 pounds, was 5 feet 11 inches tall, of light complexion with a pencil mustache, wearing a dark blue double-breasted overcoat. The third was characterized as twenty years of age, 135 pounds, 5 feet 6 inches tall, and wearing a short jacket. The fourth man, who stayed at the wheel of a waiting car, was said to be wearing a light green coat. Bystanders described the car itself as a green Plymouth four-door sedan.[28]

On the morning of Friday, February 6, an irascible Negro in his late fifties was released on bail from the Mercer County Jail. Police had detained George English for criminally assaulting the eleven-year-old daughter of his wife, Rubie. He had previously spent a year in prison for molesting another stepdaughter, Bessie. He arrived home at 12 Behm Street in Trenton, furious with his first wife, Emma, and son, Collis. They had refused to go along with his scheme to raise his bail money, as it would have required putting their own house in jeopardy. Upon arriving home, he learned that Collis had used his car, a two-door black Ford sedan, for his own jaunts, as well as the errands that George had asked him to do. For two hours he stomped about his house, bellowing, throwing things, threatening to teach his son a lesson he would not forget. Finally, George asked the police to arrest his son for using his car for three weeks without his permission and for driving without a license. At 5:30 P.M. two patrolmen arrived at 247 Church Street, Emma and Collis's residence. Collis was not at home. The police explained to Mrs. English that because of George's complaint they would have to take Collis to the station for questioning. They returned several hours later, by which time Collis was there waiting for them. The two patrolmen said they thought he would be held just for an hour or two and waited while he went upstairs to get his galoshes.[29]

The patrolmen took Collis English to the Chancery Lane First Precinct police station at 8:30 on Friday evening. From then until Wednesday morning, he saw no one but members of the Trenton police force. When the officers brought English in, they passed a man being returned to his cell, badly beaten about the face. Lieutenant Nicholas Lichtfuhs placed English in an interrogation room, saying: "You're going in here, and you're going to answer some questions we're going to ask you, or either [sic] you're going to get the same thing he got." English stated at his trial that he clearly understood he would be beaten if he did not cooperate.[30]

Collis English lived with his mother, Emma English, in a battered frame house at 247 Church Street; the toilet, bathtub, and sleeping quarters were all in one upstairs room.[31] He was twenty-three years old when he was arrested and had served in the navy for two and a half years during and after World War II, receiving an honorable discharge on May 20, 1946. During his military service he acquired malaria, as well as rheumatic fever, which damaged his heart. During a particularly severe bout of malaria in 1947 he spent a month at the Veterans Administration hospital at Fort Dix and was subsequently ordered to rest, so he did not have a job. Born and raised in Trenton, English went to school through part of the tenth grade and could read and write fairly well. George English deserted the family when Collis was still a baby.[32]

When English was in jail over the weekend, police asked what he had been doing on January 27. He mentioned the names of Ralph Cooper and "Buddy" Wilson. So, at 8:00 A.M. on Saturday, February 7, police picked up Ralph Cooper from Horace Wilson's rented apartment house in Robbinsville and took him to the Chancery Lane police station. Born and raised in Fitzgerald, Georgia, Cooper never knew his father. His grandparents raised him; at age ten he had to leave school to do whatever odd jobs he could find. Ralph could read and write a little. He found work picking cotton and spent two short stints in prison for committing larceny and forgery. Cooper hitchhiked his way to Trenton in July 1947, part of the postwar exodus north, and found work digging potatoes on a farm in Robbinsville. He met Melrose Diggs, the daughter of Mrs. Rubie English, George English's second wife, and decided to find work in Trenton to be near her. He obtained a job at Winner Manufacturing Company, but it lasted only a short time. He spent nonworking hours at the home of George English, visiting Melrose, while he roomed nearby.

At the same time that police picked up Ralph Cooper, they also arrested Horace Wilson, living in the upstairs apartment in a cement-block house in Robbinsville. English and Ralph Cooper had visited the downstairs occupant, Leanna Turner, in the afternoon of the day of the murder. Wilson, thirty-seven years old, worked as a field hand, often picking potatoes, bagging them, and loading them onto trucks. Born in Heineman, South Carolina, he came north in July 1939 to live in New Jersey after living briefly in Norfolk, Virginia. His father had died in 1935 and his mother in 1932. There were twelve children in the family, with eight still living in 1939. He had married and had a child in South Carolina, but neither wife nor child came north with him. He had been in school for two months only, could not read at all and could write only his name. But Horace Wilson carried himself with great dignity and composure.

By Saturday, February 7, 1948, Collis English's mother, Emma, was alarmed that her son had not returned home. She asked her son-in-law, McKinley Forrest, who lived with her, to go to the police station and find out what had happened and to deliver an extra set of keys to George English's car that had been in her possession. Thirty-seven-year-old Forrest worked for Trenton's largest employer, John A. Roebling and Sons, as a boiler room attendant. Born in Richland, Georgia, on December 21, 1918, son of "Boss" and Ida, Forrest had two sisters and eight brothers. The family moved to Americus, Georgia, shortly after his birth and remained there for fourteen years. Forrest never went beyond first grade and could not read or write. Other children made fun of him because of his noticeable stutter. He worked as a golf caddy and also picked cotton. When he was fifteen, with his mother and brothers all in the North, he came north, too, with funds provided by his brother Robert. He brought with him his nephew, John MacKenzie. He first found work digging potatoes near Trenton. In 1930 he began at the butcher firm of Katzeff and Wieners full-time until he began his wartime work at Roeblings. On his days off he continued to work in Isaac Katzeff's shop. At this time only three of his siblings remained alive, Robert and Alfred in Newark, and Jonas in Stamford, Connecticut. In 1935 he married Delia English, Collis's sister, who died in 1947. They had one child, Jean Ida, thirteen years old, who lived with her father in the English household. When McKinley Forrest arrived at the station, police detained him.

Mercer County Prosecutor Mario H. Volpe issued a press statement announcing that with the arrest of four new suspects authorities were on the verge of cracking the Horner murder case. Unknown to Volpe, about an hour before his press conference, police had brought Elizabeth Horner to the

Chancery Lane station to see the four men in jail. After carefully examining them, she stated, "Those are not the men."[33]

After receiving garbled information provided by Collis English, as he kept changing his story, police entered an East Trenton saloon at 5:00 P.M. the same day looking for men named Shorty or Long John. They arrested James H. Thorpe Jr., age twenty-four, who lived with his grandparents at 24 Grant Street. In 1947 his right arm had been badly smashed in a car accident. On January 7, 1948, it had been amputated, and Thorpe left the hospital on January 19. Born in Warren, North Carolina, in August 1923, Thorpe could not read or write, having attended a country school only to second grade. He was raised by his grandparents, who were sharecroppers on a farm growing cotton, tobacco, and corn, working on the farm starting at age seven. He came north with his father and grandparents in December 1939. He worked as a day laborer until he landed a job with the C & R Paper Company as a truck driver and held that job for five years, until his car accident. His father, James Henry Thorpe, his uncle Robert, and his brother Raymond all lived in Trenton, near where James lived with his grandparents. Called by the nickname of Red, he was quite light-complexioned compared to the other four men arrested that weekend for Horner's murder, and had a serious speech impediment, making him difficult to understand.[34] Police took him to Chancery Lane, placing him in a cell where he remained until being questioned on Monday morning.[35]

Mrs. Emma English, more concerned about McKinley Forrest's continued absence with each passing hour, decided she needed her daughter's help. From interviews by journalist William Reuben of the *National Guardian*, we know the details of what occurred at this point. Emma called her daughter, Bessie Mitchell, a garment worker in New York City, saying, "You'd better come down here, there's something wrong. Collis was arrested Friday and he hasn't come home yet and then this morning Mac [McKinley Forrest] went down to see what happened to Collis and he hasn't come back neither."[36]

Bessie Mitchell was thirty-six years old, born in Trenton in 1913. She began part-time work after school when she was just eight, washing dishes for twenty-five cents a day, which meant she had money to go to the movies on Saturday. She had made it through the tenth grade in Trenton's segregated schools when her mother had a stroke, forcing Bessie to find full-time employment. She worked as a domestic servant from 1928 until 1942, marrying James Mitchell in 1938. She attempted to improve her lot in life by taking evening courses at the Apex Beauty Culture School in Newark.

She finished the course and graduated but could never scrape together the forty-four dollars required to obtain her certificate.[37]

In 1942 James and Bessie moved to New York City, where she found work at a dress manufacturer, turning collars and cuffs. She earned fourteen dollars a week, six dollars a week more than she had ever made before. At the end of the first week she spent half her salary to join the International Ladies' Garment Workers Union. Bessie described herself as stubborn, telling journalist William Reuben: "If I felt I was right about something, I just made up my mind and stuck to it, no matter what happened." To illustrate, Bessie told him of her employment in the summer of 1936. In her first experience out of Trenton, she took a job at Sea Girt, New Jersey, with a Judge Nichols and his family. One day the judge's wife irately flourished Bessie's apron, found in the bathroom, asking, "Bessie, have you been using our bath?" Bessie answered, "Why, naturally. When you and the family are out on the beach, I always take my bath." Mrs. Nichols snapped back, "Well, hereafter, you take a towel and soap and go out to the ocean for your bath." In reply Bessie went into her room, put on her best dress, packed her suitcase, strode through the living room, where ten dinner guests waited, and stalked out the front door. She announced: "No bath, no work," and left, even though she had so little money she was unsure how she would return to Trenton. The next summer Mrs. Nichols tried to get Bessie to work for her again, telling her she could have her very own bath.[38] This stubbornness and perseverance were all that Bessie would have on her side in the trying days to come, in her struggle to help her brother and the five others locked up alongside him.

When Bessie arrived on an early train from New York City on Sunday, February 8, she stopped by her mother's house, then went to the Chancery Lane First District police station with McKinley Forrest's brother, Robert, and his wife. They asked the officer on duty to allow them to see their brothers and received no answer. Finally, the policeman told them to come back at 2:00 P.M. when Acting Captain Andrew Delate would be there. When they returned, the silver-haired, paunchy Delate said Bessie would be able to see McKinley Forrest. She, of course, asked Forrest why he was being held. He responded, "I don't know, Bessie. Me and Jack were sitting in the house with Collis Friday night when the policemen come and said they had to take him down to the station house because his father complained about Collis using the car. Then your mother asked me to come down to see what happened. I asked the policeman at the desk where I could find out about Collis English, and he told me to go on in to the courtroom. In about ten minutes another cop come up to me in the courtroom and asked me if my name was 'Chancy.' I told him no, my name's McKinley Forrest, and I showed him my pocketbook." The officer then took McKinley into Delate's office, booked him, and as he bewilderedly explained, "They still haven't told me what for." These events perplexed Bessie, but she told her mother, "I don't see what we can do. The police couldn't arrest a person for no reason at all." Bessie returned to New York that evening.[39]

On Monday, February 9, 1948, a short article on the front page of the *Trenton Evening Times* carried the headline "Break Awaited in Murder Case" and began with "An air of expectancy continued at Police Headquarters today, giving rise to reports there might be an early break in the holdup-slaying of William Horner . . . but there was no information from official police sources."

The next day a front-page headline of the *Trenton Evening Times* screamed "Five Confess Brutal Killing of Merchant"; it was accompanied by a large photo of Collis English, Ralph Cooper, Horace Wilson, McKinley Forrest, and James Thorpe taken at police headquarters. A smaller headline read "Suspects Recount Details in Death-Beating of Horner: Chance Arrest Leads to Solution of Crime." The *Times* proclaimed that "[e]ffective work on the part of city police and officials of Prosecutor Mario H. Volpe's office solved one of the most brutal crimes committed here in recent years," as police officials claimed the five men had confessed to the crime. The paper went on: "The first break in the case occurred last Friday night when Patrolmen Lichtfuhs and Amman together with Sergeant Creeden stopped a motor vehicle violator on Perry Street. The driver gave his name as Collis English. During the questioning it was developed that English was involved in the Horner murder. English in turn gave the names of Wilson and Cooper to the officers. . . . The first break in the case came on Sunday morning when Collis English and Cooper admitted their guilt. They involved the other three. When Forrest, Thorpe, and Wilson were confronted by Cooper and English they also admitted taking part in the brutal holdup, police said."

The appearance of the *Trenton Evening Times* story caused a number of things to happen. First, it explained to Mrs. Emma English why neither Collis nor Mac had returned home. She again called Bessie and asked her to come to Trenton, saying, "Come down here right away, Bessie, there's trouble," but refused to give any further details over the phone. When Bessie Mitchell arrived several hours later, she found her mother overwhelmed by grief, as neighbors crowded into the tiny house, some sobbing. They showed her the newspaper, and Bessie went to her wailing mother, saying, "Mama, you might just as well stop your crying right now. If our men had anything to do with this, they'll have to pay for it, that's all." Frustrated neighbors stayed late into the evening explaining to Bessie the facts they did know, which did not agree with the newspaper account.[40]

The second effect of the *Trenton Evening Times* story was the immediate difficulty that Prosecutor Volpe and Chief Detective Frank Naples found themselves in. The headline stated in broad, bold type that they had five confessions, but at that point they actually had none. They dealt with this in the dead of night, by holding a "confession session" at midnight in the jail for the five men. Wilson refused to make a confession, leaving Chief Detective Naples with four confessions, but the newspaper headline blared that they had five.

At 5:00 A.M. on Wednesday, February 11, police again knocked on the door of 247 Church Street, home of Collis English and McKinley Forrest, interrupting Bessie's sleep. They asked for James Martin or Jack Kelly but discovered no one by those names in residence. They then took the only remaining male, John MacKenzie (called Jack by his family), nephew of McKinley Forrest, back with them to the First Precinct police station. John MacKenzie, born in Americus, Georgia, on February 14, 1923, was the oldest son of one of Forrest's two sisters. After John's parents died, McKinley brought him north when he was just five years old. John attended school in Trenton until eighth grade and could read and write fairly well. He worked for eighteen months in the Civilian Conservation Corps camp in Chatsworth, New Jersey. After that he returned to Trenton and worked as a hotel cook and in construction. He served thirty-three months in the army during World War II, receiving an honorable discharge as well as two battle stars for serving under fire in northern France and along the Rhine. After his discharge on January 1, 1946, he began work at Community Slaughterhouse on Union Street, adjacent to Forrest's employer Katzeff and Wieners. John's sister, Vera, married to Alphonso Strauss, also lived in Trenton, and he saw her frequently.

It is important to note that John MacKenzie was the only one of the six men without a major disability. Collis English had a bad heart. McKinley Forrest and James Thorpe had serious speech impediments, and James Thorpe was still recovering from the amputation of an arm. Only English and MacKenzie could read and write competently. None of the men had any idea of their constitutional rights under American law, such as the right to remain silent and the right to an attorney.

Once Bessie Mitchell absorbed the traumatic fact that the police had now taken all the family males from the home, she composed herself and set to work. She spent two hours calling every man who might possibly come to the house, telling them to stay away. This included her husband, her brother-in-law, other relatives, and friends. After that she took her mother and niece, Jean, McKinley Forrest's daughter, downtown to make necessary arrangements. She changed her mother's bank account to a joint account and went to the relief office to apply for home relief. While they were waiting for a bus home a neighbor told them that John had also been charged with murder. This made no sense to Bessie; if John was guilty why would he have spent five days at home waiting to be arrested?

Bessie needed more information, so she and Jean went to the public library to examine recent issues of the local newspaper. She found two things especially troubling. The original description of the suspects given by the police, two light-skinned Negroes, did not fit Collis, Mac, or John, Collis and Mac being especially dark-skinned. In amazement she studied the photo of the five arrested men in the *Trenton Evening Times* and thought it must have been doctored somehow; in it Collis and Mac looked light-skinned. She was also concerned that the newspaper stated Collis had been arrested in an auto, driving on Perry Street, something she knew to be untrue from the accounts told by her mother and others.[41]

After her library research, Bessie collected John MacKenzie's sister, Vera Strauss, and went to the Chancery Lane First Precinct police station to show Acting Captain Delate her notes. She assumed that the police would want to know about their mistake. Instead, the captain told them, "Those boys were well treated, they had plenty of food and cigarettes. The police don't have no more to do with that case." With that, he turned his back on them, refusing to say more.[42]

That day the *Trenton Evening Times* ran an editorial that began: "For a time the brutal murder of William Horner, 72-year-old second-hand dealer of North Broad Street, and the attack on his wife baffled all efforts toward solution. Although the crime was committed in daylight and in the very heart of the city the murderers seemed to have left no trace of identity. Now, after two weeks of effort, five men have been rounded up and have confessed their guilt." It concluded with kudos all around: "Solution of this crime mystery is the result of police work of an exceptional character and the superior officers and patrolmen who worked on the case so effectively are entitled to generous commendation. . . . Prosecutor Volpe, who has paid generous tribute to the police, and members of his staff aided in breaking this case. They, too, are deserving of a share of the credit."[43]

On Thursday, February 12, police transferred Collis English, McKinley Forrest, Ralph Cooper, Horace Wilson, and James Thorpe to the Mercer County Jail to await trial. Guard James Brearley put Forrest into a segregation cell because he was "talking irrationally, mumbling unintelligibly, making considerable unnecessary noise and upsetting the rest of the inmates."[44] They did not move John MacKenzie at this time, as police had not arrested him until the day before. Instead, Acting Captain Delate questioned him further; Clerk Henry W. Miller recorded his complete statement regarding his movements and innocence. Police then returned him to his cell, where guards gave him cigarettes. He then signed a confession about which he remembered nothing.[45] Possible explanations for this would be brought out at the trial. Police moved him to the Mercer County Jail on Saturday, February 14, where he was put in a segregation cell due to his erratic behavior.

On Friday, February 13, Robert Forrest, brother of McKinley Forrest, visited his brother at the Mercer County Jail. Robert had with him Harold Simmandl, a former judge, and Arthur Salvatore, a Trenton attorney and head of the Trenton Bar Association. Robert had his own contracting business in Newark and had provided McKinley the funds necessary to come north. As the three testified at trial, they found McKinley to be disoriented, incoherent, and unable to recognize his own brother. They witnessed him "laying on the floor like a pig with vomit all over him."[46]

On Tuesday, February 17, the *Trenton Evening Times* announced that during its January term the Mercer County grand jury had indicted the six men for murder. The court record stated:

Ralph Cooper and Collis English and McKinley Forrest and John MacKenzie and James H. Thorpe and Horace Wilson, late of the City of Trenton in the said County of Mercer, on the twenty-seventh day of January in the year of our Lord one thousand nine hundred and forty-eight, with force and arms, at the City aforesaid, in the county aforesaid, and within the jurisdiction of this Court, one William Horner, in the peace of God and of this State then and there being willfully, feloniously and of their malice aforethought did kill and murder, contrary to the form of the statute in such case made and provided, and against the peace of this State, the government and dignity of the same. By Mario H. Volpe, Prosecutor of the Pleas.[47]

McKinley Forrest's bizarre behavior finally ceased on February 19; on February 20 the jail warden transferred him to a regular cell. Forrest did not recognize a trustee at the jail, Daniel Duke, with whom he had worked at Roebling Company, until after he "came to himself"; then he recognized Daniel Duke immediately.[48] The significance of his behavior would be a focus of both the prosecution and defense during the coming trial.

Bessie Mitchell soon realized that her brother Collis and the other five men desperately needed good legal assistance. She also realized that none of them had funds to pay for it. Thus, she reasoned it would be most effective for the six to band together in obtaining legal help. She was thwarted in this goal when the other relatives told her that Irving Lewis, attorney for George English, had told them that Collis was guilty and the rest would not have gotten into trouble but for his actions. Bessie went to see Irving Lewis, who immediately told her, "That Collis is no damn good, he's guilty as hell. He's as good as in the chair, there's nothing to do but pull the switch." Bessie stated her belief that Collis was innocent, as were all of the men. Since Irving was the only lawyer Bessie knew, she begged him to take the case. He told her to go out and raise some money, "not chicken feed." She returned in one week with three hundred dollars, most of it the money her husband, Jimmy, had received from his military discharge pay and overseas bonus, as well as twenty-five dollars collected from members of her mother's church. Irving Lewis told her to forget it, she would never raise enough money and besides, "Your brother's guilty."[49]

Bessie persisted, getting recommendations of lawyers through people that either she or her mother had worked for. Not one would take the case for less than two thousand dollars, an impossible sum. Someone suggested that the NAACP could help. Emma English, Bessie's mother, had been to see Dr. Charles Broadus, head of the Trenton NAACP, just one week after Collis had been arrested. Bessie tried again; he listened to her sympathetically but said there was nothing he could do to assist. She went to the Veterans Administration, hoping her brother's benefits entitled him to legal advice. She wrote to magazines and newspapers. She sent letters to Governor Alfred Driscoll and the editor of the *Trenton Evening Times*. She made the rounds of Trenton's black churches; the pastors all agreed to pray for the men but seemed to feel, as the Reverend Grayson, pastor of Union Baptist Church, told her, "These men wouldn't be down there if they weren't guilty."[50]

Next she tried the Federal Bureau of Investigation (FBI), having once heard the radio crime drama *This Is Your FBI*. She went to FBI headquarters in Foley Square in New York City, was sent to Long Island City, where she was referred to Newark, New Jersey, then to the FBI in Trenton, and then back to Foley Square. Finally, only several weeks before the trial was to begin, an agent in the Newark office explained that the FBI could not do anything, "but if the men aren't acquitted, get in touch with us after the trial and we'll see what we can do then."[51] She followed up on any and all suggestions but came up empty-handed.

Robert Forrest, brother of McKinley, obviously knew some lawyers; two, Arthur A. Salvatore and Harold Simmandl, accompanied Robert on his visit to McKinley in jail. However, the court determined that Robert Forrest did not have sufficient funds to pay counsel for a lengthy trial. He had retained Salvatore's law partner, Frank S. Katzenbach III, for a short period, so the court now appointed him to represent McKinley. Katzenbach was a member of a prominent family active in Democratic politics in New Jersey; like other family members, he supported civil rights and was highly regarded in the black community.[52] He had been a judge in Mercer County from 1940 to 1945, had served three sessions in the state assembly, and attended the Democratic National Convention as a delegate in 1940. After clerking for his uncle, he formed the law firm of Katzenbach and Salvatore.[53]

Katzenbach's father, Frank Snowden Katzenbach Jr., was the first cousin of the best-known family member, Nicholas Katzenbach. Nicholas Katzenbach served as a bomber pilot in World War II, graduated from Princeton University in 1945, earned a law degree at Yale, and went to Oxford University as a Rhodes Scholar. After stints teaching law at Yale and the University of Chicago, he was appointed deputy attorney general by U.S. Attorney General Robert F. Kennedy in 1962; he then played a prominent civil rights role in the South, confronting governors George Wallace of Alabama and Ross Barnett of Mississippi as they attempted to keep African Americans from attending previously all-white public colleges. Nicholas Katzenbach drafted the Voting Rights Act of 1965 and served as Lyndon Johnson's attorney general in 1965 and 1966.[54]

Upon investigation, it became clear that none of the other five had funds for counsel, so the court appointed lawyers for them on March 29, 1948. James S. Turp headed the defense team, receiving four thousand dollars for his efforts, while representing James Thorpe Jr. and John MacKenzie. Turp had worked long and hard to achieve his position in life, having quit school at age fourteen for work in a cotton mill to help support his family. He attended night school, graduated from business school, and in 1920 received his law degree with honors from George Washington University in Washington, D.C. He practiced law in Trenton from 1921 to 1943, then opened his own law office in Hightstown, New Jersey. From 1932 to 1934 he served as mayor of Hightstown. From 1935 to 1940 he was judge of the Court of Common Pleas in Mercer County. Thus, during the trial Judge Hutchinson frequently referred to Turp as "Judge."[55]

James Waldron, son of one of the five Trenton city commissioners, represented Collis English. Waldron attended the Temple University School of Law , worked briefly for the FBI, then volunteered for the Office of Strategic Services during World War II. After the war he began his law practice, becoming a partner in Backes, Waldron, and Hill in Trenton.[56] He was the youngest member of the defense team.

Robert Queen, one of two black attorneys in Trenton and executive director of New Jersey's NAACP, assisted with MacKenzie and represented Ralph Cooper. Robert Queen began his work with the NAACP in 1913, only four years after its founding, when local leaders started a Trenton branch of the organization.[57] Historian Jack Washington described him this way: "Perhaps the person who was the staunchest supporter of the N.A.A.C.P. and civil rights for the Black community of Trenton was Robert Queen, attorney at law. Queen championed the quest for civil rights in Trenton and, indeed, was the guiding legal mind behind the strategy. Robert Queen dedicated his career to civil rights causes and was in the forefront of every major fight to attain a measure of equality for the Black community in the city."[58] In 1932, when the new, integrated Trenton High School opened, black students could swim in the school swimming pool only once a week, when whites were not there. Gaining the support of the national NAACP, Robert Queen argued the case with the city. Trenton's attorney ruled that such segregation was blatantly illegal, and the swimming pool opened to all students equally.[59]

While Trenton School Board policy led to an integrated high school, the junior high schools remained segregated. In 1943 parents Gladys Hedgepeth and Berline Williams filed suit against the school board for a policy that did not allow their children to attend the neighborhood school, but forced them to walk a considerable distance to the black Lincoln School. Robert Queen argued the case before the New Jersey Supreme Court. He questioned Trenton School District superintendent Paul Loser, asking if the two children had been excluded on grounds of color. Mr. Loser responded yes, saying it was done "in accordance with a policy in keeping with the philosophy of education . . . [as] it was considered most likely that Negro pupils could develop better opportunities for leadership when they are segregated." Surprising many at the time, the Mercer County Teacher's

Union issued this statement: "One of the basic principles of our Union is the policy of not discriminating against any individual or group because of race, color, or creed. This is based upon the letter and intent of the Constitution of the United States. Consequently, we must protest against the Board of Education's refusal to allow two Black children to attend a nearby school, and its insistence upon their attending Lincoln School."[60] On January 31, 1944, the state supreme court ruled unanimously in favor of Mrs. Hedgepeth and Mrs. Williams. Chief Justice Newton Potter declared, "It is unlawful for boards of education to exclude children from any public school on the ground that they are of the Negro race." Ten years later NAACP lawyer Thurgood Marshall cited New Jersey's ruling, among others, in argument before the U.S. Supreme Court in *Brown v. Board of Education*; the Court's decision outlawed racial segregation in America's schools.[61] Thus, in Robert Queen the defense team had a lawyer experienced in combating racial prejudice. Katzenbach, Waldron, and Queen each received three thousand dollars for their work.[62]

Just as the postwar mood in the city played a role in these events, so did key Trenton politicians. Trenton's mayor, Donal Connolly, described as a dapper and wisecracking Irishman, began his career in Democratic Party politics at a young age. His boyish good looks and ever-extended glad hand helped him become the youngest member of the New Jersey State Assembly, to which he was elected in 1937 at the age of twenty-nine. In 1942 Democrats appointed him secretary of the State Beauty Culture Control Board, and he returned to this job after World War II. Connolly's political rise seemed in jeopardy in the spring of 1947 when he faced grand jury charges that he had accepted bribes and kickbacks in issuing beauty shop licenses. The grand jury failed to indict him; immediately afterward the son of the jury foreman received a well-paid city job. Republicans pressed on, and Connolly faced the charges again in October 1947. This time Connolly created a strategic diversion. The Civil Rights Congress, an arm of the Communist Party USA, had been issued a permit to hold a public meeting in Trenton, at which Gerhart Eisler, recently indicted for contempt of Congress by the House Un-American Activities Committee, was to speak. Several days after Connolly's troubles reemerged and a month after all the arrangements for Eisler's appearance had been made, Connolly launched an all-out Red Scare. In a statement picked up quickly by local newspapers, Connolly warned that Trenton's fine people faced serious peril in allowing members of the Communist Party USA to speak in their city, and permission was thereby denied. When the organizers appeared at city hall to protest, the mayor had them physically removed, with local press photographers recording the events. Connolly announced "We do not give Communists the right to be heard here."[63]

Sponsors of the meeting sought, and received, a court order enjoining the mayor and city commissioners from hindering the meeting. Again in view of press photographers, Connolly tore up the injunction. Police Chief William Dooling announced that anyone attempting to enter the meeting hall would be arrested. On the meeting day, October 26, a mob of five thousand, many armed, surrounded the hall. They threatened to kill anyone who tried to enter. Governor Alfred Driscoll joined in, holding a press conference saying that protesters, as he referred to the mob, had a right to object to the activities of the Communist Party. Finally, the Chancery Court, at the request of local Communists, issued an injunction restraining all officials from interfering "through the use of intimidation, coercion, instructions, orders, or other means," with the Communists' constitutional right to assemble peaceably. All of this kept Connolly's legal troubles off the front pages of local newspapers. Connolly's problems resurfaced when the court set his trial date for January 26, 1948. Shortly before the trial was to begin, however, the court postponed it until March 22. This occurred after two jury members told the court that a detective agency representing Mayor Connolly had sent someone to see them for a friendly little chat. The *Trenton Evening Times* assured its readers that this was not evidence of jury tampering, but merely the result of "well-meaning, but mistaken, action on the part of friends of the mayor."[64] Then, the January 27 murder of William Horner drew the attention of local citizens away from the mayor's legal difficulties.[65]

A politician much too clever to end up with troubles like those of the mayor, Andrew J. Duch, the blatantly racist director of public safety and creator of the submachine gun–toting police squad, played a role in the fate of the Trenton Six. A Trenton native, he graduated from the University of Pennsylvania's law school in 1917 and served as a lieutenant in World War I. After the war he entered local Republican politics and was rewarded by the party quickly, being appointed clerk of the police court in 1923. He soon became police court judge and in 1937 was appointed Mercer County prosecutor. As prosecutor he once ordered every black in the city brought in for questioning and fingerprinting for a murder in which the only known facts were that the murderer was an African American who fled the scene in a car. On one occasion, he decided that groups of blacks standing on streets presented a threat; he had nineteen young blacks arrested for doing so. However, his most infamous act as prosecutor involved the manner in which he solved six murders that occurred over a five-year period in local lovers' lanes. In 1938, and once a year thereafter, a pair of lovers was attacked by a man wielding a shotgun at close range. In each case one of those involved was married and committing adultery. One witness survived long enough to describe the assailant as "a short, stocky colored man." Duch decided they were looking for "a lunatic, a man obsessed with sex mania, probably a religious fanatic." When the killer struck again, in 1942, the couple escaped, and described their attacker as "a tall, thin black man, about fifty." Using a piece of wood from the shotgun that contained a partial serial number, police came up with Clarence Hill, a short and stocky black man, perhaps fitting the description of the 1938 killer. He had no police record and was a thirty-four-year-old Sunday school teacher, a native of Trenton, currently serving in the army. The army sent him to Fort Dix, where he was forced to stand naked night and day and was beaten periodically by the military police. After a month he was told that his suffering would end if he confessed to the lovers' lane killings; otherwise he would be turned over to a lynch mob. He finally confessed. No physical evidence linked him to the murders, and he had an unbroken alibi for the night in question. The prosecution, perhaps realizing the weakness of its case, charged him only with the first murder. The all-white jury found him guilty but recommended life in prison instead of the death penalty. After twenty years the parole board freed him, at which time he was dying of throat cancer.[66]

After becoming mayor, Duch continued in a similar vein. He threw advocates of minorities out of public hearings. A woman reporter who questioned Duch's selection of a site for Negro veterans' housing located "squarely between the city's garbage incinerator and the Pennsylvania Railroad switchyard," while the site for white veterans was in a quiet, residential section of Trenton, found herself forcibly ejected from a meeting. The Trenton Committee for Unity called Duch biased against colored veterans, a charge he ignored.[67] In 1946 a cross burning occurred in Hamilton Township, near Trenton, to intimidate a black family planning to move into a previously all-white area. Two members of the Communist Party, Manuel Cantor and Alfred Wishart, appealed for a permit to rally against the increasing influence of the Ku Klux Klan in New Jersey. Duch refused permission unless the Communists would also be censured. He told them, "Anyone who believes in the Communist Party does not belong in this country."[68]

Duch's worldview revealed a fear then circulating in the American national psyche. Senator Joseph McCarthy made his career accusing government employees and others of being Communist spies and sympathizers. He smoothly convinced Americans to accept his declarations as truth, and he remained at the height of his influence exactly when the trials and travails of the Trenton Six occurred, a backdrop to this story.

The *Trenton Evening Times* played its own crucial part in city politics. Owned by James Kerney, who edited and published the paper until his death in 1934, it was carried on by his widow and three children and edited by James Jr., the oldest son. On December 18, 1947, the paper ran an editorial on "The Right to Citizenship," stating, "So long as we deny equal citizenship with all its privileges to some of our citizens, we put all our freedoms in jeopardy." Despite such high-minded proclamations, the paper's premature report of the five confessions seemingly catalyzed the chain of events that ultimately led to indictments. Thus, the paper created events as much as it reported on them.[69]

At the time that the police were interrogating the Trenton Six, other suspects appeared to be under consideration. On June 23, 1948, about a week after the trial began, police took a statement from Garrett "Jerry" Griswold, a thirty-eight-year-old single white man. Griswold periodically worked for Mr. Horner, helping with deliveries, moving furniture, and repairing stoves for sale. When he worked for Horner he lived in the shop, sleeping on the bed in the back room where Horner was fatally injured on January 27. Griswold claimed he had left Trenton two days before the murder to go to Baltimore, returning the afternoon of January 27. He maintained that a few days after the murder he was able to get his clothes from the shop and that was all he knew about it, but locals suspected that he was present at Horner's murder.[70] He had moved into his father's place in Asbury Park, New Jersey after the murder, where police found him.[71] Officers had been interested in Griswold since shortly after the crime. In February they brought him from Asbury Park to Trenton for questioning. Detectives showed him photos of the six suspects, and he stated he knew none of them and had not seen any of them at the store. Police kept Griswold in a small room in the courthouse for the duration of the trial, paying him two or three dollars a day, perhaps to stay out of sight. Griswold eventually admitted that he knew details of the murder, not because he did it but because a man named Pete had told him all about it.

Quiet rumors eventually reached journalist William Reuben that this Pete and a man named Eddie Poulis had actually committed the crime. Reuben could not find proof either way. Attorney Robert Queen sent a memo to William Patterson, later involved in the appeal to the New Jersey Supreme Court, asserting that information had come to him that a man named Robert

Polas had been at a local tavern, drinking and talking: "He knew more about what happened to Horner than anybody they had ever heard talk. Only one who had been there could have known so much. . . . He knew where Horner kept his money; he knew how much Horner had on him; where Horner was struck and with what."[72]

Finally, harking back to the man who started it all, the *Trenton Evening Times* ran a story on April 13, 1948, telling readers that George English, who had originally pleaded not guilty to the crime of molesting his stepdaughter, had changed his plea and received a three-to-five-year sentence on a morals charge from Judge Charles P. Hutchinson. He began serving his sentence in the state prison, where soon he would be joined by his son, and the five other men who eventually became known to the world as the Trenton Six.

CHAPTER 2

THE TRIAL, PROSECUTION

The process of jury selection took place with Judge Charles P. Hutchinson presiding. The twelve-person jury, with two alternates, eventually consisted of nine women, all housewives, and three businessmen. The group was white and middle class. The defendants noted the obvious absence of any blacks, laborers, and foreign-born or low-income individuals. Even before the trial began, John MacKenzie astutely told journalist William Reuben, "I knew we were cooked when I seen that jury."[1]

The trial of the Trenton Six, the longest and most expensive in New Jersey history up to that time, began on June 15, 1948, and lasted until August 6, generating a 6,200-page trial transcript. The length of the trial would not be the only challenge that jurors, sequestered for the duration, had to face. With six men tried at once, featuring 127 witnesses over so long a time period, it required intense concentration. The factor that caused the most difficulty for the Six was the lack of cultural and social comprehension of the white jury. No matter how understanding the jurors attempted to be, the everyday lives of poor, uneducated men of color in Trenton remained a mystery to them. This revealed itself in critical courtroom testimony when the Six had no notion of the precise time when things occurred, did not exhibit typical white middle-class manners, and did not understand questions in the language in which they were asked.

Prosecutor Mario H. Volpe played the central role for the state in all trials and appeals of the Trenton Six. His father had been the only one of nine siblings to leave Italy for the United States, and Mario Volpe grew up in Trenton and attended Rutgers University on a scholarship from the *Trenton Evening Times*; he remained one of the newspapers' favorite subjects. He graduated from law school in 1933 and soon entered politics; he was elected to the state assembly in 1940. He entered the army as a private in 1941 but was commissioned as a second lieutenant while overseas. At some point during his time in Europe he worked for the Office of Strategic Services, forerunner to the Central Intelligence Agency. In May 1945, the army awarded him a Bronze Star. He was serving with the U.S. legation in Switzerland when Governor Walter Evans Edge appointed him a Mercer County district court judge.

As a district court judge, Volpe heard arguments in a race discrimination suit filed against the Lenox Restaurant by Leslie Hayling and Samuel Dorsey, two blacks who were refused service on December 17, 1945. Such refusal was clearly contrary to New Jersey law. Robert Queen represented the two men before Volpe and described the result: "We had a very strong case but Volpe decided against us. We had the evidence and there was a state law prohibiting discrimination, but Volpe used some legal double talk to rule against my clients, in favor of the restaurant that discriminated against them because they were Negroes."[2]

In January 1947, the newly elected governor, Alfred E. Driscoll, appointed Volpe as Mercer County prosecutor. His first successful prosecution involved two black Fort Dix soldiers found guilty of robbery. Another case, in the summer of 1947, involved nineteen-year-old Harvey Hoagland, a black man whose head was blown off by a shotgun blast fired at close range in a public park, a violence committed by James Roberts, a white southerner visiting Princeton. Volpe brought no charges until a Negro minister who had witnessed the shooting collected 1,600 signatures demanding that he take action. Roberts was found guilty but received a light sentence. Short, stocky, neatly groomed, and ambitious, Volpe was forty years old when the trial began; he was single and lived with his mother in Trenton.[3]

Charles P. Hutchinson had been appointed to the Mercer County Court of Common Pleas in 1945. Before that he had been Mercer County clerk and an assistant United States attorney. He graduated from Princeton in 1909 and received a law degree from New York Law School in 1912. During World War I he served as an army captain in France. A newspaper article on his service as judge noted that he was very patient, "sympathetic to the ills and shortcomings of humans, but he can grow stern and severe when the occasion demands. His court is always a model of dignity and decorum. He allows no personal squabbling between counsel. Spectators toe the line in the matter of proper conduct. There is a friendly feeling at his court sessions."[4]

Tuesday, June 15, 1948

The typical court day lasted from 10:00 A.M. to 4:00 P.M., with a one-hour recess for lunch and short morning and afternoon recesses. As soon as Judge Hutchinson officially assembled the jury, Prosecutor Volpe began the state's opening. He listed what the state would prove: that William Horner carried large amounts of cash upon his person, that Ralph Cooper picked up Collis English, then Horace Wilson and James Thorpe, and finally John MacKenzie and McKinley Forrest, and that John served as the lookout man while the others entered the store. Then Horace Wilson cracked Mrs. Horner over the head with a soda bottle while McKinley Forrest did the same to William Horner. Collis English delved into Horner's pocket, pulling out a handful of bills. The men then hurried back to their vehicle and left the scene.[5] Volpe concluded: "[T]he State will prove beyond a reasonable doubt that after their apprehension, purely by a stroke of luck and by the excellent work of the Police Department, that they made those admissions as to their participation in this crime, each implicating the other, with the exception of one man: Horace Wilson, who was implicated by the other five." (Wilson's involvement as described by the others was hearsay evidence, which Volpe knew.) Volpe emphasized the most crucial point: "Ladies and gentlemen, we will prove to you that those statements were voluntarily signed and given by these men. We will prove to you that no group of men charged with crime have got as good treatment as these men received while they were in the custody of the police."[6]

The defense opening began with attorney Frank Katzenbach representing McKinley Forrest. He announced that he would prove McKinley was elsewhere when the crime was committed. He pointed out that the men's apprehension took place "when the city was crying out for action, when suspects were being interviewed right and left . . . I will prove to you they were kept for five days without benefit of any legal advice at all or anybody to defend them." He asked the jury to be patient when the defense asked witnesses for details, such as how many police officers were present, how long they questioned the men, as "that will be the actual crux of this case." He pointed out that these men were "of a race who a hundred years ago were between decks that weren't big enough for men to stand up in, and brought into this country from an aboriginal state, men who are afraid of the law."[7]

Counsel James S. Turp then explained that he, Mr. Queen, and Mr. Waldron had been appointed to defend the other five men, which he hoped the jury would not find confusing. (The lawyers addressed each other as "Mr." in court, so this form of address will appear in court testimony.) Several of them had also been judges previously and referred to each other this way, which perhaps would have been confusing to the jury. He commented that the defense had never seen any of the statements made by the defendants. Nevertheless, he emphasized that the statements were made involuntarily and therefore were not properly admissible as evidence. Further, "they were made while the defendants were illegally held with no warrants, as we understand, for their arrest, and no authority for even their detention, merely being held by force in jail in the First Precinct, and were made after long periods of questioning, after the defendants were struck or threatened or given promises of hope or reward for making such statements."[8] Turp pointedly told the jury that while state and federal laws theoretically protect everyone, these rights are not universally applied. Using the case of Collis English as an example, he described how English remained in confinement without charge or arraignment well beyond the forty-eight hours allowed by New Jersey law. English had no knowledge of his rights or money to obtain a lawyer and thus was deprived of his liberty without due process of law. In light of his severe heart problems and having been struck and threatened by the police, "to such a person who does not know his rights, and so confined without any ideas as to how or when he can get out of jail, the situation is terrifying, and a statement made under those conditions above outlined would be, we contend, involuntary." Each side made it clear from the outset that the confessions would be central to the trial. Turp further noted, "All and each of the defendants deny any participation in or any knowledge of this alleged crime, and some of the defendants did not even know others of the defendants until after their arrest."[9]

WEDNESDAY, JUNE 16, 1948

Prosecutor Volpe opened the state's case with Police Officer Sterling Pettit showing the jury a map he had drawn of the crime scene, William Horner's secondhand store. Detective Anthony L. Magrelli exhibited his photos capturing the crowded interior of the main room and the tiny back room (see figure 2). Police Officer Elvin K. Sharpe demonstrated his exterior shots of the store and several views of the block on which it was located. He also displayed, over the objections of the defense, his photos of a black, two-door Ford sedan owned by George English, which had been towed to a police parking garage.

Sharpe concluded by presenting the jury with several images of the deceased taken at the morgue.[10]

Prosecutor Volpe then called Dr. David Eckstein, who had performed the autopsy on William Horner at 9:00 P.M. on January 27, 1948, the day Horner died. Volpe asked Eckstein whether the victim's fractured skull could have been caused by a soda bottle, and Eckstein responded yes, it could have. When questioned by defense lawyer Turp, however, Eckstein admitted he had no idea what the actual implement used in the murder had been.[11]

Next on the witness stand was Laura C. Anderson, eldest child of the deceased. She had identified her father's body. Under questioning by the defense, Anderson acknowledged that her father had not lived with her mother, Ellen A. Horner, for the past thirty years, since 1916, although he had not obtained a divorce.[12]

The star witness for the prosecution, Elizabeth McGuire, who had been known as Elizabeth Horner, then took the stand. She agreed with Volpe that William Horner always carried large amounts of cash on his person and that they never drank soda and thus never had soda bottles at the store. Volpe led her through her testimony, which was reported by the *Trenton Evening Times*: "In a dramatic scene, witnessed by a tense courtroom, Mrs. Horner descended from the witness stand after Prosecutor Volpe had asked her a question. She walked briskly over to where Collis English was seated at a defense table. She pointed to him and said, 'That's one.' Then she walked around the same table to McKinley Forrest, explaining 'That's one.' She hesitated a moment as she scanned the faces of the other defendants and then walked to a second table where she pointed to Horace Wilson, 'And this one here,' she said in a clear voice." This was in stark contrast to her earlier statements that she did not recognize the men. The *Times* writer observed: "Attired in a black and white dress and a pert hat, she looked younger than the fifty-nine years she admitted to." Mrs. Horner described the three men as entering the store on January 16, 1948, asking to see a mattress. She clearly stated that McKinley Forrest did the talking and put a two-dollar deposit on the mattress; she then gave him a receipt. On Monday, January 26, the men returned, saying the mattress had a hole in it and they didn't want it after all. Mr. Horner gave Forrest two dollars back and Mrs. Horner had him sign a receipt that he had received the money. Defense lawyer Katzenbach briefly intervened to make sure she meant McKinley Forrest signed his name to the receipt and she indicated yes, that had occurred.

On the morning of January 27, Mrs. Horner continued, Collis English and McKinley Forrest returned and went into the back room again to see the mattress, while Horace Wilson appeared asking about a stove. When she leaned over to demonstrate its features, she received a terrific blow to her head, then another on the side of her face. She struggled to the front door, where she screamed for help. The attackers had broken several of her ribs and fractured her cheekbone.[13]

THURSDAY, JUNE 17, 1948

Defense lawyer Turp began the cross-examination of Elizabeth McGuire Horner by delving into her history with Mr. Horner. Mrs. Horner revealed that she had only learned that he was married to Ellen Horner after living with him for two months. She was twenty-seven at the time she moved in with the forty-year-old Horner. She gave Turp only vague answers about how she knew that the first time she saw English, Forrest, and Wilson was on January 16. He then asked her if she had gone over the story with the prosecutor and the police. At first she said, "No, I haven't." Under further questioning she admitted, "Once in a while," and finally, "Yes." Then Turp turned to the issue of identifying the suspects. First he asked if she had been shown photos of the suspects. "No," she said. Under persistent questioning, she admitted, "Yes, I have been shown, but I knew them before." Turp continued to press her. She agreed that she had been at police headquarters on February 7 to see a lineup of the men, at which time she identified none of them, but explained, "I couldn't quite recognize them, because my eyes were all puffed up. But after I got home their faces came to me." He asked if she had lost consciousness during the attack, as she had stated during direct examination, and she said yes, even though Turp pointed out that she had told a doctor upon her admission to the hospital that she had not lost consciousness at any time.[14] Turp also raised the subject of Jerry Griswold, the part-time helper in the store; she had no idea of his whereabouts.

Next Turp addressed the issue of lighting in the crowded store, presumably questioning Mrs. Horner's ability to identify individuals. The store had large front windows, but only one forty-watt bulb in the main room. He asked about her description of the three men to the police: "I told the police they were sort of light-skinned, one was a light-skinned colored man, and one of them had a sort of a high cheekbones, the other one had sort of a slanty eyes." Under questioning, Mrs. Horner admitted that she had not seen the person who struck her but assumed it must be the individual she named as Horace Wilson, because he was the only one nearby at the time. Turp also elicited that fact that on two occasions she refused to talk with defense lawyer Waldron, "so that we didn't know what you were going to say until you told it here today, did you?" Her answer: "No, I didn't care to talk about it. With anybody." Question: "Well, you had discussed it with the police, hadn't you?" Answer: "Yes."[15]

Next defense lawyer Katzenbach, representing McKinley Forrest, took his turn. He focused on her identification of the men, having the following exchange: "So, the first time you felt that you could tell any of these men from anybody else was when you were in court here, then you made up your mind that you knew them; isn't that so?" "No, I knew them before I put my foot inside this courtroom." "From the pictures; isn't that right?" "Yes." She admitted she had not identified them in person, at the police station, but insisted this was due to her "puffy eyes." Katzenbach continued his questioning about the men's appearance. Mrs. Horner described McKinley Forrest as wearing a dark blue coat and no hat, Collis English as wearing khaki-colored clothes, a short coat, with leggings or boots, with the trousers stuffed in the boots, and a cap with a peak. She guessed the men were about twenty years old. She remained insistent in her identification of McKinley Forrest, even though he was thirty-five years old, did not own a navy blue jacket, and could not write, even his name, so could not have signed the receipt for money returned to him.[16]

Assistant Prosecutor Frank Lawton, a tall, blond man going bald prematurely, with a wispy mustache and excellent tailoring, began his line of questioning. He assisted Volpe throughout all trials and appeals of the Six and at this point brought forward the patrolmen who participated in the events of January 27. Officer Arthur Dennis explained that he helped carry William Horner to the front of the store where he could be put on a stretcher, then returned to the tiny back room to locate and examine the apparent murder weapon. He discovered a full green bottle of Step-Up soda lying on the mattress, plus pieces of a brown soda bottle lying scattered on the floor. He gave all of these to police Detective William Stanley who placed them in an evidence bag.[17]

Lawton called cigar salesman Frank A. Eldracher to the witness stand. Eldracher had seen "two colored fellows" come out of the Horner store. The first he described as about his height, light complexioned, wearing a short gray jacket, something like an army jacket, and wearing a cap. The second, whom he described as a little taller and a little darker, emerged from the store in a leisurely manner, carefully turning around and closing the door. He thought they must be purchasing furniture and ceased paying attention to them as they slowly walked up North Broad Street. A minute or two later he heard someone screaming for help, observed Elizabeth Horner slumped in the door of the Horner store, face covered in blood, and ran to get the policeman he had earlier observed nearby. Defense attorney Katzenbach asked him about the ages of the two men; Eldracher thought they looked between twenty and thirty years of age.[18]

Detective Donald F. Toft testified that as a result of speaking with Frank Eldracher he called in a general alarm for police to be on the alert for the two men seen leaving the store. He then interrogated Mrs. Horner at the hospital and sent out a teletype, an eight-state alarm, for the apprehension of three men. After receiving further information from her, he went to the Horner living quarters above the store and retrieved a receipt that she had placed on a nail above the kitchen table. "From other information I received as to the name on the receipt, I was given the name of Jessop or Jessam—the name on that receipt is not legible; I went through our files to determine who this Jessop or Jessam was, but had no success in that line."[19]

FRIDAY, JUNE 18, 1948

Prosecutor Volpe began the day with testimony by Dr. Edmund R. Cytowic, an intern at McKinley Memorial Hospital who treated Mrs. Horner. The doctor described her injuries, including the fact that her left eye was completely closed and her right eye partially so. On cross-examination Waldron brought out that her vision had improved by the time she left the hospital, as the swelling had gone down. Katzenbach asked if she could recognize shapes and objects, and Dr. Cytowic answered that she could.[20]

Detective William T. Stanley took the witness stand to describe his participation at the crime scene. Volpe offered the full soda bottle and the broken bottle for identification and Stanley testified that he had taken them to the Identification Bureau at police headquarters. During cross-examination Katzenbach asked about the description of the suspects given to Stanley by Mrs. Horner. Volpe objected, saying such information would be hearsay testimony. The judge sustained Volpe's objection and Katzenbach did not get the description.[21]

Volpe then questioned Patrolman Michael LaRossa, who was called to the scene at 11:00 A.M. on January 27. He had been assigned to scour the neighborhood in search of a place that sold Step-Up soda. He found one such location, the New Life Restaurant at North Broad Street and Perry. Defense lawyer Katzenbach objected to this testimony: "If Mrs. Kokenakes [proprietor of the New Life Restaurant] can say she sold Step-Up to any of the defendants here sitting at this table, it may have some bearing on their guilt or innocence. But the fact that they sell Step-Up in that store has no effect on this case. And I really seriously press this point." Judge Hutchinson responded, "The testimony is admitted, and the objection is overruled." Mrs. Agnes Kokenakes sold two bottles of soda to two African Americans, whom she said she would not recognize as she paid no attention to their appearance.[22]

Sergeant Laurence A. Bloking, questioned by Assistant Prosecutor Lawton, described going through Mr. Horner's pockets in the presence of Acting Captain Delate and Police Clerk Henry W. Miller as the man lay unconscious at Mercer Hospital. Bloking found a roll of bills in the left trouser pocket and another in the left hip pocket. He also found some coins and cuff links with a small diamond chip in the center. The money totaled $1,642, which he then gave to Acting Captain Delate. Defense attorney Waldron brought out the fact that the money found in each pocket was still neatly folded in an orderly fashion.[23]

Lawton called Patrolman James A. Connor to the stand and turned the testimony toward Collis English. At 5:30 P.M. on February 6 he had arrived at 247 Church Street, the home of Collis English. Mrs. Emma English, Collis's mother, told Connor to come back later when Collis would be home, so Connor returned at 8:30 P.M. At that time he placed English under arrest and sent him in the wagon to police headquarters. Defense lawyer Turp made clear that Connor had no warrant for English's arrest. Lawton maintained that a warrant was unnecessary for Connor to bring English in for investigation.[24]

Next Volpe called Patrolman Nicholas Lichtfuhs to the stand. Lichtfuhs questioned English from the time of his arrival at police headquarters at 8:30 P.M. until 11:00 P.M. that evening. Lichtfuhs's testimony led to a confrontation between Volpe and the defense lawyers over the admissibility of the statements, oral and written, made by the defendants while in the Chancery Lane First Precinct police station. Katzenbach emphasized to Judge Hutchinson, after Hutchinson's ruling that the jury could stay and hear the testimony: "The practice has always been to exert discretion in favor of 'Out of the jury hearing' to determine the voluntary character. Now my experience, I admit, has been limited, but insofar as I have had any experience in such matters, I can't recall a single case where the motion has been denied." The judge responded, "Well, I do, I can recall cases. It is within the sound discretion of the Court, and is, of course, reviewable only for abuse of that discretion; at this time I can see no injury to the defendants as a result of its being heard; that is, the testimony being heard before the jury. You may proceed."[25] Thus Judge Hutchinson ruled that the prosecution could present the testimony regarding police questioning and the subsequent confessions without deciding first whether the confessions had been voluntary and were thus admissible into evidence.

When Lichtfuhs questioned English at police headquarters, English had explained, "I think my father is having me brought in here for using his car without his consent." He elaborated that he went to Robbinsville with Ralph Cooper two or three times a week to get potatoes, which Cooper brought into the city to sell. Lichtfuhs told English, "Collis, you are not telling me everything I want to know, and there is only you and I here, you can tell me what you want to, or you don't have to tell me a thing, you can suit yourself, but—I says: I would advise you to tell me anything you want to tell me, or just stop lying about anything." Patrolman Amman then entered the room. He asked "You know me, don't you, Collis? I know your family." And he said, "Yes." Then Amman asked "Didn't you hit that woman on North Broad Street? Collis English replied, "I did not hit the woman." Patrolman Amman continued, "Well, then, you hit the man." English said: "I did not hit anybody." Lichtfuhs and Amman then decided to call in a sergeant in order to have him hear this line of questioning.[26]

At this point defense lawyer Turp could contain himself no longer: "If your Honor please, we are getting in all the evidence before we hear whether it was voluntarily made or involuntarily, before that decision is made. There is no statement here that he was apprised of his rights or anything of that kind. We have only at the present time that he was taken there without any warrant, and nothing that he was appraised of his rights." Volpe responded, "There is nothing in the world which says that a Police Officer must caution in any way."[27] In 1948, courts made the assumption, correctly or not, that suspects knew they had the right to remain silent and the right to an attorney. It was not until the 1963 case of *Miranda v. Arizona* that the U.S. Supreme Court made clear that suspects needed to be told the following, in these or similar words: "You have the right to remain silent. Anything you say can and will be used against you in a court of law. You have the right to speak to an attorney, and to have an attorney present during any questioning. If you cannot afford a lawyer, one will be provided for you at government expense."[28] It is doubtful that Collis English knew of his constitutional rights, and Lichtfuhs made no effort to invoke them. Turp and Volpe repeatedly sparred over the rights issue as Lichtfuhs's testimony continued. When Volpe asked if he had cautioned English in any way before talking to him, Lichtfuhs responded, "He was only asked by me to tell the truth, and he was promised nothing in return for what he said. I said: 'If you are going to tell me a lot of lies, you don't have to tell me anything.'" Volpe asked if the witness was cooperative, and Lichtfuhs responded: "He answered the questions readily and willingly, but they were mostly lies." At this both Katzenbach and Turp leapt to their feet, objecting vehemently. Judge Hutchinson agreed that the answer should be stricken, while Turp commented, "He didn't say what you wanted him to say, isn't that it?"[29]

After further objections from Turp, Volpe suggested a recess to consider the question of the witness statements, saying that arguments made in front of a jury could be prejudicial. Judge Hutchinson agreed to a recess, and when he and the lawyers emerged, he ruled, "The Court can see the possibilities of danger in hearing the question as to the voluntary or involuntary character of any admissions or statements that may be offered—by testimony or in written form—before the jury. The danger being that some improper prejudice might be caused to the defendants or some of them. And so at this point the jury will be excluded until sent for. It is unfortunate, but it seems to be necessary."[30] The jury left the court on June 18; it did not return until July 5, and members stayed sequestered at the Hotel Hildebrandt. In its coverage of the case, the *Trenton Evening Times* revealed that the jury was typically taken out of town for lunch on Saturday, and went on sightseeing excursions on Sunday. Strictly guarded by sheriff's aides, jury members could play cards and listen to the radio, but the radio selections were carefully monitored.[31]

MONDAY, JUNE 21, 1948

When court resumed without the jury, Turp brought up a new defense objection to the statements: when the defendants referred to each other, that testimony would be hearsay and should not be admitted. Judge Hutchinson overruled this objection and Lichtfuhs finished his testimony.[32] Defense lawyer Waldron then cited rulings by the U.S. Supreme Court on the application of the Due Process Clause of the Fourteenth Amendment. The Fourteenth Amendment, enacted after the Civil War, articulates, "No State shall make or enforce any law which shall abridge the privileges or immunities of citizens of the United States; nor shall any State deprive any person of life, liberty, or property, without due process of law; nor deny to any person within its jurisdiction the equal protection of the laws."[33] The clause "without due process of law" has provoked much litigation. Quoting Justice Felix Frankfurter, Waldron stated, "Legislation throughout

the country reflects a similar belief that detention for purposes of elic-
iting confessions through secret, persistent, long-continued interrogation
violated sentiments deeply imbedded in the feelings of our people." He also
quoted Justice William O. Douglas: "The Fourteenth Amendment prohibits
the police from using the private, secret custody of either man or child as a
device for wringing confessions from them."[34] The defendants' lawyers were
thus arguing that their clients' rights under the Fourteenth Amendment
had been violated by the Trenton police.

JUNE 22, 1948–JUNE 25, 1948

In the absence of the jury, Prosecutor Volpe continued to lead policemen
through their stories. Defense lawyer Turp, during his cross-examination
of Acting Police Captain Andrew F. Delate, attempted to demonstrate that
police officers concocted a story that they then presented to Collis English.
Turp summarized: "Collis English was arrested on the sixth, Friday night,
and Friday night he was questioned and taken out to Robbinsville, and
with practically no sleep, or very little rest, very little, and he was brought
back from Robbinsville; he went there on two trips, and he was brought
back from Robbinsville Saturday morning, and he was taken right in and
right away started being questioned again. And Saturday afternoon he was
questioned, and then this gentleman says he was not questioned Saturday
night. And Sunday morning this gentleman says he told him the story. And
then the man admitted. Now, if this has no bearing on the voluntariness, I
missed the point." Judge Hutchinson refused to allow the attorneys to question Acting Captain Delate about whether he and other officers together
had formulated a story.[35] Throughout the trial Hutchinson appeared, at
times, to be protective of the prosecution and the police. Further in this
cross-examination, Turp pointed out that when Cooper's statement was
taken there were at least seven police officers present, the obvious purpose
being to intimidate Cooper.[36]

Prosecutor Volpe wished to introduce mug shots of each defendant and
link them to each witness's statement. Presumably the mug shots, always
unflattering, made the men look like typical criminals, an association Volpe
wished to encourage. Katzenbach called them unnecessary and highly prejudicial; he declared, "If these pictures are waved in front of the jurors I will
move for a mistrial." Judge Hutchinson dismissed Katzenbach's argument
as "untimely and premature."[37]

JUNE 28, 1948–JULY 2, 1948

On Monday morning, still without the jury, Volpe called each of the Six to the witness stand to tell the stories of their arrest and the taking of their statements. Trenton was sweltering during a heat wave, and people in the courtroom baked as the hot sun streamed through the windows, to the point that Judge Hutchinson told witnesses they could remove their suit jackets.[38]

During his questioning of Ralph Cooper, Volpe reintroduced the police photos taken of the Horner store. Earlier, when questioning Collis English, Volpe had pointed out English's signature on the back of one of the photos. He asked Ralph Cooper about his signature on the back of a photo, presumably because this would somehow link Cooper to the store, and thus to the murder. At this point Turp began objecting strenuously: "We offered no objection [to the photos being entered into evidence] and we were told it was for the purpose of showing the store, that it was in for one purpose; and your Honor would not uphold the Prosecutor in misleading—." Volpe: "I have not misled anyone." Turp: "I say you have. The Prosecutor has misled us, if your Honor please—the Prosecutor either deliberately or otherwise misled us as to the introduction of these pictures. I claim that, if your Honor please, there was nothing said about the names on there, nothing said about them. They were not proved as being on there until English was on there and they started to mention it. That was the first intimation I had had, and now it comes up with Ralph Cooper. I had no intimation and there was no proof of any kind that it was the signature of these people, and now it is brought out, and it was not put in for that purpose. And I don't think the Court would encourage the Prosecutor—. . . I say deliberately or otherwise the Prosecutor has misled us." Volpe claimed he would never mislead the court and highly resented Turp's remarks. Turp responded: "Oh, we should have detected the trick?" Volpe: "I should not have to point it out to you." The next morning Judge Hutchinson overruled all objections, allowing the photographs with signatures into evidence.[39] After lunch the court moved to an air-conditioned room for the duration of the trial. Even in this cooler space, half the seats reserved for the public were often empty. Relatives and friends of the accused seemed to be the only ones interested in watching and listening day after day as the weeks passed.[40] The trial received no publicity outside Trenton, so no one else seemed to care what became of the six men.

After finishing with the Six, Prosecutor Volpe presented further police testimony. In the afternoon Judge Hutchinson heard objections to using the statements; the first objection was offered by Waldron on behalf of Collis English.[41] Waldron relied on the Fifth Amendment, which says no person shall be compelled to be a witness against himself. He summarized by saying, "The Supreme Court has, on constitutional grounds set aside convictions, both in the Federal and State courts, which were based upon confessions secured by protracted and repeated questioning of ignorant and untutored persons, in whose minds the power of officers was greatly magnified, or who have been unlawfully held incommunicado without advice of friends or counsel."[42] Waldron cited a number of specific cases that upheld his statement. The defense tried to demonstrate that the manner in which the men's confessions were obtained violated their rights under the Fifth Amendment.

Next, defense attorney Queen addressed the confession of Ralph Cooper, who claimed to have been repeatedly threatened. Queen also pointed out that nothing had been offered to connect Cooper with the crime other than his confession and that he been induced to smoke "reefers" until he signed the confession. Cooper claimed that Chief Detective Naples had told him that if he did not write what he was told it would not be good for him; thus his confession was produced by fear, rendering it inadmissible. Next Queen turned to defendant John MacKenzie, whose first statement denied all participation in the crime. Subsequently, he made a statement, under promises that things would "come out easy" for him, and, under the influence of drugs, he signed another statement, the one at issue.[43]

Defense lawyer Turp spoke on behalf of James Thorpe, stating that he concurred with legal arguments made by Waldron and Queen. Thorpe had testified that Chief Naples had told him to go ahead and talk and "it would be easier with him." Turp emphasized that this type of statement was used in the New Jersey case of *Roesel v. State*, in which it was ruled that such language made a confession invalid. Because Thorpe signed his statement even while saying it was not true, Turp pleaded with Judge Hutchinson: "It hardly appeared possible to me that people engaged in the prosecution of crime and taking statements from these people in communities would go ahead and permit a man to sign it when he says it is not true. That is the time when these people should have gotten up in arms and said 'If that is not true, you are not going to sign that statement,' especially people engaged in the prosecution of crime, whose duty it is to be fair and impartial, or at least fair." Turp concluded by pointing out that nothing except for their statements connected Thorpe, MacKenzie, or Cooper with Horner's murder.[44]

Katzenbach then spoke on behalf of his client, McKinley Forrest. He stressed that Forrest's statement could not be considered voluntary since he had been "in a mental state in which he had no understanding of his acts or statements or the questions propounded to him." He described McKinley as having an "attack of hysteria" that left him incapable of dealing with police questioning. Katzenbach concluded that Forrest's statement should not be admitted "because it is not even worth the paper that it is written upon."[45]

After a recess, Prosecutor Volpe asked for the admission of all oral and written statements made by the defendants "upon the ground that it [the prosecution] has proven every requisite necessary in accordance with the legal procedure, and requirements for the admission of such documents and statements." He told Judge Hutchinson that with six defendants involved, and a limited number of officers working on the case, it naturally took longer than if fewer defendants had been on trial. He denied that any of the six had been mistreated. He then quoted a court ruling that cautioning "was not required if the confession was not obtained by illegal practices."[46] He cited another ruling to the effect that defense counsel was not required for defendants when they decided whether to confess. He concluded that most of the court cases cited by defense counsel had been federal rulings, while he himself cited New Jersey decisions. Judge Hutchinson took all citations with him and recessed until the next Tuesday, allowing a day off for the Fourth of July.

The *Trenton Evening Times* reported on a different facet of the trial: the fast-growing expense. At a weekly meeting, the Mercer County Board of Freeholders unanimously passed an emergency appropriation of $50,000 to cover the cost of maintaining the jury, fees for witnesses, and paying defense counsel, commenting that these funds may be "only the beginning."[47]

TUESDAY, JULY 6, 1948

On Tuesday morning Judge Hutchinson ruled that all of the defendants' statements had been made voluntarily and would thus be admitted as evidence: "The statements have a far greater ring of truth than the testimony of defendants to disprove them." On the constitutional issues brought up by the defense, he found that the cases cited did not bear on the current trial. In response the defense attorneys asked that portions of the statements made by one defendant about another not be read to the jury, as those would be hearsay. Judge Hutchinson felt that this would not be possible but agreed to caution the jury, repeatedly if necessary, about the proper use of the statements. He then asked that the jury be returned. He explained to the jury that the defendants' statements would be admitted but "I caution and instruct you that when considering any of the statements, whether oral or written, you are to consider that portion only of each statement which relates to what each particular defendant making that statement says therein that he did or said." He also pointed out that Horace Wilson had made no statement and that any mention of him by the other defendants in their statements was to be disregarded. The trial resumed at the point it had stopped so abruptly two weeks earlier with Patrolman Lichtfuhs about to question Collis English.[48]

Lichtfuhs took the stand and Prosecutor Volpe led him through his paces, thus beginning the examination of the defendants' statements before the jury. Lichtfuhs explained that he had begun questioning English at about 8:30 P.M. on Friday, February 6, specifically about his use of his father's car. Patrolman Lou Amman came into the courtroom at 9:30 P.M. and asked, "Has Collis told you anything?" Lichtfuhs responded, "Nope, he told us something, but not just what we want to know." Amman accused English of hitting the woman on North Broad Street, and when he denied it Amman stated, "You must have hit the man," which English also denied. Lichtfuhs said he interrupted at that point to inform Collis, "Look, anything you tell us now is going to be of your own free will, because anything you say now is likely to be held against you later, at a trial if it goes to Court." (Lichtfuhs did not report this when he testified without the jury, but he apparently wished to assure the jury of his care of defendants' rights.) At this point in their questioning of English, Lichtfuhs and Amman called in Lieutenant Dawson and Sergeant Fagan and by 11:00 P.M. or so they had the following story, as related by Patrolman Lichtfuhs:

> The morning of January 27th, about 9:45, he told us he parked his car in front of the Alps [a restaurant], when he got out, and was told by Cooper to go into Klein's to get a watch for him, he was told by Mr. Klein that there was no watch for Cooper and Cooper would have to have a ticket if he did leave a watch there. And as he came out of the jewelry store he noticed three men come running from the furniture store towards his father's car, which at that time was parked in front of the furniture store, double parked. He told us that there was a colored man behind the wheel wearing a green coat whom he didn't know, with the motor running of the car. He said as he approached the car these men ran past him, pushed him aside, and started up the car towards Perry Street, made a left-hand turn on Perry Street to go east. We asked Collis English if he knew these

men. He said he recognized them to be Ralph Cooper, Spud Green, and Buddy Wilson. The next time he repeated the story he was dragged into the car; when they got to the red light at Stockton and Perry he asked them what was the matter; and he didn't know, they didn't tell him.[49]

After English indicated that Ralph Cooper and Buddy Wilson could be found at Flock's farm in Robbinsville, a group formed to apprehend them. At 12:30 A.M. Chief of Detectives Naples, Captain Ryan, Lieutenant Dawson, Sergeant Fagan, Patrolman Amman, Sergeant Creeden, and Patrolman Lichtfuhs departed in three cars. They got lost in heavy snow and returned to Chancery Lane First Precinct police station at about 2:45 A.M. They tried again to reach the farm at 5:00 A.M. and, when it was light, searched about fifteen of thirty or so bleak and tottering shacks in the area. Chief Detective Naples and others found and detained Ralph Cooper and Buddy Wilson in the second floor of Horace Wilson's cement-block house, and the cavalcade returned to the police station about 8:30 A.M. At 10:00 A.M. Lichtfuhs again questioned English, and at 1:00 P.M. he brought English to Acting Captain Delate's office, where Prosecutor Volpe, Assistant Prosecutor Lawton, Chief Detective Naples, Acting Captain Delate, Clerk Miller, and Sergeant Creeden all waited. Delate charged English with the robbery and murder of Horner at 213 North Broad Street.

At this time English agreed to make a statement. However, Acting Captain Delate interrupted him: "You are not telling us the truth, Collis. There's no use of telling us anything further, we don't want to hear anything more." Delate then asked, "Would you confront Ralph Cooper and tell us in front of him what you told us?" English agreed to do so, so Cooper was brought into the room. Lichtfuhs testified that English at that point said, "That's Ralph Cooper, he's the man that struck the woman." Then a patrolman brought Horace Wilson in and English stated, "That is Horace Wilson, that is not the Buddy Wilson I mean." At about noon on Saturday an officer finally returned English to his cell.[50] Thus, the police used one arrested man to accuse and confront the others, with English agreeing to accuse Cooper, but not Wilson.

Lichtfuhs explained that on the morning of Monday, February 9, Acting Captain Delate asked that Lichtfuhs handcuff himself to Collis English and be driven to the store at 213 North Broad Street. Clerk Miller removed the handcuffs and led English to the tiny room at the rear of the store so he could see the ancient, stained mattress where Mr. Horner had been lying, skull cracked and already swelling, left for dead. Then he indicated where Mrs. Horner had been found, screaming and bleeding, propped against the front door. Lichtfuhs again handcuffed himself to English and returned with him to the station Detention Room. At the end of his testimony, responding to questions by Volpe, Lichtfuhs testified that English had not been beaten and that no one had promised him anything in return for his statement, which he had given freely. Defense lawyer Turp led the cross-examination of Patrolman Lichtfuhs: "Then when Amman came in you told Amman, 'He's told us something [about going to Robbinsville for potatoes] but he hasn't told us yet what we want to know'?" "Yes, sir." "You had something specific that you wanted him to say, didn't you?" "I don't know that I wanted him to say anything specific, but I know what was in my mind and the way I was questioning him." Turp asked about solving the Horner murder: "Is that what you were interested in?" "I think every policeman in the department was interested in that, that's all we had in our mind."[51] Under Turp's questioning it became clear that the story of Spud Green and the others did not emerge until Patrolman Amman and Sergeant Creeden had both entered the room. Lichtfuhs described English as normal and calm until Patrolman Amman asked him about striking the woman, whereupon English "seemed to be uneasy and perspiring freely."[52]

WEDNESDAY, JULY 7, 1948

At Volpe's lead, Patrolman James E. Creeden described his time questioning English and noted that the statement was not yet successfully completed: "Acting Captain Delate said to Collis: 'Collis, you are not telling us the truth, at least not the whole truth, because that back door is nailed shut and no one could have gone out there.' And Collis hung his head and he indicated that he wasn't telling the truth."[53] When taken to the Horner store by police, English had obviously not noticed that no one could use the rear door.

Next, Patrolman Charles H. Dawson told of his taking over English's questioning at 11:00 P.M. on Friday, February 6. He explained that English gave him three different stories. "The first story he gave me was, he said he went into Klein's store to get a watch for a fellow by the name of Cooper, and when he came out to the car he had ridden there in, it was gone." He continued:

And I told him that it didn't sound right, why the car should have left him, and I asked him why, and then he turned around and changed his story, and he said that he ran after the car and he was pushed into the car. And I asked why he was pushed into the car, and then he turned around and told me a different story. And he said he was driving the car and three men came up the street and jumped into the car and he drove the three men up to the Swamp Angel and let them out. And he stated that one of the men had blood stains on his shirt and he found a blood-stained handkerchief in the car and he disposed of it in the garbage. He gave me three names. He gave me the name of Spud Green and a fellow by the name of Buddy Wilson and Ralph Cooper.[54]

After Dawson's testimony, Police Clerk Henry W. Miller took the stand. Well-spoken and still boyish-looking in middle age, Miller described the admissions that English made on Monday, February 9. English for the first time said he was at the store and when the police took him to the store he demonstrated how he had taken money from Mr. Horner's pockets.

Next Volpe turned his attention to the statement of James Thorpe, which was recorded the morning of Tuesday, February 10. Charged with murder, Thorpe responded, "All I can say is I didn't kill nobody." The gist of Thorpe's statement, as read in court by Clerk Miller, was that Thorpe was standing just inside the front door at the time of the murder. He had met Cooper, English, Wilson, and Forrest in Sam Cutter's saloon on Monday evening, January 26, to plan the crime, and English had asked him to be part of the group. "They talked about a man having a roll of money." After they hatched their plot in the saloon they drove to the store, where Wilson entered to ask about a mattress. They ultimately decided not to rob the place that day as there were many people in the area, plus a nearby traffic cop. Wilson came out and "said we would go back again tomorrow."

The statement continued with Thorpe waiting at the corner of State and Broad streets the next morning at 9:00 as English had instructed. English picked him up and they drove to the Horner store. English and Forrest went into the back room with Mr. Horner while Wilson talked to Mrs. Horner. Cooper stood near Wilson, and Thorpe remained at the door, making sure no one entered. Thorpe explained that when he heard the woman scream he ran out the front door to the car, with the others right behind him. English drove through East Trenton, letting the others out one at a time. Thorpe heard later, from his uncle, that a man had been killed in this store, but he did not go to the police because he was afraid to do so. Under questioning, he agreed that he could not read but could write his name "pretty good." He signed his statement on February 11, 1948, acknowledging that it was "a true, free and voluntary statement."[55]

Next Volpe asked Clerk Miller to read McKinley Forrest's statement, made on Tuesday, February 10. Miller had told Forrest of the charges against him and Forrest answered, "I didn't kill nobody. I hit him with a bottle over the head." Forrest did not join the others at Cutter's Saloon because he had just worked sixteen hours at Roebling. Instead they picked him up at Union and Fall streets, directly from the Roebling bus. Collis drove, and the other three present were "Ralph, Red, and Horace." After aimlessly milling around, they pulled up by the secondhand store. They all entered the store and Forrest, Cooper, and English went into the back with Mr. Horner. "Ralph told me to take the bottle out of my pocket. As I raised my hand to hit the man with the bottle, Horace Wilson grabbed my arm and helped me to bring the bottle down on the man's head. I'm not so sure which way he fell. I went in one of the pockets and Ralph went in the other. I got about $50 or something like that." They all raced out the door and into the car, with English driving. Forrest gave English half of the money and spent his own half. When asked if the bottle broke when he hit Horner with it, Forrest answered, "I don't remember. I let go of the bottle when Ralph said go for the pockets." When shown a bottle in evidence Forrest agreed, "It was shaped something like that." When shown photographs of Horner, and the back room, Forrest agreed that he recognized the individual he had hit and where it had been done. He further stated that he could not read or write and that the statement was true.[56]

THURSDAY, JULY 8, 1948

The day began with Clerk Miller again in the witness box, continuing to read the defendants' statements in a clear ringing voice.[57] Journalist William Reuben, observing the trial, felt that Police Clerk Miller "was the most effective, convincing, unshakeable and reliable witness to testify for the State."[58] First this day was Ralph Cooper's confession, made on February 10, 1948. Upon being officially charged with murder and asked, "What do you have to say to the above charge?" Cooper answered, "I'll tell you what I knows about it." He proceeded to relate that he called English at home on January 27 at 8:00 A.M. and asked him to go with him to State and Broad streets, to accompany him to the loan office. English instead asked Cooper to meet him at Perry and Broad streets at 9:00 A.M. English picked up Cooper first, driving his father's car; then they picked up Thorpe, Wilson, and Forrest. After driving around East Trenton they pulled up in front of the Horner store and went inside. Horace Wilson inquired about a mattress, and when Mrs. Horner turned around, "Horace Wilson struck her with a brick or a bottle or something which he had in a sock like. She screamed and fell. I looked around when she screamed and she was falling and I told Horace, 'You hit that lady and killed her.' Then I walked out of the store."[59] The others also hurried out of the store and got in the car. Cooper got in the back seat with Wilson, while English drove; Forrest sat next to him, and Thorpe next to Forrest. Then, Cooper said, "I laid down on the back seat and went to sleep and when they woke me up about 1:30 in the afternoon I was in front of 18 Sheridan Avenue. I got out of the car and went into the house and went to bed." All of the others were still in the car. Cooper ended by agreeing that he could read and write a little, and when he signed the statement, acknowledged it was a "true, free and voluntary statement."[60]

When Volpe finished questioning Miller about Cooper's statement, he turned to English's, whose story had changed greatly between the time he gave it on February 6 and when Miller typed it on February 10. According to English's statement, the four men—Thorpe, Wilson, Forrest and Cooper—planned the robbery together at Sam Cutter's saloon. The previous Friday Cooper and Wilson had been in the store to buy a mattress, but they didn't have enough money to place a deposit on it. On the day before the crime they went back, but too many people were around for them to carry out their plans. On the morning of the crime, English and Cooper picked up Forrest, Thorpe, and Wilson. They parked the car at 219 Broad Street, near the secondhand store. The others went into the store and English turned the car around, parking it across the street toward Battle Monument, near the Alps restaurant. According to English, "McKinley said to the old man, 'I want all the money you got.'" Horner was untying a mattress to show them when McKinley hit him on the head with a beer bottle he had gotten out of the back of the car. English claimed they were supposed to use the bottles as imitation guns in their pockets. At Wilson's order English went through Horner's right-hand pocket and got a few dollars, but "was too shaky" to do the other pocket. Wilson impatiently pushed him away, saying "Get out of here, you're too damn slow." According to English, "Wilson said he should hit me on the head too, and leave me there."[61]

English drove the car as it sped away; Thorpe and Cooper were up front with him and McKinley and Wilson were in the back. When they were in the car English reported this conversation: "After we got a little ways from the store Wilson said, 'What's the matter are you too yellow to go through a man's pockets.' I told him I didn't like going through anybody's pockets while they was unconscious. I told the other boys McKinley had hit the old man and I told McKinley I didn't like the idea of him hitting the old man. McKinley he gave me some money and Wilson he had a hand full of money all balled up. Wilson said 'If it was up to me, you wouldn't get nothing.'" In answer to the question "What did you do with the money McKinley gave you?" English answered, "I put some gas in the car and bought some beers and went to a couple of movies."[62] Upon being shown a photograph of a bottle used in the crime and photos of the store interior, English agreed that this was the weapon and the location of the crime. He acknowledged that he could read and write and that he signed the statement voluntarily.

When asked to do so by the prosecutor, Miller read the brief statement by Horace Wilson, which indicated he had not participated in the Horner crime.[63] Volpe came last to the statement of John MacKenzie, given on February 12, 1948. Upon being formally charged with the crime of murder, he agreed that he had been the lookout man. The others picked him up where he worked at the Community Slaughterhouse and drove around Trenton, finally ending up parked in front of the secondhand store. Cooper told MacKenzie to get out of the car and watch out for cops at the corner of Perry and Broad streets. When the others left the car MacKenzie saw Forrest and Cooper put soda bottles into their pockets. After serving as lookout man for ten minutes, MacKenzie walked back toward the Horner store. He noted three or four of the group rush out and get into the car. He witnessed the car driving up North Broad Street toward Battle Monument. MacKenzie walked back to work, arriving about 11:15 or 11:30 A.M. He never received any money from the robbery, from either McKinley Forrest or Collis English. After agreeing that he could read and write and that he had made the statement freely and voluntarily, MacKenzie signed it on February 13.[64]

During his cross-examination of Miller, Turp elicited the information that Ralph Cooper, while reading aloud the statement he supposedly had written, could not pronounce some of the words and had to have help.[65] It also became apparent that on February 12, MacKenzie had made a first statement denying any part in the crime. Then, at 10:00 o'clock that night he made another statement, the final one, in which he said he was the lookout.[66] Turp further extracted the fact that when Collis English was taken to the Horner store on the morning of February 9 he made no mention of McKinley Forrest being in the store.[67] After numerous questions to Police Clerk Miller, it became clear that Forrest, after emphatically denying any part in the crime on that same Monday morning, was confronted with Cooper and English, who both confirmed that he was the one who hit Mr.

Horner. Forrest responded loudly and disgustedly: "Blame it on me; I hit him. I didn't kill anybody. Let the other guys go. Blame it all on me."[68]

FRIDAY, JULY 9, 1948

Andrew F. Delate, graying, with glasses, spent the entire day on the witness stand, answering questions in such a low tone that Judge Hutchinson repeatedly asked him to speak up so the court reporter could hear. He had been acting captain of the Chancery Lane First Precinct police station at the time of the Horner murder but his rank was now reduced to lieutenant, although Judge Hutchinson continued to refer to him as captain. His testimony added some new pieces of information. When Thorpe was still insisting he had no part in the Horner crime, Delate related that one day while he was at the desk talking to the lieutenant on duty, Thorpe passed him, telling him, "Captain, those men in there are trying to frame me." Thorpe spoke of being confronted with Ralph Cooper and McKinley Forrest, who both insisted he had been involved.

Delate also disclosed that police brought Wilson in to be confronted by Cooper. Cooper insisted that Wilson had taken part in the crime, which Wilson adamantly denied. Cooper stated, "You are telling me you weren't there, have you got a twin brother?" Wilson answered, "Lord have mercy, I wasn't there."[69] In his cross-examination of Delate, Turp focused on the way police maneuvered to obtain the men's statements: "That is the way the statements were gotten, as a matter of fact, isn't it, Captain: by telling each other what the other had said and telling or at least suggesting them the stories?" Answer: "That's the way the statements were gotten: by confronting one another with them."[70]

Katzenbach now took his turn cross-examining Delate: "As acting captain was it your duty to take over homicides?" Answering somewhat bitterly: "Was it mine? No, it was not, to tell you the truth. It's the captain of detectives job to do that. But it was wished on me, Mr. Katzenbach."[71] Delate thus indicated some possible tension within the Trenton Police Department.

MONDAY, JULY 12, 1948

Court opened late due to the illness of one of the jurors, Mrs. Lola A. Knoblauch. Her physician advised Judge Hutchinson that she should not continue as a juror, so the sequestered group became thirteen in number, reduced from fourteen, which had included two alternates. As Mrs. Knoblauch left, Sheriff

Sido L. Ridolfi told her to speak to no one about the trial.[72] Then Katzenbach continued his cross-examination of Acting Captain Delate regarding the timing of the signing and witnessing of the statements: "They were not read to them and signed until late at night, were they?" "That's right, yes." "And the process went into the early hours of the morning?" "That's right." "Was there any particular business of the police department on the following day which might have interfered with your taking the signatures the following day?" "No, sir."[73]

Katzenbach then attempted to question Delate on the possible innocence of the suspects, but repeated objections from Volpe made this difficult. Katzenbach: "If you took a statement from them, and it indicated so far as important details are concerned, that they didn't know the scene, didn't know what must have happened, you could believe only two things, couldn't you: one, they weren't telling the truth; or else they weren't there, and they were innocent?" Then followed objection and discussion between the judge and prosecutor. Questioning continued: "Now, as a matter of fact, when Collis English was first being questioned and made a statement, which only occupied one sheet of paper, he stated certain things in there which didn't check, isn't that so?" "That's right." "He told you that he, or somebody else, went out the back door; and you knew it was locked, and you knew that detail was wrong. Now that could have indicated to you either that he didn't know the place he was in, and therefore had not been there, or else that he was holding out on you and wasn't telling you the truth, one or the other?" "That is true." "And you decided that he wasn't telling you the truth?" "That's right." "Your duty is to bring persons to the bar of justice who have committed crimes?" "That's right." "It is also to eliminate the innocent, isn't it?" "That's right." "So if you had been convinced that Collis English as a matter of fact didn't know anything about the details of how this crime was committed or the inside of the place you would have thought you had the wrong man, wouldn't you?" "If I was convinced? Yes. I would. But I wasn't convinced."[74]

After further discussion with Judge Hutchinson, Katzenbach explained what he wished to accomplish: "My suggestion is that I can demonstrably prove that many of these men should have been eliminated because they didn't know the details." Judge Hutchinson: "Well, their statements speak for themselves, don't they, Judge?" (Since Katzenbach had previously been a judge, Hutchinson used his former title when addressing him.) Katzenbach responded: "And I also want to show that they didn't even question some of these people about some of the important details which might have eliminated them." Katzenbach then assured Judge Hutchinson that he would "try to shorten it up as much as possible."[75] He questioned Delate about the variety of implements apparently used in the attack. Different statements included a beer bottle, a Seven-Up bottle, and a Step- Up bottle, all different in shape and color, in a sock or not, perhaps even a brick. Delate agreed that this was true. "Then you saw no details in these various statements which were so conflicting and so important that you felt the matter should be re-investigated after these statements were made?" Said Delate, "Mr. Katzenbach, whether I did or not, I couldn't eliminate anyone." Then Judge Hutchinson: "The question was not that. The question was whether you did." Delate: "No, I did not."[76] Next Katzenbach asked Delate about two possible witnesses: Mrs. Kokenakes, the woman who sold two bottles of Step-Up soda shortly before the murder, and the cigar salesman, Fred Eldracher. Delate agreed that police had taken neither witness to the Chancery Lane First Precinct police station to look at the six men. Additionally, Katzenbach pointed out that the patrolman on the corner, Fred Sigafoos, had never been asked if he could recognize John MacKenzie, the supposed lookout man. Police also never brought Mrs. Virginia Barclay, who witnessed the flight of the men and car, to see if she could identify any of the Six.[77]

The major witness of the afternoon was Dr. James Minor Sullivan III, a young Negro physician in Trenton who had been called to the First District police station on February 10, 1948, by Prosecutor Volpe. Dr. Sullivan had asked a local political character, also black, Peyton "Scrappy" Manning, to accompany him. Dr. Sullivan may not have realized that Scrappy knew both Prosecutor Volpe and Acting Captain Delate quite well. They arrived about 11:00 P.M. as requested. Police took Dr. Sullivan to Acting Captain Delate's office, where Detective Toft, Detective Stanley, Prosecutor Volpe, Assistant Prosecutor Lawton, Clerk Miller, and two other physicians, George A. Corio and a Dr. Cardelia, as well as Chief Detective Naples were present, in a room described under cross-examination as being only about five feet by nine feet. All had copies of the defendants' statements. A turnkey brought in James Thorpe, and his statement was read to him. Dr. Sullivan then asked Thorpe if he had had any part in the crime of which he was being accused. He said no. Dr. Sullivan asked if he had been mistreated or beaten. Sullivan recounted, "I asked if he had been denied food or kept awake, denied cigarettes if he smoked. And he said no. I think I recall asking him if he wasn't guilty of this—of the crime why was he going to sign the statement. To which he said well, he would get a few days and serve out his time. And then I told him this wasn't just a few days, this was murder, and he didn't have to sign it. At that, I believe the Prosecutor arose and said 'We aren't making any promises here. You sign this of your own free will' or something of that effect." Thorpe then signed the confession.[78] Dr. Sullivan, assisted by Dr. Corio, who was a close personal friend of Prosecutor Volpe and a member of the New Jersey State Boxing Commission, then gave Thorpe a physical exam, especially looking to see if he had any marks or bruises from having been beaten.[79] He found none.

The same procedure was followed with Collis English. Dr. Sullivan asked him if he had had any part in the crime of which he was accused, and English replied that he had. Sullivan asked if he had adequate food, sleep, and cigarettes, and English signed the statement. Dr. Sullivan then gave him a physical exam, noting that he had a heart murmur. McKinley Forrest appeared next, answered questions, signed his statement, and had a physical exam. Ralph Cooper read his own statement, answered questions, and signed his statement. Dr. Sullivan noted that Cooper's eyes appeared red and that he seemed drowsy. Next the turnkey brought in Horace Wilson; his statement of innocence was read to him and he signed it. Dr. Sullivan then questioned and examined him. The session ended at 2:30 A.M. on February 11, 1948. On February 12 at 11:30 P.M. police recalled Sullivan to go through the same procedure with John MacKenzie. The identical cast of characters observed as Dr. Sullivan asked questions and MacKenzie agreed that he had been treated properly.[80]

TUESDAY, JULY 13, 1948

Dr. Sullivan returned to the witness stand for cross-examination. Defense lawyer Turp extracted the information that Thorpe had said he was afraid and when Sullivan asked him what he was afraid of, he answered "Of the boys." Turp did not pursue this answer.[81] Turp then asked Dr. Sullivan if he remembered the day, April 1, when Mr. Katzenbach, Mr. Waldron, Mr. Queen, and himself visited with Dr. Sullivan in Queen's office. During the interview Turp asked him about the purpose of his presence at the police station: "I thought my purpose was that I would be asked [sic] concerning the health mainly, and I didn't know about all these other questions. I was surprised to be a trial witness at all." Turp made certain the jury realized that the city of Trenton was Dr. Sullivan's employer.[82]

Next, McKinley Forrest's lawyer, Katzenbach, questioned Dr. Sullivan specifically about his client,. He carefully drew a description from Dr. Sullivan that Forrest was nervous, in a state of excitement, with his hands shaking so badly that he needed help in removing his clothes for the physical exam. No one had told Dr. Sullivan that a physician had been called in for Forrest earlier in the day.[83]

Dr. Corio, the City Poor physician, took his place on the stand to relate the same events described by Dr. Sullivan. He, too, had been invited to be present by Prosecutor Volpe. Dr. Corio never addressed the defendants, but he did assist in the physical exams. He recalled Dr. Sullivan saying to defendant Thorpe, "Do you know if you sign this statement that you're liable to get the electric chair?" Thorpe had just mumbled something in response.[84] Dr. Corio described Collis English as having "a marked heart condition. A marked murmur. And I believe in questioning, I believe he gave a history of a rheumatic condition. But he had a very bad heart condition."[85] During cross-examination by Turp, Dr. Corio explained his understanding of why he was called in that night. "For a two-fold purpose, to my knowledge, by the Prosecutor. One, to see these men were not physically or mentally tortured into signing these confessions. That was one. And, secondly, to see if there was any evidence of any physical violence or mental torture. That was the two-fold purpose."[86]

Frank A. Naples, chief of county detectives for five years, with twenty-five years experience as a detective, came next. At fifty-one years of age, he was described as having the manner of a mafia crime boss rather than an officer of the law.[87] Assistant Prosecutor Lawson took him through his litany, as he described the questioning of the defendants in the same way those in the courtroom had heard many times previously. He did elaborate on Wilson's comment when Wilson was confronted with Cooper insisting that Wilson had taken part in the crime. Naples described Wilson as exclaiming: "Mercy—God have mercy on my soul. I wouldn't kill no white man."[88]

Defense lawyer Katzenbach, during his cross-examination of Naples, worked to bring out further discrepancies in the statements. Initial information had been that only one individual had hit Mr. Horner with a bottle, but Collis English said both Wilson and Cooper had hit him. English had originally indicated the involvement of a Spud Green but quit mentioning him in favor of Wilson and Cooper. Naples resolutely denied that the search in Robbinsville was for a Buddy Wilson and said he never heard Horace explain that he was not Buddy Wilson, but Horace Wilson, even though he was the first inside the tiny home in Robbinsville. Naples agreed that "everybody got put in the crime as a result of something that English said." Katzenbach showed that English put Forrest, Cooper, Wilson, and Thorpe all in the Horner store with himself, thus five people total. But it took twenty-nine questions by Katzenbach, interrupted repeatedly by objections from Assistant Prosecutor Lawton, before Katzenbach got Naples to answer "How many people did witnesses say were in the store?" Answer: "I was told by Lieutenant Delate of three."[89]

Having finally achieved this point, Katzenbach asked, "You were so interested in getting confessions or statements or implications that you didn't check to see if any of these descriptions fitted any of these men, did you?" "Yes, I checked—we did, rather." "And you found they didn't jibe with the descriptions you had received from Mrs. Horner; did you?" "No, they did not."[90] Driving this point home, he further inquired: "Did you do anything to check on these various statements which you had gotten, you and your assistants, in this investigation to find out if it couldn't be the fact that some of them weren't true?" "After the statements were obtained I don't think there were stronger statements made." "This is your own personal opinion, isn't it?" "Well, that's how we work." Judge Hutchinson then asked a question, very unusual for him: "The question is: what did you do, Chief, to find out whether they were true in fact after you got them?" "There wasn't nothing we could do: we had the six implicated." Judge Hutchinson: "That is the answer, I guess: you didn't do anything. A long time reaching that point."[91]

Katzenbach then asked what actions Naples took when the men all denied having anything to do with the crime: "Aside from the fact that somebody else whom you had questioned before implicated them, you had no particular reason to believe that the person who denied it was not telling truth, isn't that so?" "That's right." "So then you sent them back to the cell and told them to think it over; isn't that about right?" "That's right." "And you didn't say whether they would have to think it over for just that day or for the next week, or for the next year; did you?"[92] The Six had no knowledge of their legal rights, and as far as they knew, could simply be locked up forever. Katzenbach also clarified that Chief Naples remained at the station for four straight days and nights while detaining and questioning the first five men.[93]

WEDNESDAY, JULY 14, 1948

On this last day of the prosecution's case, Chief of Detectives Naples returned to the witness stand to be cross-examined by defense lawyer Turp.[94] Turp wrested from Naples the fact that although others had done the questioning of the six men, Naples had been alone with Ralph Cooper for twenty minutes right before Cooper decided to write out his testimony. This was at lunch time, and Naples provided Cooper with lunch and cigarettes. In fact, Naples himself provided "plenty of cigarettes" for the men. He was also alone with Thorpe right before Thorpe decided to sign his statement. Turp asked what the men slept on in the cells, learning that it was a plain, unadorned board. They were taken from the cells repeatedly, day and night, for their questioning. Turp also brought forth from Naples that when English provided the story of meeting to plan the robbery in Sam Cutter's Saloon, he was alone with Chief Detective Naples.[95] Turp's very last question concerned fingerprint evidence on the bottles used in the murder. Naples said that no prints could have been obtained since the men stated they had used a sock over the bottles; however, no sock had been found at the crime scene.[96]

Naples's testimony ended the case brought by the state against the six defendants. However, the defense had a plan ready to go. Defense lawyer Turp rose, stating, "I move for the direction of a verdict on behalf of all of the defendants on the ground that the corpus delicti has not been proved sufficiently." In other words, he claimed that the state had not proven that the crime of robbery had actually taken place. He further quoted a New Jersey case that showed that "so many people confess to crimes that they do not do, that as a simple precaution the Court in this State adopted a rule they would not convict a man on the confession alone, unless there is proof of a corpus delicti independent of the confession." Turp pointed out the obvious discrepancies among the statements, and the apparent weakness of Mrs. Horner's eyewitness testimony. Defense lawyer Katzenbach then added that the main evidence, the confessions, were not obtained with suitable regard for the Fourteenth and Fifth amendments of the U.S. Constitution, and thus the rights of the six men had been violated.[97] Prosecutor Volpe responded forcefully, indicating that the state had proven all elements successfully and sufficiently.[98] Judge Hutchinson denied all motions. It appeared to some observers watching the trial over many weeks that Judge Hutchinson favored the prosecution over the defense in his rulings, tilting the balance in its favor. At this point in the proceedings, the main focus of the prosecution's presentation to the jury was the confessions of all the men but Horace Wilson, making the case look very bad for the defendants. On July 14 the state rested its case. The Six would finally have the opportunity to tell their side of the story.

CHAPTER 3

THE TRIAL, DEFENSE

After a month of stifling days in court listening to Prosecutor Volpe, Chief Detective Frank Naples, and Police Clerk Henry Miller, the time finally came for the Trenton Six to tell their stories, both about their actions on January 27 and about their questioning at the Chancery Lane First Precinct police station. The defense began by putting Horace Wilson on the witness stand to be questioned by defense lawyer James S. Turp. Turp established that Wilson came north in July 1939, having lived in South Carolina until then. In 1948 he was thirty-seven years old, could not read, and wrote only his name. Since coming north he had worked on farms outside Trenton, harvesting wheat, rye, potatoes, tomatoes, corn, and cauliflower. Members of the court and jury had difficulty understanding him, and Turp repeatedly asked him to speak both more loudly and more slowly. Turp took Wilson through each element of the crime, asking the defendant if he was there, took part in the crime, hit Mrs. Horner; each time Wilson firmly answered "No, sir." Then Turp went through each statement made about Wilson by the others, with Wilson emphatically denying all of them.

Next his counsel led Wilson through his day on January 27, 1948. Wilson explained that he had been working in Robbinsville at the Edward Dilatush Company, under the supervision of foreman Johnny Murphy from 8:30 A.M. to 12:30 P.M. Under Turp's continued probing he revealed that he first met Ralph Cooper and Collis English at his house on January 27 at approximately 1:30 P.M. when he went home for lunch and found them there, visiting Leanna Turner. He saw them again on January 30 when they returned to the house. He had never met McKinley Forrest, James Thorpe, or John MacKenzie before his arrest. Now Turp focused on what occurred when Chief of Detectives Frank Naples arrested him. As Wilson told it: "Well, they come in the house and stood and looked at me and asked what my name—was my name Buddy Wilson. I said 'No, Sir, my name is Horace Wilson.'" According to Wilson, Naples replied: "Yes, you are the man, Buddy Wilson; get up and get dressed, and give me the pistol you got." Wilson denied having a pistol; police searched the house and found no weapon. Naples made no answer when Wilson questioned why he needed to get dressed, where he was being taken, and what he was accused of. Wilson heard someone yell toward the police cars parked outside "Is this the man?" but could not understand the answer. He did hear someone say "Bring them along; we will take them anyway."[1]

Turp led Wilson through the story of his questioning at the Chancery Lane First Precinct police station by Naples, Prosecutor Volpe, Assistant Prosecutor Lawton, Acting Captain Delate, and Clerk Miller, at about 10:30 A.M., regarding the murder on Broad Street. Wilson explained, "Captain Delate, he told me: 'Yes, you was there.' So Clerk Miller said: 'Why don't you go on and tell the truth? That English, he has already put you in it, why don't you tell the truth.' And I said: 'English couldn't put me in no thing. I don't know nothing about it.'" Delate responded, "Take him back to the cell, he ain't doing nothing but lying. I don't believe anything he said."[2]

At about noon police took Wilson from his cell and brought him to Acting Captain Delate's office for further questioning. Chief Detective Naples asked Wilson where he had been on Monday and Tuesday. Thinking he meant the previous Monday and Tuesday, Wilson told him he was working for Mr. Koppel. They then returned Wilson to his cell, taking him out briefly in the afternoon to be fingerprinted. The rest of that weekend police left him alone. On Monday the same group questioned him at about 11:30 A.M., 5:00 P.M., and 10:00 P.M. They confronted him again at 9:30 A.M. on Tuesday, at 7:00 P.M., and then late on Tuesday evening, into Wednesday morning. He told the court about his examination by Dr. Sullivan and that he signed a statement saying that he was not guilty.[3]

THURSDAY, JULY 15, 1948

Volpe began the by day cross-examining Horace Wilson, starting with the initial questioning on Saturday morning. Wilson explained that Volpe himself "cussed and stomped up and down—. You told me I wasn't doing nothing but telling lies. You said I was as lying a son-of-a-bitch as you have ever seen." Then Clerk Miller said, "He is lying, you can tell by the way he is sweating." Wilson didn't want to use Miller's words in court, as the language was not proper, but Volpe persisted, so Wilson quoted Miller as calling him "a lousy cock-sucker."[4] This evoked an audible gasp from the jury and precipitated an uproar in the courtroom. Spectators broke into conversation, causing court attendants to rush throughout the room demanding quiet.[5] Volpe then asked Wilson to go through details of his questioning, which days, what times, and what was said by whom, pointing out when he told the story differently than the day before. Wilson explained, "There was so many times—I can't remember every time, just over and over, I can't remember."[6]

Volpe then turned to Wilson's conversation with Dr. Sullivan: "Well, Dr. Sullivan asked me was I in with the boys on the Horner murder case. I told him no, I wasn't. He asked me why the boys would put me in it if I wasn't there. I told him I don't know, I only know the boys said back in the cell they were whipped and made to say that."[7]

When Volpe finished with Wilson, Turp introduced Wilson's defense witnesses. First on the stand was John M. Murphy, his supervisor. Murphy stated that Wilson had worked from 8:00 A.M. to noon on January 26 and 27. Wilson had worked for the company for five or six years, hired as an extra man when needed. The prosecution had taken the foreman's hourly work record from him on February 16 and kept it. Turp asked Murphy to look at the book: "Now, is the book in the same condition that it was in when you gave it to the Prosecutor, having particular reference to either the 26th or the 27th record?" His answer: "It has been marked, or something, on the 27th." Murphy indicated a mark in red, plus something that looked like an erasure, that had not been present originally.[8] Under cross-examination by Volpe, Murphy revealed that the actual work record did not indicate what hours a person worked, just the number of hours. Thus, Horace Wilson could conceivably have had time both to murder William Horner and work four hours for Murphy.

FRIDAY, JULY 16, 1948

Turp continued to call defense witnesses for Wilson. He began with Verona M. Carheart, the pay clerk at Dilatush. She testified that she herself had paid Horace Wilson for his work on January 26 and January 27, in cash, at the rate of seventy-five cents an hour. Under cross-examination she stated that the potatoes had been loaded in the morning of January 27, but she admitted that she did not personally see them being loaded.[9] Farmer Ural Koppel testified that Wilson frequently worked for him, especially in the afternoons, including the afternoon of January 27, when he worked from 1:00 to 3:30. However, his records indicated simply two and one-half hours worked, not the actual times. In response to Turp's question, he answered that he had never heard Horace Wilson referred to as Buddy Wilson in the eight years he had known him.[10] Elmer R. H. Hutchinson, owner of two farms in Robbinsville, stated that he worked directly with all the men he hired and that Wilson was a good worker and respected in the community.[11]

Evelyn Smith, the final witness for Horace Wilson, explained that while she knew Ralph Cooper, Horace had not known Ralph Cooper or Collis English until they visited him in Robbinsville. On the day police arrested Wilson and Cooper, Evelyn explained what Chief Detective Naples told her and Leanna Turner, "If you will tell the truth, you won't go to jail; if you don't tell the truth, we will haul you both in jail. Horace has a gun, and some of the children are likely to get hurt." Evelyn protested that she had never seen a gun in the home, but Naples insisted that they look for it; none was found.[12]

With Wilson's defense concluded, James Waldron began the defense of Collis English, taking him carefully through his story. At the beginning of his testimony, English's soft speech differed from that of the other defendants, being more grammatically correct. The Trenton-born English had the advantage of a tenth-grade education; he had left school to help his mother, who had had a stroke and could not continue her work taking in laundry by herself. However, as his testimony continued and he described what happened to him at the Chancery Lane First Precinct police station, his speech increasingly resembled that of the other five. His veneer of education slipped as his fear increased. Waldron took English slowly through the events of the morning of January 27, 1948, in which he had assisted his mother with the weekly laundry she took in and then cashed his disability check, which he received for the heart condition that resulted from a bout of rheumatic fever he suffered during his navy service in World War II.[13] In the afternoon he went to his father's house to see if his stepmother, Rubie English, needed any wood or coal. His father, then in jail, had left the keys to his car at home so Collis could run errands for Rubie. That afternoon Collis and Ralph Cooper, who was there to visit Melrose Diggs, Rubie's daughter, decided to take the car and go for a ride, "just riding around." They went to Robbinsville, where they saw a boy that Cooper recognized as a son of Leanna Turner, so they stopped in to visit, staying several hours. English returned a couple of times to visit Evelyn Smith, also living in the home.

Next Waldron turned his focus to the day of English's arrest, February 6, 1948. When English arrived home that evening his mother told him to remain there because the police were looking for him. Two officers arrived about 8:00 P.M. and took him to the police station, where they removed his belt and shoestrings and placed him in a cell. After just a few minutes they took him to the courtroom, pausing in the anteroom, where someone, leaving, passed them. Officer Lichtfuhs asked English, "Would I like what that boy had got?" referring to a beating. English reiterated, "They told me if I didn't tell the truth, I would get beaten." Then Patrolman Amman as well as Lichtfuhs questioned English. Both policemen were wearing guns and carrying blackjacks; soon Lieutenant Dawson came in and joined the questioning. Waldron established that they screamed at and threatened English. English described one incident: "Dawson told me to stand up, he would 'search 'im again, make sure he ain't got nothing on him'; and I stood up, when he was talking—when I stood up he was talking to Amman or Lichtfuhs, one of them, and the next thing I know he's backhand slapped me—I fell in a chair, over the chair I went."[14] Later, police took English to the detention room, where someone came up from behind and hit him on the back of his head with what he guessed was a rubber hose.[15] After English spent his night going on two trips to Robbinsville, police brought in both Cooper and Wilson, asking English to identify them, which he did. Naples asked if these two had been part of the Horner murder and English answered, "'I don't know. I can't keep no track of them.' They started to take them back out. They said 'Either you identify them, or else you ain't going back home.'" They then returned English to his cell.[16] Later in the day, when English was brought in again, Naples commanded him to make a statement. English answered "I told him I didn't know whether I could make a statement or not, that I didn't know anything about it." When English did not answer any of their questions Delate said, "Send him back to the cell and let him think it over."[17]

MONDAY, JULY 19, 1948

English continued on the witness stand, explaining to his attorney that he did not open his mouth except to say he never hit anyone, but the police told him a number of things, such as knowing a person named Spud Green, and that his father's car sat in front of the Horner store during the robbery. Police questioned him "all at once, all right behind one another."[18] Waldron focused on the evening of Sunday, February 8, when the prosecutor questioned English for two and a half hours. English reported that Volpe told him "[t]hat if I didn't talk I'd be made to talk, sent around to the detective bureau, they'd get it the other way, they'd get it the hard way."[19] Police Clerk Miller took his statement on Tuesday evening and English signed it at 12:30 A.M. Wednesday. Waldron asked, "[W]hy did you sign this statement, Collis?" English responded that if he didn't he knew he would get a beating. He had been "worked over" previously, in 1942, when wrongly accused of stealing chickens. Waldron asked Collis, "Why didn't you tell Dr. Sullivan and Dr. Manning?" He answered, "Why tell them? If I told them and they asked the policemen the policemen would deny it."[20]

Waldron had English describe his cell: about ten feet by twelve feet, a board to sleep on, a small sink and a toilet. The cell contained no window and no light. Waldron led English through every question and answer in his statement, asking if each were true; English retorted a decided no to each question.[21]

Prosecutor Volpe's cross-examination of English took two and a half days, with Volpe "alternately shouting, threatening, and taunting."[22] Volpe confronted English with small differences between his current testimony and that given when the jury had not been present. At one point English responded in a frustrated manner that he had seen no calendars in the police station and did not have a watch. Volpe asked what he had been wearing January 27, 1948, and English described a field jacket, a cap, and rubbers. He denied wearing a navy jacket or leggings.[23] When Volpe asked about English's conversations with various policemen, he replied, "I didn't talk to them, they talked to me."[24]

TUESDAY, JULY 20, 1948

Volpe continued with a barrage of questions until English said he was not feeling well. Judge Hutchinson asked if he would like to rest until 2:00 P.M., and he agreed. Waldron then called defense witness Mrs. Emma English, Collis English's mother. Waldron focused on names that had been bandied about by the police. Mrs. English had never heard John MacKenzie called Brint Kelly or Leon Wright and had never heard McKinley Forrest referred to as Chancy.[25]

At 2:00 P.M. English resumed the stand for further cross-examination. At one point Waldron felt compelled to rescue him, telling Judge Hutchinson:

"I object to the Prosecutor's brow-beating loud manner; he is confusing the witness." Judge Hutchinson responded, "Your objection is overruled." Waldron couldn't help himself and continued. "I think the witness should be protected." The judge replied, "The court will do its best to protect the witness."[26]

WEDNESDAY, JULY 21, 1948

The defense of McKinley Forrest began with his direct testimony sandwiched between a parade of defense witnesses. He had thirty-four witnesses appearing on his behalf, whereas English had three, Cooper six, MacKenzie four, and Thorpe and Wilson each nine. This was partially due to Forrest's greater participation in the community: he worked two jobs, voted, and was married, providing more records for examination. However, it could have also resulted from the fact that he had one lawyer devoted solely to his case, while the other defendants shared representation. Four of Forrest's defense witnesses were white, as were five of Wilson's.[27]

Defense lawyer Frank Katzenbach began by asking Robert Forrest to describe his visit with his brother on February 13, 1948. Robert described McKinley as lying in a cell at the Chancery Lane police station, covered with vomit. McKinley asked Robert, "Is this my brother?" which he kept repeating, as he felt Robert's legs, arms, and face.[28] He spoke gibberish, but then would say, "Wait until I get myself together." Robert described it: "His mind would go loose and come back again." McKinley kept saying "Wait, somebody is talking over my head." His visitors gave him water, which he looked at, examined, and sniffed carefully before he drank five glasses in rapid succession; they also gave him a cigarette, but Forrest examined it closely, smelled it, and then tossed it away, saying, "This cigarette's got something in it. I don't want it." Under cross-examination by Prosecutor Volpe, Robert stated his brother kept saying, in his rational interludes, that he had no idea why he was in jail.[29]

Forrest himself spent the rest of the day on the witness stand, telling his own story. He had a stutter, which made him somewhat difficult for the jury to understand. Katzenbach led him through his visit to the police station and arrest on Saturday, February 7. On that day Acting Captain Delate, Chief Naples, and Clerk Miller asked him about riding in George English's car with Collis English, and Forrest responded that he had never been in George's car. When Forrest asked them why he was being held and questioned, they made no answer. He remained in his cell until Monday morning at 8:00, when police took him for a mug shot and fingerprinting. Then Acting Captain Delate brought him into his office, where Collis English and Ralph Cooper waited. Delate asked English and Cooper if Forrest "was the fellow." English responded, "Yes, he was the fellow that hit the man." Forrest was about to ask what his brother-in-law was talking about when Chief Naples told the officers "That is all that is necessary, as long as he says so, that is all right to take him out." Cooper also identified him, saying, "Yes, that is the boy." Forrest explained that as of Monday morning he still had no idea why he was being held.[30]

Only a few minutes after Forrest was returned to his cell, the turnkey brought him to Acting Captain Delate's office, where Delate, Naples, and Miller peppered him with questions, one after another, until 2:00 P.M. As Forrest put it "Well—they started to ask me about what do you know about this murder on Broad Street? And we knows that English said you hit the man, and so on, and I don't know. I got so nervous and so scared that I wanted to tell them where I was. And Captain Delate told me 'You are not telling us, we are telling you.'" Forrest continued, "Chief Naples said to me about where I was 'Will you swear to it?' And I said 'Yes, I will swear to it.' And I got down on my knees, and I swore that I didn't know anything about it, what they were talking about, this murder. And I swears as to where I was. And when I got on my knees, Naples said 'Get off your knees, there is no use to your swearing to a damn lie.'"[31] After a brief stop for lunch the questioning continued with all three men hollering at him, as Forrest described it, but "I never did say I was on North Broad Street." At this point Delate brought him a paper cup of water, which, Forrest noticed as he drank it, had a pill dissolving in the bottom.[32]

Katzenbach then began an exploration of Forrest's movements on January 27, 1948. Forrest explained that he started at Katzeff's at 22 Union Street at 8:00 A.M. that day. Both the chicken market and the adjacent meat market used kosher means of butchering, which Forrest explained. At about 10:30 A.M. Mr. Katzeff sent Forrest to the bank, with his wife's Christmas Club account book, to make a deposit, and with sixteen dollars to bring back as change for use in the shop. Forrest thought he must have been at the bank at approximately 10:45 A.M. He continued working for Mr. Katzeff the rest of the day, spending the afternoon cleaning calves' feet. Katzenbach also asked Forrest about his work on January 26, 1948; he worked at Roebling's making wire from 8:00 A.M. until midnight.[33]

THURSDAY, JULY 22, 1948

Forrest resumed the stand and Katzenbach led him through his "confession." He denied everything in it, answering Katzenbach with a nearly shouted "No sir!" when his lawyer asked him "Did you go into 213 North Broad Street on January 27 and hit an old man on the head with a bottle?"[34] Forrest underscored that he had no memory of anything from Monday afternoon at the Chancery Lane First Precinct police station shortly after he took the pill, until Sunday, February 15, when he came to himself while showering in the Mercer County Jail. Upon being shown his statement, which prosecutors pointed out had his initials, Forrest immediately responded that since he could not write, he signed with an X, not with his initials. He also described his first conversation with Chief Detective Naples. "I was just walking in the door into the Captain's office. He say 'Come on, Chancy.' So I said, 'My name ain't Chancy.' So I reached into my pocket and showed him my pocketbook; my name ain't Chancy, my name is McKinley Forrest."[35]

During cross-examination Assistant Prosecutor Lawson handed Forrest a photo of Horner, and Forrest, after taking a long look, retorted, "I never saw him before." Lawson showed him a soda bottle used in the murder and Forrest stated, "I never saw it before I came to this courtroom." Lawton presented a photograph of the interior of Horner's store and Forrest insisted, "I was never there in my life."[36]

FRIDAY, JULY 23, 1948

Katzenbach brought forth witnesses who had seen Forrest on January 27, beginning with the owners of the several meat markets in downtown Trenton, as well as individuals he worked with. The testimony of Isaac Katzeff proved particularly important, as his Christmas Club account showed clearly that Forrest made the deposit on that day, and Katzeff definitely remembered it being before lunch. Katzeff described Forrest as "a quiet boy, never was out of order, he was always nice to the customers, he never insulted nobody, he never was drunk, he was real nice." Both Katzeff and other witnesses spoke of Forrest's good character.[37]

MONDAY, JULY 26, 1948

On Monday morning, the start of the eighth week of the trial, attorney Queen began the defense of Ralph Cooper, whom he called to the witness stand.

Through his questions, Queen brought out that while Cooper had known Collis English and met Horace Wilson, he had not met the other defendants until placed in the Chancery Lane First Precinct police station. Next they went through the details of Cooper's day on January 27, during which he spent the morning at 12 Behm Street, visiting his girlfriend Melrose Diggs, and then went to Robbinsville at English's invitation.[38] Cooper recounted the details of his arrest and his questioning on the weekend of February 7 and 8. Surrounded by Acting Captain Delate, Prosecutor Volpe, Chief Detective Naples, and Clerk Miller, Cooper repeatedly claimed he had no idea what they were talking about and knew nothing about any murder, even though they told him English had said he was involved. Cooper detailed a particular event on Saturday afternoon, when Clerk Miller, in the presence of Prosecutor Volpe, swore at Cooper and hit him in the face with his fist. On Sunday Delate and Miller questioned Cooper for two hours: "They told me that Collis English and I was there and I hit the lady. Kept telling me over and over, just keep telling me over and over."[39]

In jail on Monday, a little before lunchtime, Chief Detective Naples provided Cooper with paper and pencil and told him to write a statement "and that if I didn't it wouldn't be good for me."[40] Cooper told the court that he began a statement "in fear."[41] At lunchtime Naples gave him a carton of coffee, a roast beef sandwich, and a cigarette, and then left. As Cooper described it "After I drink the coffee and smoked the cigarette, about ten or fifteen minutes I started to feeling right sleepy." After that point, he had no memory of events until Friday, including Tuesday evening when Dr. Sullivan asked him, "What is the matter with you, boy, have you been smoking reefers?" He had no memory of making a statement that was then typed up by Clerk Miller. Queen led him through the statement question by question, with Cooper vehemently denying that any of it was true.[42] At this point Judge Hutchinson interrupted, as a witness in ill health had come to court and needed to be accommodated.

This witness, Mrs. Virginia Barclay, described the car she saw from her window, the morning of January 27, just down the street from the Horner store. It was a 1936 four-door blue green Plymouth with a driver sitting in the vehicle; this occurred at about 11:00 A.M. She saw three Negro men dash to the car; two got in on the street side and one from the sidewalk. They drove off so fast that the right rear door had not yet closed when the car began moving, which caught her attention. The three she saw looked to her as if they were in their teens, with one wearing metal-rim glasses. She knew this happened on January 27 because her husband was on the street below, trying to get his car started; he did not succeed and had to walk to work. Katzenbach showed her three photos, already in evidence, of a black 1935 two-door Ford that belonged to George English, and she asserted emphatically that it was not the car she had seen.[43]

Next, postman Russell John Cullen Jr. testified, questioned by Queen. He told of seeing Ralph Cooper while delivering mail to 12 Behm Street for Melrose Diggs at 11:00 A.M. on January 27. However, under cross-examination by Volpe it became clear that while he guessed it had been 11:00 A.M., it could have been as late as noon.[44] Cigar salesman Frank A. Eldracher took the stand, remarking, "I have been here much before." Katzenbach had asked him back on this day specifically to have him look at McKinley Forrest; Eldracher replied that Forrest looked older than the men he had seen leaving the Horner store on the morning of January 27. Lawyer Turp had him look at Wilson and he made the same reply. Then, over vociferous and repeated objections by defense counsel, but with the consent of Judge Hutchinson, Volpe brought forth the facts that Collis English and John MacKenzie looked the age of the men he had seen, but James Thorpe was too old. Katzenbach wished to ask Eldracher a key question but had to overcome numerous objections by Volpe. Having finally convinced Judge Hutchinson to let him ask the question, Katzenbach found out from Eldracher that he had never been asked by police to identify the defendants, seemingly a key omission.[45]

At this point Ralph Cooper returned to the witness stand to be examined by Queen. Cooper testified that he had no memory of signing his statement. He also explained that he knew Leanna Turner's little boy in Robbinsville because he and Leanna had worked on the same farm for a while. During cross-examination, when Volpe asked Cooper a question, he would add, "No blankout at that time, Cooper?" When Cooper answered a question by saying he knew nothing about it, Volpe responded, "You have done a lot of things that you don't know when your mind went blank." This caused Queen to object and Judge Hutchinson to agree that it be stricken from the record.[46]

TUESDAY, JULY 27, 1948

When Ralph Cooper resumed the stand, Prosecutor Volpe shouted question after question at him, but Cooper remained calm, steadfastly disclaiming any part in the crime, almost chanting his recurring denials.[47] Volpe demanded, regarding his statement: "Now, up to this point, Cooper, where you got to East Trenton on your statement, the middle of page 2, had you written all this by yourself?" Cooper explained that he was writing it by hand, but that Chief Naples "was standing there telling me what to put on there."[48]

Cooper further explained that after Naples left, the patrolman still in the room continued to tell him what to say. He had no memory of the last page of the statement.[49] Volpe asked, while wagging his finger in Cooper's face, "Weren't you running away when you went to Robbinsville, and weren't you taking it on the lam because you knew Collis English had been arrested for murder and you were afraid he would involve you?" Cooper shouted, "No, that's not true."[50]

After defense witnesses for Cooper and Wilson, the defense of John "Jack" MacKenzie began, with the defendant himself on the stand, questioned by Queen. Queen took MacKenzie through his movements the day of January 27, 1948, where he worked at Community Slaughterhouse from 7:30 A.M. until noon, when he visited his sister's house for lunch. Then he returned to work until 6:00 P.M. Next Queen talked him through his arrest on Wednesday morning, February 11. When officers came to the English home at 247 Church Street they asked for a Martin or Kelly. MacKenzie showed them his social security card to verify his identity, but was taken to the Chancery Lane First Precinct police station anyway "because Captain Delate wished to speak with him." They brought in Collis English, who stated that MacKenzie had been "the lookout man on the corner." At this point MacKenzie objected that he had no idea what Collis was talking about. He was taken before Judge Albert Cooper to be arraigned for murder, never even having been questioned. After MacKenzie was booked, Acting Captain Delate and Clerk Miller took him into Delate's office, where they started to take a statement. However, after just a few minutes they sent him back to his cell, saying that he was lying. On Thursday morning they confronted him again and he provided a statement regarding his whereabouts and actions on January 27.[51] After he signed it, police brought in a chaplain to see him. The chaplain asked if everything in the statement was true and MacKenzie assured him that it was. The chaplain then asked "why the other boys put me in it, and I said I wasn't; I said I didn't know." Then the turnkey returned MacKenzie to his cell.[52] After supper the turnkey reappeared and asked if he wanted any cigarettes. MacKenzie answered that he did. MacKenzie then revealed that after smoking four or five cigarettes, he "started seeing things. It seems as though I could see a cop pointing a gun through the ventilator in the cell. Nothing but a whole lot of shooting going on and all that stuff like that."[53] MacKenzie did not come to himself until a week later at the Mercer County Jail, where he was in the segregation cell, the "hole." He had no memory of dictating a statement, seeing Dr. Sullivan, or signing a statement. When Queen took him through the statement, line by line, MacKenzie insisted it was completely untrue.[54]

MacKenzie resumed the stand for a grilling by Volpe, which continued all morning and for some time after lunch; during questioning he persistently and completely denied any participation in the Horner murder.[55] George B. Glasco, warden of the Mercer County Jail, testified that MacKenzie remained in the isolation cell from February 14 to February 20. He described MacKenzie as walking, talking, muttering in the cell, behaving abnormally.[56]

Late in the day, James Thorpe, the last defendant, took the stand in his own defense, questioned by Turp. Thorpe's speech impediment made him difficult to understand. Turp and Judge Hutchinson repeatedly asked him to speak both more slowly and more loudly. Turp began with Thorpe in early 1947 when he severely injured his right arm in a car accident; it was removed on January 7, 1948, with Thorpe leaving the hospital on January 19.[57] Turp took Thorpe through the events of February 7, 1948, a Saturday, when he was arrested in Palaschak's Saloon at 5:00 P.M. Two officers approached Thorpe, asking him if he was Shorty, or Long John. He showed them his social security card, but they still took him to the police station. Next a policeman brought Collis English in and asked if he knew Thorpe, and English responded in the negative. Thorpe remained in his cell until Monday morning, when English claimed that Thorpe was Shorty. Then Ralph Cooper placed Thorpe at the crime, saying he was the lookout man. On Monday evening a turnkey brought Thorpe to Delate's office, which was already filled with Prosecutor Volpe, Assistant Prosecutor Lawton, Chief of Detectives Naples, Acting Captain Delate, Clerk Miller, and defendants English, Cooper, and Forrest. "They taken me in and asked me was I the lookout man; and I said no; and they turned around and throwed me right out," Thorpe said.[58] As the turnkey took him out the door, Prosecutor Volpe hollered, "Bring him back, I'll make the sonofabitch talk." At this point Chief Naples threw Thorpe a pack of cigarettes and said "If I talk he make it easier on me." Thorpe did not smoke the cigarettes, saying he was afraid of them because "McKinley Forrest was acting funny." He also explained that he did not sleep well, as McKinley Forrest was in the adjoining cell "making noise, going on, and kicking the side of the wall, going on and hollering and saying different kind of words. Kept me awake."[59]

On Tuesday morning a turnkey returned Thorpe to Delate's office, where the prosecutor, Volpe, told him to "[t]ell what part I took in this killing. And I told him I didn't take no part in no killing; I wasn't there; I didn't have nothing to do with it. Then he said, 'Well, you shut up, and let me tell you,' and then he started again telling me." They took a statement in which Volpe asked a question, answered it, and kept going, with Thorpe not saying a word. On Tuesday evening he joined the group with the doctors, Scrappy Manning, detectives, and prosecutors. Dr. Sullivan asked him if his statement was true and he replied no. Sullivan asked him why he was going to sign it, and Thorpe responded that he was not going to sign. Then Turp followed up: "Why did you sign it?" "I signed it because I was afraid. Afraid of being whupped. I heard people hollering there, that is why I was afraid—people hollering in daytime and at night, so that people were hollering, and that is why I was afraid."[60] Turp took him through his statement, line by line, with Thorpe denying that any of it was true. Thorpe also made clear that he had never in his life been known as either Shorty or Long John.

THURSDAY, JULY 29, 1948

The morning began with Turp continuing to question Thorpe. They went through his movements at the time of the murder, when he spent the morning helping his uncle work on his father's car, which was parked in front of the house. Assistant Prosecutor Lawson took him through his statement again, when some new information emerged. Lawson asked, "Now, do you remember this question: 'Did the others also come out of the store?'" And your answer: "Shorty English, he came out and then McKinley, Wilson, and Cooper came out." Thorpe replied: "No, but I know how he [Clerk Miller] got that in there. When they were questioning me on Monday, and Collis English was saying I was 'Shorty' and I said if anybody was 'Shorty,' Collis English was. And that is all, they got that in there from that. I was walking toward English as he called me 'Shorty,' the lookout man, and I was walking over toward him and I said: 'If anybody is Shorty you are Shorty.' And I was going to hit him, and the man made me get back and they made me shut-up. I was going to hit him for calling me that. And that is how that got in there."[61]

After several witnesses, both relatives and neighbors, told of seeing Thorpe in front of his home working on a car that day, Frank Katzenbach stepped forward with several witnesses he had called on behalf of McKinley Forrest: Andrew Duch, the director of public safety; William Dooling, the chief of police; and [Acting] Captain Andrew Delate. He had subpoenaed the three to produce documents that had not been forthcoming even though requested. Judge Hutchinson had the sheriff remove the jury while the ensuing legal discussion took place. Prosecutor Volpe asked the judge to quash the subpoenas, saying they were merely a fishing expedition, bringing in a number of legal references to indicate they were too broad. Katzenbach replied, "I have stated with particularity, that I wanted records as to fingerprints. There has been some foundation laid for that. Someone has said something about—well—there couldn't have been any fingerprints upon the bottle because they are supposed to have used a sock. Now no sock has been introduced in evidence. There is evidence that the bottles were referred to the fingerprint man, and I don't know who it is. The only people who would know, who would have any records about this, would be the people in the police department, and I have asked the people I believe to be custodians of the records, to let me know, and let me examine, and produce them in Court."

Judge Hutchinson answered, "Well, your thought is that you might show that there were fingerprints actually on the bottle, and those of other persons than these defendants?" Katzenbach responded, "Yes, your Honor. The bottle was treated with some sort of a chemical to bring out fingerprints, it shows, you can see it right on the bottle top, your Honor." Katzenbach also requested records pertaining to the descriptions of the men who committed the crime, provided in eyewitness accounts, that he had never been able to get, the evidence always being rejected as hearsay. As Katzenbach went on, the judge interrupted: "That really leads to what the Prosecutor expects—exactly what he expects: a fishing expedition." Katzenbach: "Sir, when I go fishing I do not expect to find anything." Judge Hutchinson: "You are a very pessimistic fisher." Katzenbach: "But I feel quite confident in this case that when I subpoena fingerprint identification records that fingerprint identification records will be produced; and that when I ask for police blotters, in an effort to find out whether there were persons apprehended whose fingerprints might possibly have been taken and coincide with the ones found in evidence in this case, I know that there will be blotters." Judge Hutchinson quashed all the motions and the three witnesses did not testify.[62]

FRIDAY, JULY 30, 1948

A further round of defense witnesses took their turn on the stand. Lawyer Turp asked Leanna Turner, who lived with Horace Wilson: "Do you have a clock in your house?" "No," she responded. The defendants repeatedly appeared at a disadvantage when pressed for precise times when events occurred; they simply did not know the times.[63]

Katzenbach issued a subpoena for E. Paul Sjostrom, supervisor of the State Bureau of Identification, who handled fingerprint records. When Katzenbach asked if any evidence in the Horner murder case had been sent to his office, Volpe promptly rose to quash the subpoena. Katzenbach appealed to Judge Hutchinson, justifying his request for information specifically about the broken and unbroken bottles found in the Horner store and apparently used as weapons. The judge ruled that the motion to quash would be granted. Katzenbach responded, "Well, may I take exception to the ruling. First, upon the ground that this is not the state's witness; this is a defense witness. The Prosecutor has no place to make a motion to quash his subpoena." He also remonstrated that they could not do their own tests as the judge suggested, because having been tested once, the bottles would no longer be suitable. Judge Hutchinson allowed Katzenbach to ask if they did have evidence, and Sjostrom answered, "There was evidence submitted up there for examination, that I know."[64] Court ended for the week. This would be the last weekend the jurors had to stay in seclusion.

MONDAY, AUGUST 2, 1948

Katzenbach ended his case for McKinley Forrest with witnesses bringing in official records, such as Forrest's marriage license, draft records, and work records. Each showed that he signed with an X, not with his initials, as appeared on his confession. Next Katzenbach called on J. Howard Haring, a nationally known handwriting specialist from New York City. He had been asked to look at the confession and the initials that Forrest signed on back of the photos and on the bottle, to give his opinion about the emotional state of the person who initialed them. Haring's testimony proceeded slowly as a result of continual sparring between Volpe and Katzenbach, mediated by Judge Hutchinson. Haring felt very strongly that the confession and photos had been signed by one person and the bottle by someone else. He showed and explained the differences to the jury on enlarged samples that he had made. Next Katzenbach showed Haring the receipt for the mattress, saying $2.00, with a signature, which Mrs. Horner said had been signed by McKinley Forrest. He responded, "It is my opinion that the name appearing below the three lines of writing was not written by McKinley Forrest. Was not, and could not have been written by him." He felt that the initials on the confession and photos demonstrated such a tremor or nervousness that "the person was in such a state that they could not make that which they sought to make, namely, the pattern which they had in their mind." When pressed by Volpe during cross-examination, Haring declared, "It is absolutely impossible that that man could have signed that label on the bottle that you now hold in your hand."[65] With the completion of Haring's testimony, the defense rested its case for all six defendants.

Volpe now led into his twenty rebuttal witnesses. John P. Duffy, a chemist with the New Jersey State Police, had conducted a chemical experiment on the book containing Horace Wilson's pay record for January 27, which he had been given by the Trenton police. He applied a chemical called Grapho-Detector to an area with an apparent abrasion, or erasure. He then took a photograph of the result, which showed a darker area near Wilson's name. It left behind a reddish residue, which was what Wilson's foreman, John M. Murphy, had found so puzzling when he examined it, as well as the erasure that Murphy had not observed previously. Defense lawyer Turp objected furiously to having the photograph introduced as evidence, but Judge Hutchinson allowed it. Turp extracted the fact that the number "4," which showed how many hours Wilson worked, had no abrasion present.[66] At the end of the day, Judge Hutchinson announced they would go until 5:00 P.M. each day in order to conclude the trial by the end of the week.

TUESDAY, AUGUST 3, 1948

Prosecutor Volpe paraded the police officers involved in the case through testimony in which they denied any threats to the defendants, any swearing at defendants, any striking of the defendants, any promises to the defendants; they asserted that all defendants appeared normal and that crying, screaming, and "hollering" did not occur at the police station. A lengthy argument ensued between Katzenbach and Volpe over admitting the photographs, commonly known as mug shots, taken of the prisoners after they had been in custody several days, sleeping in their clothes, without access to showers. Katzenbach called them "highly prejudicial" and completely unnecessary but Judge Hutchinson eventually ruled that they could be admitted.[67] Delate denied ever giving McKinley Forrest a cup of water with a pill in it. Delate also brought with him a short coat, a pair of leggings, and a cap, claiming them to be what Collis English wore during the commission of the crime. Turp objected forcefully that while they might be English's clothing, there was no proof he wore them on January 27, 1948. Judge Hutchinson allowed them to be entered as evidence.[68] After Volpe finished his rebuttal witnesses, the state rested its case.

Defense lawyer Turp then rose to make the same motions he had made when the state initially rested its case, saying that no proof of a robbery had ever been presented. Regarding Wilson, he stated that there was "not sufficient evidence in the case to warrant sending it to the jury." Regarding MacKenzie, Cooper, and Thorpe, he argued there was no evidence of a common purpose. And on behalf of all the defendants he urged the judge to consider that "the State of the case and the condition of the evidence is in such confusion that it is impossible for the jury to determine wherein the truth lies." Katzenbach then pointed out that the chief witness in the state's case clearly said three men were in the tiny store, and the confessions indicated five people on the premises. Thus, "With this conflict, it leaves the jury in the impossible condition where it cannot pick out from five sets of evidence, all offered by the Prosecutor, as to the ones which are actually true, or could be actually true." He also added about McKinley Forrest: "[T]he state has presented no evidence pointing to his guilt which is proper evidence for the jury to consider. The witness who identified him as being in the building at the time of the crime was thoroughly impeached. It was quite obvious that the person that she saw was another person, because the person she saw could write; the defendant McKinley Forrest could not write." Prosecutor Volpe rebutted these arguments and Judge Hutchinson denied all motions.[69] Only two days of trial remained.

WEDNESDAY, AUGUST 4, 1948

Defense attorneys spent the day "ripping and hacking" at the state's evidence, as described by this day's *Trenton Evening Times*. First Waldron spoke for an hour, about the case in general, and Collis English in particular.[70] He began by pointing out the basis of American law: that a man is presumed innocent until he is proven guilty. The state bears the burden of making its case beyond a reasonable doubt, not the other way around. He then asked, "Now, has the State met this burden of proof beyond a reasonable doubt? The defense makes the flat and emphatic declaration that the State has failed utterly and completely to prove the charges that it has made against these men." He went on to illustrate his contention; first he charged that the state put on much extraneous testimony to muddy the issues. For example, the defense conceded willingly that Mr. Horner died of a skull fracture. But the state presented six witnesses regarding Horner's cause of death. Next Waldron pointed out that only two kinds of evidence connected these defendants to the Horner murder: the testimony of Mrs. Horner, and the statements. When police brought Elizabeth Horner to the Chancery Lane First Precinct police station on February 7 she could identify none of the men. When she was brought back again, Delate gave her six photos to identify. As Waldron put it: "They didn't give her 25 pictures of people who might possibly be suspected or not suspected and say, 'All right, now let's see; pick out from that group which of the ones were on the premises.' They didn't do that, according to her testimony. All that they did was give her six pictures. The six defendants. How could she miss?"[71]

Next Waldron addressed the question of other eyewitnesses. The prosecution never took Frank Eldracher, Virginia Barclay, or shopkeeper Argiros Kokenakes to see the defendants. Eldracher had testified in court that he felt only English and MacKenzie could be in the correct age range, and MacKenzie was charged solely with being a lookout man down the street. Virginia Barclay told the jury that one of the men she saw wore steel-rimmed glasses, whereas none of the defendants did. Her description of the getaway car bore no resemblance to George English's two-door black Ford. Next Waldron dealt with the question of whether a robbery even occurred. According to the various confessions, four different men went through Mr. Horner's pockets, yet at the hospital police found $1,642 in neatly folded bills in three pockets. Moving on to the question of fingerprints, one of which was clearly visible on the bottle, the defense had never been able to access the fingerprint test results. And the sock that supposedly covered the bottle was never seen, or found. Then Waldron asked, "And, speaking of fingerprints, was there any testimony that the police had gone in there and dusted the place for fingerprints?" The store had been immediately secured, but police made no effort to check for prints, not even on the outside doorknob that Mr. Eldracher clearly stated they touched. Waldron considered the men's statements, giving examples of their inconsistencies.[72]

Lastly, he concentrated on Collis English, pointing out that he was a navy veteran of World War II, had suffered from malaria and was disabled by heart disease, and helped his mother with the laundry. English had testified that he had a fear of police ever since they beat him in 1942 and charged him with stealing chickens. As to the police witnesses all testifying that they spoke to English in a conversational tone, Waldron pointed out that Prosecutor Volpe hammered at the defendants so loudly in the courtroom he practically lost his voice. Referring to English's occasional confusion about time and dates when in the police station, where he had neither watch nor calendar, Waldron rebutted by referring to a number of inaccuracies revealed by Chief Detective Naples in his testimony, particularly regarding the name of Buddy Wilson.

Waldron summarized by asking the jury to imagine a man who has a heart condition, is threatened with beatings, questioned at all hours of the day and night, and surrounded by thirteen screaming men in a room the size of the jury box: could signing a statement possibly have been voluntary? Waldron concluded: "Justice without wisdom is impossible; we request that you bring in a verdict of not guilty as to all of the defendants."[73]

After a short recess, Queen began his peroration, speaking on behalf of Ralph Cooper and John MacKenzie. After bringing up a number of contradictions in their statements, Queen commented, "I am afraid that the police did not consult the eye witnesses before they made these statements. It would seem that the eye witnesses should have consulted the prosecution, those who investigated this case, so that in some way the statements of eye witnesses would agree with the case, with the theory of the case, and as perceived and conceived by Acting Captain Delate and the other investigating officers."[74] Queen summarized what both men said they did on January 27, 1948, their statements, and their character witnesses. He concluded that the men would never have willingly agreed to sign unless they felt themselves to be under tremendous threat of some kind. He went on: "The only thing that could beat signing these statements, members of the jury, would be for a man to ask the Governor to provide him with one of those automatic electric chairs, by which he can get in there voluntarily, strap himself in, and ask for a button that he could push, to kill himself. That is the next step to what has been done here."[75] Queen asked the jury to find all the defendants not guilty.

After lunch, Katzenbach began his summation on behalf of McKinley Forrest. He admitted, "This has been a very long trial. I am tired, and I know that you probably are tired." He affirmed, "I do have confidence, utter confidence, in the innocence of McKinley Forrest, and I believe that in the time I take I will be able to demonstrate his innocence."[76] He brought up the inconsistencies in the statements, his inability to find out the results of the fingerprint tests, and the eyewitness descriptions that did not match either the defendants or George English's car. Then he veered in a new direction, bringing up the subject of Jerry Griswold, who worked for Mr. Horner on occasion, and who would have known that Horner carried large amounts of cash on his person. Mrs. Horner had made clear her animosity toward Griswold when she testified as a witness for the state. Katzenbach commented, "There's no evidence about whether he was ever apprehended by the police, ever questioned or interrogated at all."[77] Of course, Katzenbach did not know what would come out at the second trial: that police had paid

Griswold several dollars a day to stay out of the way during the trial, keeping him in the very building in which the trial itself was soon to be concluded.[78] Katzenbach then brought up a previously unaddressed point: none of the defendants appeared to come into sudden wealth after the supposed robbery. None had any money on their persons or had been observed spending any but small amounts of cash.

Katzenbach attempted to teach the jury a basic difference between themselves and those on trial. When the defendants found themselves in police custody, alone, questioned day and night, charged with murder, their reactions seemed to be of unreasoning terror. But, as Katzenbach said of himself: "I wouldn't have been scared. Fortunately I have had some education and know some things about my constitutional rights, and I would know that in the end in the long run, I would be able to communicate with the outside, and I would be able to get an attorney, and I wouldn't be the least scared; and I might even make some accusations about false arrest, and false imprisonment. And the police might get scared enough to let me go. But that isn't the situation with these men." He described how the police enmeshed the men in lies, confronted them with each other, gradually building up the statements to the conclusions they sought. Katzenbach then turned specifically to facts regarding his client, McKinley Forrest, such as Mrs. Horner saying she had given him a receipt to read and sign although in fact he could not read or write. Mrs. Horner had described a brief conversation she had with him, yet never mentioned that he stuttered, one of the first things a stranger describing Forrest would note.[79] Then Katzenbach went through Forrest's alibi witnesses, who could clearly account for his movements the entire day of January 27, 1948. He summed up McKinley Forrest as a hardworking individual, a widower devoted to his only child. Finally, he concluded with his belief that McKinley Forrest was not a murderer, and "I know that some day when his days come to an end and earth to earth returneth, as it must to everybody, in the still hours of the morning when the leaves stir, he'll go out to meet his Maker a good man: a man that is not a murderer, out on the wings of the morning. I'm confident of it; and I ask your consideration in his behalf."[80]

After a short recess, it was Turp's turn to address the jury. As head of the defense team, he began by thanking Waldron, Queen, and Katzenbach for their efforts, as well as their teamwork. He then explained to the jury that the "[p]rosecutor has a great advantage in this case in that he closes. He has all night to see what we have said and come back tomorrow and attack it. And I would like you to keep that advantage in mind." He then pressed the jury to consider Mrs. Horner: "This is not a case where the woman should command the deep sympathy of the jury which might be shown had she been his lawfully wedded wife and had they been living there at 213 North Broad Street as a lawful family, properly united in the sacred bonds of matrimony." He reminded the jury, "It is the duty of our law enforcing agencies to investigate crime and eliminate those people who can show that they are being accused without due grounds. The only reason given by the Captain [Delate] was that the sworn statements of other defendants were responsible and therefore he could not eliminate any one of the defendants. Yet you have heard the judge time and time again say to you that these statements cannot be used as evidence against anyone except the one who made the statement."[81] Turp then moved on to something that continued to puzzle him. At the very beginning of the investigation, two detectives, Lieutenant Detective Stanley and Detective Toft, had been assigned to help Delate with the case, and they seemingly worked on the case all the way through. Yet the prosecutor only called them to the witness stand for preliminary work they had done. Why? Turp's answer: "I surmise it is because their testimony would not corroborate in all instances the testimony that had previously been given."[82] Turp recalled for the jury that Thorpe had had his arm amputated recently and had been out of the hospital less than three weeks when arrested. "One can imagine his feeling; his arm stump sore and painful, his spirits correspondingly low. Everything seemed to be against him. He heard noises that caused him to believe prisoners were being beaten. Officers were everywhere and he was afraid of officers."[83] He asked the jury to remember that Thorpe insisted he was innocent even up to and when signing his statement and to focus on the fact that the police not only made no effort to keep Thorpe from signing the statement but actively encouraged him to do so.[84] In discussing all six defendants, Turp expressed his feeling that most individuals being tried for a crime like the Horner murder would have a long arrest record. Yet only Cooper had served time, and that was in the South. As to English, since Volpe never produced his court record, he must never have been tried, "for otherwise the Prosecutor would surely have found it."[85]

Turp revealed that he had just recently understood a puzzling aspect of the defendants' testimony. Each had spoken of being brought to a room and told to look out a window, but it was a window through which they could see nothing. Right on the other side stood Mrs. Horner, looking at them through smoked glass. Turp commented, "You know that the fairest way would be for the defendants to be in line with other prisoners, with the witness attempting to identify them. But be that as it may, Mrs. Horner did not identify any of them at that time, even though she had the advantage of looking just at these particular defendants." He elaborated: "I sincerely trust that you would not, under any circumstances, consider the possibility of trying to send any of these people to the electric chair on the identification of this witness."[86]

Turp next considered Wilson's case. He highlighted the fact that Wilson never made any self-incriminating statements and that what the other five said about him could not be considered as evidence against him. In fact, the state's entire case against Wilson rested on Mrs. Horner's identification.[87] He asked the jury to remember all of Wilson's alibi witnesses, then pointed out cultural differences between the defendants and the others in the courtroom, especially regarding manners and awareness of time. An element Volpe had made a great showing of was the defendants' lack of introduction or official acknowledgment of each other. As Turp explained it, "They accept each other, more or less matter-of-factly." He concluded his summation, and that of his entire team, saying, "I ask you in all sincerity to consider your verdict carefully and bring in a verdict of not guilty with respect to each defendant."[88]

Thursday, August 5, 1948

Prosecutor Volpe began the day by thanking the jurors for their sacrifice; they had been separated from their families for nine weeks. He also complimented them on their intelligence, saying he felt assured that they would have no difficulties in sorting out the confusion described by the defense attorneys. He even admitted, "There have been times I suppose in the course of this trial when I might have offended your sensibilities: Yes, I've lost my head. However, don't let that prejudice the case one way or another." He observed, "I'm proud to be an American, and much more so now. Our great democracy affords these six defendants accused of a most brutal crime, giving them every opportunity to come before you men and women so that you could judge fairly and honestly as to whether the people of the State of New Jersey were justified in bringing them to trial, and to determine whether they were guilty or innocent of this most brutal killing which occurred on January 27th last."[89]

Volpe began with John MacKenzie, pointedly discussing MacKenzie's nine-day memory lapse: "I know that this type of testimony by these defendants has been an insult to the intelligence of this jury. I didn't dignify it by bringing here a Doctor, or any expert in drugs, to prove to you that such a thing could not be possible. I don't think the average person on the street, with the average intelligence, could possibly believe such a fantastic story." He informed the jury that MacKenzie acted as he did while in jail because he had been without liquor and couldn't stand it, in spite of the fact that no one had ever mentioned that MacKenzie drank to excess. Regarding the middle of the night confession session, he told the jurors, "Yes, I often pray to the Lord because he gave us the foresight that night of calling in these disinterested people," referring to Scrappy Manning and Dr. Sullivan, both black. They did not use police doctors "because we wanted disinterested persons who have absolutely no connection with law enforcement, so that it would leave no doubt in the minds of anyone that they were interested one way or another in the outcome of the case." He concluded his summation of MacKenzie's case by discussing the merits of eyewitness testimony versus admission by an individual accused of a crime, concluding that an eyewitness can be mistaken but an individual's admission is a much stronger evidence of guilt.[90]

Volpe next turned his focus on McKinley Forrest. In doing so, he remarked, "Ladies and gentlemen, there is only—the only probable testimony in this case as to what happened at the First District Police Station is the testimony of the police officers. They are not interested in convicting people who are innocent." He questioned the testimony of Forrest's defense witnesses, particularly the testimony of Mr. Haring, the handwriting expert. He reiterated the many safeguards, such as calling doctors in to verify the good condition of the defendants. Then he stressed the "best evidence of all: Forrest's own confession."[91]

In summarizing the case against James Thorpe, Volpe contrasted police statements with Thorpe's statements, making it obvious that if given a choice, any person would choose as true those of the police. He belittled Thorpe's relatives and friends, intimating that they were not of great intelligence.[92] Volpe proceeded along the same lines with Horace Wilson, managing to impugn Wilson's character in that he did not sign a confession, which the rest of the men had been honest enough to do. In discussing Ralph Cooper he used the same technique. When arrested at Horace Wilson's block house, Cooper did not protest but did what police told him to do. Whereas Volpe stated, "An innocent man doesn't react that way. An innocent man would have stood up, and said 'What right do you have to be here?'" On commenting on Cooper's and the others' fear of the police, Volpe advanced this thought: "I submit, ladies and gentlemen, there is no fear of the police unless there is fear in your conscience; if you are a law-abiding citizen there is no fear of the police."[93]

Volpe turned at last to the first man arrested, Collis English. He described bringing English in for driving his father's car without permission. Then: "We had a lead on the murderer. The police were on the move to protect your lives. The most brutal murder committed in this City of Trenton. Yes, the police were on the move. They worked four continuous nights, no sleep; and they were on the move."[94] He discounted both English's alibi witnesses and his statements in his own defense.[95]

Volpe concluded his summation by asking whom the jury should believe, the defendants or the police department? Should they believe Captain Delate and Chief Detective Naples, or these six men?

> Clerk Miller, yes, Clerk Miller on that stand, a Clerk. Why would he have to lie? Why should he have on his conscience that he caused six men to go to the chair? What gratification is there to the Police Department in sending innocent men away? Do they get promoted on that basis? They are civil service men. They have no personal gains—there is no bonus with these things. And yet they say to you that the whole Police Department in their frantic frenzy to apprehend these criminals and satisfy the community and to salvage their reputation, that no colored person was safe on January 27th. . . . You either find these men not innocent—or rather, innocent—and accuse the Police Department. That is what you will have to do—by an innocent verdict—of having brought in men who are innocent and trumped up a case against them. Or else you justify the excellent police work, and the excellent preparation, admitted by the defense, and bring in a verdict which the evidence warrants.[96]

Volpe cautioned against a compromise verdict. After commenting on the "incensed community" that looked to the police department to solve the Horner murder, he concluded by telling the jury: "You owe it to the Police Department."[97]

Late in the hot August afternoon, Judge Charles P. Hutchinson began his charge to the jury. First he cautioned jury members to be very careful in their deliberations given the serious nature of the charge of murder: "You are the sole judges of the facts, regardless of the recollection of either counsel or the Court itself; it is your recollection which must govern. In this, as in every criminal case, the defendants and each of them are presumed to be innocent until proved to be guilty . . . the evidence must establish the truth of the fact to a moral certainty." The jurors needed to judge the credibility of each witness, whether for the state or the defense. He then explained to the jury the three possible verdicts they could render: if guilty the defendants were to be sentenced to death, or if guilty the jury could recommend imprisonment at hard labor for life, or the jury could find them not guilty. Judge Hutchinson summed up the state's evidence against each defendant. Regarding the confessions, he explained that they "were given under circumstances testified to by the state's witnesses, or these witnesses swore falsely or were mistaken and they were given under the circumstances testified to by the five defendants themselves." He questioned Forrest's, Cooper's, and MacKenzie's loss of memory or consciousness involved in the confessions, asking how such surprising behavior could actually have taken place. Judge Hutchinson pointed out that Mrs. Horner identified Wilson, who had made no confession, as having been in her store twice. (At the end of the charge James Turp reminded the jury that Mrs. Horner identified Cooper, not Wilson, as having been in the store twice.) The judge then moved on to the alibis and defense witnesses of the accused, pointing out inconsistencies in their testimony. He concluded by reminding jurors of the three possible verdicts they could legally find: if guilty they could be sentenced to death, or, if guilty be sentenced to hard labor for life in prison, or they could be found not guilty.[98]

The court clerk, J. George Cole, then drew juror names from a box, identifying as number-one juror and thus the automatic foreman Robert F. Burroughs, a handsome young man in his middle twenties.[99] Joined by nine female jurors and two other males, with the thirteenth (alternate) jury member now able to leave, the jury retired for deliberations at 4:32 P.M. After the jury left the courtroom, Judge Hutchinson agreed to hear objections to his charge in his chambers. Attorneys Turp and Katzenbach brought up numerous errors they felt Judge Hutchinson had made and requested a motion for arrest of judgment, as Judge Hutchinson had not allowed the jury or the defendants to hear their lengthy objections. The judge denied this motion, and court finally concluded while the jury deliberated.[100]

FRIDAY, AUGUST 6, 1948

At 12:58 A.M. the jury returned to the courtroom after eight and a half hours of deliberation. Two sergeants and nine patrolmen ringed the room inside and out to prevent disturbances.[101] Court Clerk Cole asked the defendants to rise and face the jury and then asked the jury to rise also. He intoned, "Ladies and gentlemen of the jury, have you agreed upon a verdict?" The jury replied, "We have." The clerk responded, "And who shall speak for you?" They answered,

"Our foreman." The clerk asked, "Mr. Foreman, how do you find?" He replied, "We, the jury, find the defendant Ralph Cooper guilty. The defendant Collis English guilty. The defendant McKinley Forrest guilty. The defendant John MacKenzie guilty. The defendant James H. Thorpe guilty. And the defendant Horace Wilson guilty." Turp then asked, "Your Honor, please, may the jury be polled in regard to each defendant?" Cole asked each juror in turn their finding as to each defendant in turn, which led to seventy-two responses of "Guilty." The August 6 *Trenton Evening Times* reported, "The defendants received the sentence without emotion. They showed neither surprise, fear nor contempt. Each stared straight ahead and made no attempt to talk to one another. When they were being led back to the county jail, Forrest made a circle of his thumb and forefinger and raised it towards his counsel, Frank S. Katzenbach 3d in the manner generally recognized as meaning 'everything is going to be okay.'"

At this point Turp and Katzenbach requested and were granted a meeting with Judge Hutchinson in his chambers. They presented a motion for arrest of judgment on the grounds that the state did not adequately prove its case, which the judge denied. Back in the courtroom, Judge Hutchinson asked the sheriff to present the defendants before the bench. He asked Ralph Cooper, "Have you anything to say why sentence should not be pronounced against you?" Cooper answered, "No, sir." This was followed by five identical questions and answers. Judge Hutchinson then proceeded: "Ralph Cooper, Collis English, McKinley Forrest, John MacKenzie, James H. Thorpe, and Horace Wilson, the jury has found each of you and all of you guilty of murder in the first degree, without recommendation of life imprisonment. It is difficult for any of us, none of whom is without fault, to pass judgment on another, but the law has provided the penalty for your crime. And it therefore becomes my duty to impose"—here the judge halted abruptly due to a commotion in the rear of the room. A woman jumped to her feet and screamed, "How could you take everything we had, how could your own wife and son listen to such a verdict and be proud of a man like you! I wish this dirty, rotten country would rot under your dirty, filthy feet! You're a bunch of rats! You need an insect can to be sprayed on all of you! They ought to get rid of you, you murderers. Kill me if you want to, there is nothing in this country left!" Several deputy sheriffs grabbed Bessie Mitchell roughly and literally dragged her out of the courtroom.[102]

Judge Hutchinson carried on: "It therefore becomes my duty to impose the only sentences the law provides. The judgment and sentence of this Court is that you, Ralph Cooper, Collis English, McKinley Forrest, John MacKenzie,

James H. Thorpe, and Horace Wilson, each of you suffer the punishment of death at the place and in the manner provided by law, on some day of the week beginning Sunday, the nineteenth day of September, 1948—and may God have mercy upon your souls."[103]

The front page of the August 6, 1948, *Trenton Evening Times* screamed in bold type: "Six Sentenced to Die for Slaying of Horner." A police mug shot of each man was prominently displayed. Both the Trenton paper and the Associated Press wire story then pointed out the obvious strain of the trial on the jurors. "As the foreman gave the verdict for each defendant, three of the women jury members dabbed at their eyes. Later, during a poll, some of the jurors mumbled the words 'Guilty' in voices that were half sobs."[104] Both Mrs. Christina Leedom of South Logan Avenue and Mrs. Stella Silvester of Princeton broke down sobbing and received medical treatment.[105] Besides the emotional and physical toll of the trial on all involved, the paper pointed out that the forty-five-day trial had cost well over $50,000, to be paid for by Mercer County taxpayers. The article added that any appeal also would be paid for by Mercer County residents, and defense lawyers had announced immediately after the verdict that they would appeal the six death sentences. Here, however, New Jersey state law stepped in. It provided that any recipients of a death sentence automatically received a stay and an appeal to the New Jersey Supreme Court, with counsel provided.

Journalist William Reuben interviewed African Americans in the city at the trial's end and found great disquiet. Most blacks felt the Six had been entrapped by the state and had nothing to do with the Horner murder. The Reverend A. E. Martin of the Asbury Methodist Church expressed the sentiments of many in his community, when he prayed: "May God in his wisdom enable those in authority to correct their mistakes, if they are wrong." He asked that "Justice roll down like waters, and righteousness like an overflowing stream."[106]

After Bessie Mitchell's ejection from the courtroom, she wandered the streets for hours, in a daze, unable to face her mother with the trial result. Mrs. English had stayed home to cook a large celebratory meal for the six men. A friend from a butcher shop on Union Street gave them a huge steak and Mrs. English spent hours preparing the men's favorite side dishes. At 4 A.M. Bessie went home, woke her mother and announced, "Mom, they sentenced the men to the chair. But don't worry, it isn't over yet. We'll tell people what really went on in that court, and it'll come out all right."[107]

While Bessie Mitchell's was the only voice heard in protest in the courtroom itself, others soon added their cries to her anguished objection. The

Trenton Evening Times unexpectedly noted, "The jury decision finding all the defendants guilty without a recommendation of mercy seems to have stunned the entire city." Joseph H. Collins of the Progressive Party issued a statement that ran in the *Trentonian*:

> I believe I express the thoughts of thousands of Mercer County citizens when I say I was shocked at the tragic verdict rendered in the Horner case.
>
> How 12 Americans could condemn to death six young men in a case with so much conflicting evidence, without even a recommendation of mercy for any of the accused, is beyond my comprehension.
>
> As the case developed and was reported in the press, there were doubts raised in the minds of a vast number of people throughout the state as to the guilt of all or any of the accused men.
>
> I fervently hope that the attorneys for these boys and the higher court to which the appeal will be taken will rectify the apparent injustice which has been done and allay the sharp resentment which has been created in this community and throughout the state.[108]

At the trial's end, on August 6, the county sheriff transferred the six men from the Mercer County Jail to the Death House of the Trenton State Prison, making the trial result very real and immediate (see figure 3). Prison guard Harry Camisa described the Death House: "I swear a cold chill came over me as I looked to my left at those two tiers of nine cells each; I felt like I was looking at a set of cages containing some kind of animals waiting to be led out and slaughtered.... It just seemed like the chill of death hung over that wing like an oppressive, suffocating blanket. And unlike the rest of the prison, this cell block was quiet. All I could hear was the buzzing of the florescent lights and some muffled voices—a couple of the inmates talking quietly between the locked cells."[109] The men lived in barred cells eight feet square, with a light that was always on; guards witnessed their every move.[110] This was their new home.

CHAPTER 4

BESSIE MITCHELL FINDS HELP

Letters became a lifeline to the six men newly installed in New Jersey's Death House at the Trenton State Prison. Their communication with the outside world was made more difficult by the fact that most could not read or write, but they managed. Horace Wilson received letters from his sister Sallie Porter, written for her by her pastor and read to him by Collis English or John MacKenzie. Arcie Lee wrote letters to her brother McKinley Forrest, which his nephew read to him. And McKinley heard frequently from his daughter, Jean, who sent birthday and Father's Day cards, as well as frequent notes telling him neighborhood news. On April 25, 1949, Mrs. Emma English wrote to Mac, as McKinley Forrest was called by his family, reassuring him about his daughter: "Jean was a happy girl when she saw all of you all. She rest fine ever since."[1] Vera Strauss, McKinley Forrest's niece and John MacKenzie's sister, wrote to him often, keeping him up-to-date on family affairs. Alphonso Strauss wrote, urging his uncle to "keep praying because the way the situation stands for our people today, prayer is the only thing, and more powerful than anything any one can say or do."[2] Bessie Mitchell wrote to all of the men, asking for "God to watch over you." John MacKenzie, known as Jack to his family, wrote to Bessie on March 4, 1949:

> Bessie I received your letter today and was indeed glad to hear from you and also very glad to hear how much and how hard you are working for us so that we may get justice and if there is any to be got we know that you will get it for us. All of the boys say that they have faith in you and that they thank you very much for what you are trying to do for them and that they are praying and hoping that it will not be long before you and the rest of them get justice for us. Bessie for myself I am praying, also

trying to smile like you say but the smile is not the real thing because it is very hard to smile in a place like this when I have been put here for nothing. But I try not to worry so much about it because I guess it could of happened to anyone else as well as myself.[3]

Because John MacKenzie could read and write and had many relatives, he appeared to be the major correspondent of the six. He received letters from aunts and uncles, his sister, Vera, his grandmother, Nana, his cousin Abe, and from Emma English. Immediately after the sentencing, his Aunt Sarah wrote: "Jack and Mac, I am sorry that has to happen to you of all people, that was not no fair deal."[4] In December she wrote to John: "Tell Mac I say hello and stop worrying about the women folks so much. They will be here when you all come home."[5] In February Sarah told John: "We did not send you no card on your birthday not that I forgot it but why send you a card saying happy birthday to you when I no [sic] that you are not."[6] In a June letter she told him: "The chicken house boys say hello and hurry home because they miss you very much."[7] Mainly she let him know she was thinking of him: "I will be so glad when you come home. We miss you so much." And: "I am thinking about you all every day and night which you no [sic] that I can not forget you all at a time like this."[8] John MacKenzie also heard from lawyer Robert Queen, receiving a postcard from Schenectady, New York, dated October 3: "Dear Jack: Up here for a few days of rest. We are working on the appeal night and day. It is a very big job and we may not be ready until Christmas, but we will win."[9] The men could receive visits from family, many of whom tried to come once a month, all that was allowed. Robert and Sarah Forrest visited Robert's brother Mac regularly and asked John MacKenzie to send a special pass so they could come more than once a month. Families tried to keep the men's spirits up, but it was a challenging task.[10] Meanwhile, the trial results continued to reverberate.

SATURDAY, AUGUST 7, 1948

On this day, the Progressive Party issued petitions, launching a mass appeal for a full probe of the trial. However, party members were distracted by the time and effort expended on the campaign of Henry A. Wallace, the Progressive Party candidate for president.[11] Imanuel Kanter, chairman of the Mercer County Communist Party, issued a statement that began: "The Communist Party does not condone murder in any quarter. It does not condone the murder of William Horner. The guilty must be punished." But the statement added that this was yet another case in which "[s]uspects are abused and intimidated. Witnesses whose testimony casts doubt on the guilt of any defendant are attacked and discredited. . . . What a hideous commentary it is that the condemning of six young men to their death is regarded in the press as a 'victory' for the prosecutor. . . . The Communist Party pledges its fullest support to obtain full justice in this case."[12] The Communist Party had assisted in the Scottsboro case, part of its strategy to attract blacks to its cause. The Associated Press story on the trial was picked up by the *New York Times* and other New York City newspapers, providing coverage of the case in New York for the first time.

SUNDAY, AUGUST 8, 1948

The *Trenton Evening Times* published two articles on the Trenton Six after the trial ended. One provided a straightforward, eight-paragraph account of the trial, and the coming, mandatory appeal, for which the taxpayers of Mercer County would pay. The other, a twenty-four-paragraph article featured in the General News section, was headlined: "Jurors for Horner Trial Had Grueling Experience." It recounted their lengthy service, isolated from their families and friends.

MONDAY, AUGUST 9, 1948

After the trial ended, Bessie Mitchell gathered herself together and considered what to do next. Remembering that the FBI agent named Griffin at the Newark office had said to her: "If the men aren't acquitted, get in touch with us after the trial and we'll see what we can do then," she arranged to meet with him. He told her that she needed to see an agent named Waldron in the Trenton office. He turned out to be a brother of James Waldron, one of the court-appointed attorneys for the Six. Expressing his astonishment at seeing her, he asked, "What do you expect us to do?" "If you can't do anything, why'd you give me such a runaround?" she asked. Her answer caused Waldron to burst out laughing. Bessie recalled, "He made me so mad that I wanted to take up something and hit him."[13]

Next Bessie tried the Negro clergymen. Her experience with the Reverend Grayson was one that would be repeated many times. He listened patiently as she explained all of the inconsistencies and contradictions in the case, but ultimately responded, "Those men wouldn't be down there if they weren't guilty." She then brought up what Dr. Sullivan and Scrappy

Manning had told her of the case, with the different versions they used in court. Grayson responded, "We mustn't tear our leadership apart." Thus, he admonished Bessie not to criticize the part the men played. Next she tried to see Prosecutor Mario Volpe, who refused to speak with her, but she was able to see Assistant Prosecutor Frank Lawton. She tried pointing out to him the inconsistencies in the case, but he simply puffed on his cigarette and blew smoke into her face, refusing to answer. Finally, infuriated, she told him, "If there's any justice in this country, you can bet your bottom dollar I'll find it."[14]

Having little faith in the court-appointed attorneys, even though they were appealing the court's verdict, Bessie thought of where to go next and decided to try the NAACP again. She discovered that Dr. Charles Broadus, director of the Trenton branch, was a close friend of both Scrappy Manning and Dr. Sullivan. Broadus told her, "The NAACP doesn't handle murder cases."[15] So Bessie went to the office of the American Civil Liberties Union (ACLU) on lower Fifth Avenue in New York City. Clifford Forster, the staff counsel, listened to Bessie's story, read the pile of newspaper clippings she presented to him, and studied the transcript of the trial proceeding. Then he told her that there was "no indication of racial discrimination or of an abrogation of the men's civil liberties," and that therefore there was nothing the ACLU could do.[16]

Bessie refused to become discouraged. She formulated a plan to visit all the bars in Trenton that would let her in, Jim Crow laws being still in place. Someone had told her that news spread quickly in bars, so she decided to chat with bar patrons to see what she could learn. Since she was again working in New York City, her efforts were limited to evenings and weekends, but she began canvassing all the bars on the west side of Trenton. Collis English had told her that he had been beaten by policemen while in jail, but during the trial police had denied it. She asked dozens of bar patrons, mostly but not all black, who responded that accepted procedure was to "beat you up first, and then they start asking you questions."[17]

A secondary quest was for information about Dr. J. Minor Sullivan and Scrappy Manning, who had both testified for the prosecution during the trial. She was, in particular, concerned about Manning, whom she had gone to see after learning that he had been present when the confessions were signed. She told William Reuben that Manning railed at her in an ugly voice: "Listen, girlie, if you know what's good for you, you'll get on the first train back to New York. You're going to get yourself in trouble if you stay around here asking questions." The universal report she received on him from bar patrons was "That 'Scrappy' ain't no damn good, he'd sell his own mother down the country." With her search for information in bars on Trenton's west side complete, she started on the east side, reaffirming her knowledge of the blatant racial discrimination shown to blacks by those in authority in Trenton but learning little else.[18]

FRIDAY, AUGUST 20, 1948

A lone black newspaper, the New Jersey *Herald-Express*, protested the verdict, calling it a New Jersey "Scottsboro" referring to an infamous Depression-era incident.[19] During the Great Depression, many men and youths "rode the rails" in search of employment and food. On March 25, 1931, a posse of white men grabbed nine young blacks riding in a boxcar on the line from Chattanooga to Memphis, who had gotten into a fight with white youths, and took them to jail in Scottsboro, Alabama. Authorities discovered two young white women had been on the train that day; the women subsequently stated they had been raped by several of the blacks. A mob formed rapidly, causing Alabama's governor, Benjamin M. Miller, to call in the National Guard to protect the men in jail. Authorities promised speedy trials and executions in order to get the surrounding hordes to leave. The court quickly sentenced all nine to death; however, investigation revealed that the two females were prostitutes. After three rounds of trials and appeals, the men finally gained their freedom by 1950, although some had spent the entire time after conviction until then in prison.[20]

Meanwhile, the black community of Trenton began to stir; they knew enough about the Trenton Six case to be very angry. Most of the six were well known in town and had good reputations. They not only had reliable alibis, but people knew the questionable manner in which they had been rounded up.[21] Two black ministers, the Reverend D. M. Owens and Elder E. E. Jones, organized a protest meeting, which was held several weeks after the verdict on a sweltering Friday evening. Handbills had been distributed throughout the black neighborhoods announcing that the time had come to protest the police brutality familiar to them all. The Baptist church filled to capacity, with many having to be turned away. However, nothing further came of this meeting, except the ministers' willingness to assist journalist William Reuben. This they did until December, when they stopped returning his calls or answering his letters.[22]

WEDNESDAY, SEPTEMBER 1, 1948

On this first evening in September, Bessie Mitchell made her way slowly back to Trenton's train station to return home to New York City. She had been canvassing the bars on Trenton's east side, feeling that her cause was hopeless, but knowing no other way to move ahead. A flyer lying in the gutter with a large heading of "CIVIL RIGHTS" caught her eye. It described the work of the Civil Rights Congress (CRC), an organization she had never heard of, and provided an address to which Bessie wrote. She explained some of the inconsistencies in her brother's and the others' cases. By this time her expectations were low, so she was immensely surprised when her mother called to tell her that someone from the group wished to see her. She met with a young man named Arthur Brown, the New Jersey director of the Civil Rights Congress, who brought with him a white Trenton housewife named Mrs. Millie Salwen. They promised her help and for the first time, gave her hope.[23]

SUNDAY, SEPTEMBER 19, 1948

On this day, the Trenton Six waited to die. No lawyer, judge, prosecutor, warden, or jail guard ever told the men that their sentences had been automatically postponed when the appeal was filed on August 20. According to the *Daily Worker*, the Communist Party's newspaper, they had their heads shaved and pants split in preparation for the electric chair. If this is true, this action by prison guards, who knew there would be no execution, was incredibly cruel. Their day of agony was unknown to the outside world until ten months later when reporters were allowed to converse with the men. Asked in general about their forty-nine weeks in the Death House, Cooper spoke up first: "Oh, it wasn't so bad, except for that September 19 it wasn't so bad." Thorpe added: "Yeah, that September 19 was rough." Questioned about this reply, Cooper explained, "That's the day we thought we was going to be taken to the chair. We waited all day and night on September 19, expecting to be electrocuted." Cooper felt the pressure so acutely that he did not utter a word for the next two months. Collis English asked the reporters, "Why couldn't they tell us? My cell was right next to the execution room, and I saw them take three men in there. Then they carried them out, right past me. It was rough." Thorpe explained, "Right after the jury said we was guilty, Judge Hutchinson, he sentenced us to die on September 19. And that's all we knew till we heard something about a postponement days later on the radio." When asked if there was anything the prisoners wanted, Cooper stated, "Just to get out of here, that's all we want. Soon as they let me out, I'm going to get out of this town and never come back. You're not going to see me around here, not one minute. Else they'll pretend again that I do something I didn't do."[24]

MONDAY, SEPTEMBER 20, 1948

Mrs. Millie Salwen, suburban housewife and ardent champion of civil liberties, as well as a card-carrying member of the Communist Party, wrote an article in the New Jersey edition of the *Daily Worker*, which for the first time brought the defendants' side of the argument to public notice.[25] She interviewed Bessie Mitchell, who expressed her gratitude for the help now being offered by the Civil Rights Congress: "I am not going to let my brother die for something he didn't do; it is the people that is going to make the law come round and do right."[26] The Civil Rights Congress launched a campaign to win "in the court of public opinion," taking the battle for the Trenton Six to the streets, churches, and union halls. William Patterson, executive director of the Civil Rights Congress, defined his organization as "a defender of constitutional liberties, human rights, and of peace. It is the implacable enemy of every creed, philosophy, social system or way of life that denies democratic rights or one iota of human dignity to any human being because of color, creed, nationality or political belief" (see figure 4). Nothing could sound more deeply democratic, but in fact, the Communist Party USA operated the Civil Rights Congress. Its policy was to depend not on the courts, but on the people, to win justice. The CRC created petitions, letters, and resolutions to send to the governor, sent pamphlets to New Jersey legislators, created a play and a filmstrip, organized the Committee to Free the Trenton Six, and picketed at trials. The organization held parades in Harlem and huge rallies in Trenton, created highway billboards for prominent locations, and persuaded well-known people such as Paul Robeson and Eleanor Roosevelt to take action. The CRC found college campuses particularly receptive to its efforts, and got students from the City College of New York, Rutgers, Columbia, and Princeton interested. The CRC's activities undoubtedly churned up the waters; after a Free the Trenton Six rally in Union, New Jersey, on February 10, 1949, the Ku Klux Klan burned a five-foot cross in front of what was then termed a Negro school where the rally had taken place. Mrs. Millie Salwen had bullets fired through her kitchen window and a cross burned in her front yard.[27] The CRC agitated fully and completely, in many times and places; I have outlined only the major events in the material that follows.

MONDAY, OCTOBER 25, 1948

The feature article in the brand-new weekly newspaper first published on
this date, the *National Guardian*, detailed the story of the Trenton Six, as
reported by journalist William Reuben. Headlined "Is There a 'Scottsboro
Case' in Trenton, New Jersey?" the paper remained cautious on the issue of
innocence. The article concluded: "All the other evidence, every circumstance
surrounding the crime, the testimony of eye witnesses and experts, over-
whelmingly proved the innocence of two of the six, and left far more than a
reasonable doubt concerning the other four." This followed earlier conclusions
by the Civil Rights Congress, the Communist Party USA, and the Progressive
Party that Forrest, MacKenzie, and Wilson were probably innocent, with the
remaining three possibly guilty. Reuben noticed that the first three had white
witnesses providing alibis, while the other three had only black witnesses.[28]

The *National Guardian* went on to feature the Trenton Six whenever there
was the tiniest scrap of news about the case, unabashedly using it to provide
interest in and build subscriptions. It had been launched by three men, Cedric
Belfrage, James Aronson, and John T. MacManus, who hoped to cut through
the censorship of the conventional press owned by big business, in order to
"speak for you."[29] A month before the first issue appeared, William Reuben
contracted with the editors to do a series of articles featuring civil liberties; he
initially went to Trenton to check on the case of Elwood Dean. Dean, a black
member of the New Jersey Communist Party, found himself the subject of
a hate campaign carried out by the *Newark Star-Ledger* to force his eviction
from a public housing project. Reuben spoke with Arthur Brown of the CRC
about Dean; he also spoke to six postal workers dismissed from their jobs at
the Plainfield, New Jersey, post office on vague loyalty charges. He was about
to leave when Brown mentioned the case he was currently investigating in
Trenton, in which it appeared that two or three of the men were innocent.
Brown referred Reuben to the only two people he knew of to discuss the case,
McKinley Forrest's brother Robert, and Bessie Mitchell. Robert Forrest was
unavailable, so Reuben interviewed Bessie Mitchell several times, read her
stack of newspaper clippings, and his resulting story became the lead in the
first issue of the *National Guardian*.[30]

The *Guardian*'s editors, realizing they had an exclusive representing all they
hoped to stand for, sent Reuben to Trenton to uncover new aspects of the
case and track down leads to keep the story going week after week. Reuben
interviewed people up and down Union Street, where Trenton's butchers were
located. He spoke with the owners of the Liberty Meat Market, Isaac Katzeff

and Philip Wiener, at length about McKinley Forrest; they also knew John MacKenzie, who worked for them occasionally. Wiener showed Reuben a Jewish New Year's greeting card that he had just received from Forrest, imprisoned in the Death House. Wiener told Reuben, "You could trust Forrest with your life. He'd never do anything like this crime. He was a nice, honest, quiet boy, a steady worker. If he wanted to rob someone, as the police said, he had plenty of chances to do it right here. We'd always send him to the bank to make our deposits. Many times he'd have as much as $1,000 in cash." But Wiener did not believe anything could be done to aid the men at this point.[31]

At another butcher's down the street, Reuben talked with Harry Stern, who MacKenzie had worked for on the day of the murder. Stern couldn't believe MacKenzie would have anything to do with such a terrible crime, but wondered, if he was innocent, what was he doing in prison?[32] Next Reuben visited the Thorpe family. James Thorpe lived with his grandparents, Mr. and Mrs. Henry Thorpe, on Grant Avenue. Henry Thorpe, whom Reuben described as "a wonderful, handsome dignified looking man of seventy," told Reuben that just about everyone on the block had seen James there at the time of the crime, but "if that jury didn't believe the four who swore to it in court, there wouldn't be any reason for them to believe the thousand who could have." A very bitter Mrs. Thorpe told Reuben, "You get in the law's hands you just can't help yourself. I'm going to let the Lord work it out, let Him have his way.... James was a good boy. He wouldn't get you in no trouble.... He hadn't done one thing about this crime." James's father, James Henry Thorpe Sr., lived next door to his parents and stated firmly, "I know my boy didn't have anything to do with this." But he had full confidence that the Lord would see justice done. In searching for other relatives to speak with, Reuben learned that Cooper had no one except a grandmother, who was believed to be living in Fitzgerald, Georgia. Wilson had one living relative, a sister, Sally, in Brooklyn, New York; Reuben described her as inarticulate and living in "virtual conditions of bondage." She had not seen her brother in more than ten years.[33]

Of other relatives involved, John MacKenzie's sister, Vera Strauss, worked long hours before the trial with Bessie Mitchell, trying to find assistance for her brother and the others. But, after the trial she went back to caring for her husband and three children, unable or unwilling to help further. Robert Forrest believed completely in the innocence of his brother, McKinley, but resented Collis English, whom he blamed for McKinley's predicament, and would do nothing to assist the other five men. None of the lawyers involved in the case would speak to Reuben. It took him until January 1949 to obtain the trial transcript. Bessie Mitchell remained the sole individual to believe in the innocence of all six with the willingness to do anything she could to help them.[34]

MONDAY, NOVEMBER 1, 1948

This week's issue of the *National Guardian* featured a column headlined "I Swear I Never Killed That Man, Bessie." The article quoted Collis and Bessie: "I swear before God, Bessie, I never killed that man. I don't know nothing about it. I never even seen that store." "How come you told them you killed Mr. Horner, then?" Bessie asked. Collis responded, "If anyone beat you like they did me and the others, you'd a done the same thing." Bessie emphasized to Reuben, "I didn't have much schooling. Lots of big words those lawyers use I can't understand. But you don't have to be educated to tell when something smells bad." A photo with the article showed Collis's mother, Mrs. Emma English, holding a picture of him in his navy uniform. A sidebar announced "Help Wanted. Defense of the six men now in Trenton's Death House needs help. Funds must be raised, petitions signed. Send money, requests for petition forms and other communications to Arthur Brown, New Jersey state secretary of the Civil Rights Congress, Newark, N.J."

MONDAY, NOVEMBER 8, 1948

This week's *National Guardian* contained the headline "Witnesses Put Condemned Men Far from Horner Murder Scene," while a sidebar noted "Scottsboro in Trenton." The article focused on Reuben's interviews with employers and relatives of the Six, confirming that they were not at the Horner store at the time of the murder. He especially detailed Forrest's behavior while drugged and in an isolation cell. Ten months after the murder of William Horner, the outside world began to not only hear about it, but to hear the side of the defendants.

MONDAY, NOVEMBER 29, 1948

The *National Guardian* proclaimed "Press and Clergy Are Barred to Condemned Six in Trenton" and featured a photograph of James Thorpe's grandparents. It showed Mrs. Thorpe ironing in the background while Mr. Thorpe read his Bible, from which he said he drew much consolation. The warden of the Trenton State Prison, George Page, would not allow Reuben to interview the Six. However, he stated that their lawyers and clergymen would be admitted. Thus, the Reverend D. M. Owens, pastor of Mount Zion Church, described by Reuben as the largest Negro church in Trenton, attempted to see the men. He was not let in to seem them but was allowed to talk with Harry A. Van Pelt, the prison's only black chaplain. Van Pelt claimed that the men were receiving adequate spiritual guidance, but Reverend Owens protested, "Four of them are Methodists. Two are Baptists. Perhaps they need a minister of their own religion." The chaplain responded, "Sorry, but that can't be helped. It's against the law for an outside minister to go into the Death House." The Reverend E. E. Jones then attempted to visit but was also turned away. Reuben wondered, in his article, if there was a conspiracy at work to keep the convicted men from contact with all who might help them.

Even though the *National Guardian* sent press releases to every daily newspaper in New York City during this period, none picked up the story of the Trenton Six. However, at the beginning of December 1948, the Communist *Daily Worker* and several nationally circulated black papers began to document the case. The *Pittsburgh Courier* carried an extensive three-part series by black novelist William Gardner Smith.[35]

John MacKenzie received a letter that revealed the burgeoning influence of the *National Guardian*. It was from Mr. and Mrs. Bob Jones of Corpus Christi, Texas, and it began: "We, down here in Texas would like for you to know that we know of your case and the case of all the Trenton Six. . . . You probably are aware that we did not read of your fight for justice in our daily newspapers but like millions of others we have to depend on the *National Guardian* for this news. Each week we scan its pages for news of you and all the others that also seek justice in such cases."[36]

SUNDAY, DECEMBER 19, 1948

On this bleak Sunday afternoon, relatives of Collis English, John MacKenzie, McKinley Forrest, and James Thorpe, the four men with relatives living in the area and empowered to act on their behalf, gathered in the tiny living room of 247 Church Street in Trenton, home of Collis, John and McKinley. They gathered to meet William Patterson, the black executive secretary of the Civil Rights Congress. Patterson began by explaining what the CRC was, who its members were, what it believed, and how it operated. He reminisced about the famous case of the Scottsboro Boys, which he had worked on fifteen years previously. Patterson told his audience a little about himself and his legal training; he received a law degree from the University of California in 1919 and went on to work on behalf of the controversial anarchists Sacco and Vanzetti; he also defended black army veterans arrested during the Bonus Army March of 1932. Patterson announced, "We're prepared to do the same thing with your boys. I believe your men, every one of them, are innocent. The organization I represent believes in their innocence. And I've come down here today to tell you that we want to help you. Do you want our help?"[37]

Before the relatives could respond, Patterson went on to predict the reaction by others if the CRC got involved: "From the day you authorize me to represent your men, people will come to you and tell you I'm a Communist, that you should stay away from me." He felt sure that the court-appointed lawyers who never returned phone calls, would come around and "Tell you the boys will surely die if you get mixed up with me. Ministers, prominent Negroes, police and city officials, where are they now? Have any of them so much as lifted a finger to prevent your innocent men from being murdered?" He went on: "In many parts of these United States you can be jailed, shot down or lynched for no reason by a white man, who need have no fear of being punished. . . . The only things we get are the things we fight for. . . . The State certainly doesn't want these innocent men to go free; we've seen what the State has done to them. None of your so-called leaders in Trenton want them to go free. . . . I hope I have made myself clear. Your boys are going to die unless we stick together. This struggle will not be easy, but it can be won."[38]

After Patterson threw down the gauntlet, asking who would join him, silence reigned for over a minute. Bessie Mitchell then rose from her seat, prepared to encourage the others to come forward, saying, "Beggars can't be choosers." But Patterson urged Bessie to wait until he heard from her mother. After a long pause, Mrs. English, a tiny seventy-year-old, got up, aided by Bessie, and stated in a firm voice, "Yes, sir. I want to sign up with you." Then James Thorpe Sr., who earlier had told Reuben that his son's fate was in the hands of the Lord, spoke forcefully: "I want to sign too. I want to sign for my boy." MacKenzie's sister, Vera Strauss, thought she would wait to talk with her brother before doing anything. Mrs. Robert Forrest, McKinley's sister-in-law, thought her husband should speak with McKinley, so she did not sign. But Patterson made it clear that while he focused on whoever wished his representation, he would be working for all six, since he felt strongly that all six had been framed equally.[39]

After this meeting, Patterson drew up an ambitious eleven-point organizational program regarding how the nonlegal side of the case was to be approached. It was to be the CRC's "major national case to make the issue of Negro rights a central struggle for constitutional guarantees and civil liberties." A chronological memo of the case would be drawn up, and passed on to CRC state and local committees. Letters asking for support were to be sent out, "linking the case with a report on segregation in Washington, D.C., showing similarity and national scope of persecution." A special appeal would be made to churches, with "moral content of case always to forefront." Trade unions, women, and youth organizations would be targeted. A pamphlet would be prepared with black artists' work being utilized. Demonstrations, meetings, and conferences would be organized, with the press involved in all activities. This all reflected Patterson's long-term strategy: every element would be used to build the Civil Rights Congress. The document presciently warned, "Every effort will be made to split whatever unity is being developed in the process of this struggle." As the CRC continued its work to "win" in the court of public opinion, everything Patterson predicted came true. The relatives faced an outcry on every side that they were being used by the CRC for its own gain. And it was true that part of the CRC overall strategy was to work actively with minorities whenever possible. A memo circulated by the Communist Party USA provided evidence: "The Civil Rights Congress deserves our best support in this case . . . it will send circular letters, conduct a tour of relatives of the Trenton Six, run mass meetings. All this should spread the influence of the CRC. These actions will assist us in the fight to quash the indictments of the leaders of the Communist Party."[40] (At this time Communist Party leaders in the United States faced prison terms for violating the Smith Act. J. Edgar Hoover led the investigations.) Observers feared that the Trenton Six and their relatives had become pawns in a global propaganda struggle. However, the most vocal of the relatives remained clear that William Patterson presented them with the only substantive offer of assistance to come their way.

The CRC proceeded in tandem with the legal side of the case. Patterson began the process of hiring lawyers to manage the coming appeal.[41] He also hired an investigator to speak with Mr. and Mrs. Bowker, who lived in the front room above the Horner store from 1942 to 1948. Mrs. Bowker provided a signed affidavit regarding the behavior of Mrs. Horner: "Many times Mrs. Horner would stay in her room by herself all day, talking to herself, throwing things around and hitting the wall. Mrs. Horner cried frequently and spoke to herself while alone in her room, without making any sense. She was so noisy that we were required to keep our door closed. Mrs. Horner was temperamentally unpredictable. On one day she would be extremely sociable, while on the next day she would be completely unsociable and take issue with anything that was said to her." Among the many actions pouring out of the CRC office at this time was a poster with a one-thousand-dollar reward "for information leading to the arrest and conviction of the real murderer of William Horner."[42]

A breakthrough of sorts came from interest in the Six expressed by Gordon Schaffer, assistant editor of the English weekly *Reynolds News*, then published by the British Co-operative Party. The party still exists, working closely with the Labour Party to influence it toward "cooperative" principles, but the paper ceased publication in 1967. The paper published a lengthy article by William Reuben on December 19. The *Reynolds News* used the startling headline: "They Must Die for Being Black." United Press International (UPI) sent the story to its hundreds of member newspapers. Thus, this one story, printed in England, sent around the world by UPI, became the catalyst for dawning worldwide interest in the case. From England, papers throughout Europe picked up the story, which then spread to Moscow, India, the Philippines, and all corners of the world. The UPI story also refocused Trenton-based newspapers, which had been silent since the conviction, on the Six.[43]

The December 20 *Trentonian* featured a front-page editorial alongside its excerpt of the UPI story, beginning: "We have known for some time of an undercover Communist crusade to martyrize the convicted Horner killers, and to turn the Horner killing and trial into another Scottsboro case." The *Trenton Evening Times* described the *Reynolds News* as a "Socialist" paper, declaring, "A similar attack was made in the Sunday edition of the New York *Daily Worker*, U.S. Communist Party newspaper, the United Press reports." However, UPI made no mention of Communists or the *Daily Worker*. The *Trenton Evening Times* quoted Director of Public Safety Andrew Duch, who had created the fifteen-man machine-gun-armed squad that oppressed Trenton's black population after the murder, as saying, "There was absolutely no brutality on the part of Trenton police. There is no basis for that charge." Defense attorney James S. Turp declared, "The London story is unfortunate; that's all I can say at this time."[44] Now, however, when anyone pointed out the many inconsistencies in the case, an easy response was that they were obviously influenced by Communists. Soviet aggression in Europe at this time made this an easy charge to make and sustain.

Cracks were beginning to appear in the prosecution's position. Dr. J. Minor Sullivan III told the press that he thought one of the Six, Horace Wilson, was innocent. And Duch told the *Trentonian*, "I was convinced that one or two of the defendants had sound alibis but evidently the jury disagreed. The circumstances surrounding the taking of one life in this case did not, in my opinion, require the extreme death penalty for six persons."[45] Coming as these remarks did, right before Christmas, they provided perhaps small morsels of hope to relatives and friends having to spend Christmas separated from their loved ones locked in the Death House of the Trenton State Prison.

WEDNESDAY, JANUARY 5, 1949

The *Daily Worker* reported on this day "6 Trenton Negroes Ill in Death House." Prison authorities insisted that the men remain in the Death House during the appeal of their case; they were let out of their cells only once a week for a bath and exercise. Mrs. Emma English reported that both Collis and McKinley Forrest needed frequent care by prison doctors, and all the men indicated that being caged was sapping their strength.

MONDAY, JANUARY 10, 1949

After relatives of five of the Trenton Six (Ralph Cooper's only known relative, a grandmother in Georgia, refused to sign on his behalf) signed documents asking William Patterson to serve on their behalf, Patterson officially retained O. John Rogge to lead the charge. Rogge had served as assistant U.S. attorney general, heading the Criminal Division of the Department of Justice from 1943 to 1946; in 1948 he was a contender for the Progressive Party's vice-presidential nomination. A prominent champion of radical causes, he routinely defended organizations deemed subversive by the Department of Justice in which he had previously served. Associated with several Communist organizations, he once visited the U.S.S.R as Stalin's personal guest. In 1950 he served as one of two U.S. delegates, along with Paul Robeson, to the Communist-inspired World Committee of the Defenders of Peace meeting in London.[46] Solomon Golat, a prominent New Jersey labor and civil rights attorney, and Emanuel Bloch served as cocounsels.[47]

TUESDAY, JANUARY 18, 1949

An editorial on this day in the *Trenton Evening Times* revealed a split in the black community: "Mass meetings, protests, and other public demonstration such as those proposed could only be interpreted as endeavors to influence the orderly processes of justice through agitation and pressure. Unless there is reason to believe that the condemned men are being denied just treatment, such tactics are certain to do more harm than good." The editorial referred to an action by the Trenton Chapter of the Civil Rights Congress, in concert with the United Electrical Union and the Progressive Party, announcing a meeting planned for January 28 at which the gifted actor, singer, and political activist Paul Robeson would be the featured speaker. Some in the NAACP felt Robeson deserved their support, while others argued there should be no cooperation with the CRC, listed as a "subversive organization" by the U.S. attorney general. The NAACP decided not to participate. The dispute continued after a February CRC rally in Newark during which William Patterson criticized the NAACP stance. Thurgood Marshall, NAACP special counsel, blasted back, demanding a public retraction of Patterson's remarks. Patterson then publicly appealed to the NAACP to get involved.[48]

Also on this day, New Jersey Supreme Court Chief Justice Arthur T. Vanderbilt agreed that Rogge, Golat, and Bloch could confer with the men in the Death House to determine if they wished to change counsel. However, he stated that the original counsel needed to be present also. On January 25 Rogge ruefully noted in an article he wrote for the *National Guardian,* "Our group was probably the largest ever to enter any Death House anywhere. There were seven lawyers, five relatives, two prison officials—and twelve armed guards." William Patterson served as spokesman, saying he believed all six were innocent. Bessie Mitchell spoke on behalf of the relatives, while James Waldron served as spokesman for the original lawyers. Waldron explained that the CRC lawyers would not be in addition to the court-appointed attorneys, but would replace them. Just three of the Six, Collis English, James Thorpe, and Ralph Cooper, chose to go with the CRC. Vera Strauss urged her brother Jack to keep his original attorneys, which angered Bessie Mitchell and Mrs. English.[49] Bessie and her mother believed strongly that the original attorneys had been inadequate and had complete faith in Patterson, Rogge, and the Civil Rights Congress.

MONDAY, FEBRUARY 7, 1949

In an article headlined "1,000 Rally in Trenton to Aid Condemned Six," the *National Guardian* reported on a meeting hosted by the Committee to Free the Trenton Six. Union leaders and ministers as well as O. John Rogge spoke. Bessie Mitchell told the crowd, "I'm learning that we've got to keep fighting to get the peace and democracy we're supposed to be enjoying." Paul Robeson gave an impassioned oration: "I know what's been done to these boys could have been done to my own boy. But your presence here will show the Trenton authorities that my people have allies who will fight for them. We've come here to tell the enemies of democracy in Trenton and everywhere else that we're not staying 'in our place' anymore."

MONDAY, FEBRUARY 14, 1949

Representatives of the Civil Rights Congress met briefly with Governor Alfred Driscoll, who had never heard of the Trenton Six and knew nothing about the case. In response they sent him a pamphlet with the facts as compiled by the CRC. While several individuals met with Governor Driscoll, a group described as unionists, housewives, and clergymen picketed the State House, with signs demanding freedom for the Six.[50] A photograph of the demonstration ran widely in area newspapers (see figure 5). William Patterson took the fight for the Trenton Six to a new medium, television, appearing on an ABC news show.[51] Also on this date O. John Rogge began a three-part discussion of the trial record in the *National Guardian*. As planned by the CRC, and using a variety of methods, the story of the Trenton Six began to percolate into the public consciousness.

SATURDAY, FEBRUARY 26, 1949

William Patterson and the lawyers he retained for the appeal held a press conference in which Rogge stated: "I am in the case of the Trenton Six because I regard it as the northern Scottsboro case." On February 27 the *New York Times* ran a small item about the press conference, which came to the attention of New Jersey Supreme Court Chief Justice Arthur T. Vanderbilt. As Rogge explained it: "He immediately called New Jersey counsel to say that unless I submitted a letter of apology before eight-thirty of the following morning he would have me before the full bench of the Supreme Court on the next Monday." Rogge sent a letter to Judge Vanderbilt affirming that his comments were "in accordance with the Canons of Ethics" and with two cases he cited. He added, "In no way during the course of my comments did I reflect adversely upon the integrity of the Supreme Court of the State of New Jersey. On the contrary, I stated that my co-counsel and I confidently trusted in the judgment of that Court. Nor were my remarks intended or calculated to influence the decision of this Court except in accordance with the applicable principles of law." Judge Vanderbilt did not consider this an apology and demanded that the lawyers appear before the full New Jersey Supreme Court bench. After questioning

Rogge, Justice Vanderbilt revealed his views: "To allege race discrimination in this case, and to compare it to other cases in which race prejudice has been a factor, would constitute an indirect attempt to bring pressure to bear on the court. . . . Once an attorney has accepted a retainer which takes him into court, he assumes special obligations which definitely bar him from public discussion of the case." Vanderbilt concluded that he would leave the matter of Rogge's speaking in public to the attorney's sound judgment. That evening Rogge addressed a large rally in Trenton.[52]

Sunday, February 27, 1949

Drew Pearson, well-known columnist and radio journalist, discussed the Trenton Six at length in his weekly NBC radio broadcast. The executive board of the New Jersey State Congress of Industrial Organizations (CIO) voted to demand a retrial of the Six.[53] In response, the March 1 *Trenton Evening Times* published an editorial entitled "Pressure of Hysteria":

> Implicit in the decision of the New Jersey CIO to support the demand for a new trial of six men condemned to death for the brutal murder of an aged man is a lack of confidence in the fairness of the original trial and the competence of the Supreme Court to decide their appeal on its merits. In taking this position the president of the CIO explains that it is disassociating itself from "the hysterical appeal by organizations listed as subversive by the Department of Justice." Perhaps, however, it is influenced by the equally hysterical harangue of a radio commentator who has followed faithfully the line of these organizations and who has not taken the trouble to inform himself as to the scrupulous efforts by the agencies of law to safeguard the rights of these men at every stage of the proceedings from the time of their arrest to their conviction.

The publicity pot created by the CRC was stirring and boiling over.

Monday, March 7, 1949

In February the Civil Rights Congress published 150,000 copies of its pamphlet "Lynching Northern Style" and distribution began throughout the United States (see figure 6). The pamphlet had a striking cover design featuring a white judge at his bench above a group of six black men on the floor. Five of the men huddle around a central figure, heads bowed in anguish. The central figure has a long neck circled with a noose, stretched above the other men, and the lynching rope reaches above to the judge. After providing facts about the "legal lynching, Jersey style," the last page featured another image, a long rope with a noose at the bottom. Readers were urged to "Cut the lynch rope—clip the coupon" and "contribute to the Committee to Free the Trenton Six, Paul Robeson, Chairman."[54]

The CRC distributed the new pamphlets on March 7 at a massive rally in Trenton. Almost one thousand people, from trade unions and political, social, and church groups, jammed Moose Hall to hear Paul Robeson, the featured speaker, who in addition to his many other achievements was a former Rutgers football star, six feet five inches tall and weighing 260 pounds. Even before the chairman could finish the introduction, the audience "rose and began applauding, stamping their feet, shouting, shrieking and whistling." Finally quieting after Robeson stood at the podium, the audience was mesmerized. Robeson began: "I want to thank all of you for this great turn out. Your presence here tonight will show the Trenton authorities that my people have allies, allies who will fight with them for a world where everyone can walk the earth in peace and dignity. Your presence here will show these authorities, these fascist-minded, cowardly men, that they can no longer say to us, 'Nigger, stay in your place.' From now on the only place we're staying in is the place guaranteed us by the constitution of the United States!"[55]

TUESDAY, MARCH 8, 1951

Attorney O. John Rogge and folk singer Pete Seeger were scheduled to appear at a rally in a public school auditorium in Syracuse, New York. However, at the last moment that city's mayor, Frank J. Costello, revoked the permit, fearing bad publicity for the school. Syracuse University student Irving Feiner took to a soapbox, urging people to attend the rally, castigating not only the mayor who cancelled the permit, but also the local political system, and the American Legion. Police estimated that eighty whites and blacks (or twenty-five according to Feiner) had gathered and were blocking the sidewalk and becoming restive. Hecklers appeared and someone threatened Feiner. A police officer asked him to come down from the soapbox. He refused, was arrested, found guilty, and sentenced to thirty days in jail. While event organizers held a successful rally at the nearby Hotel Syracuse, the events had great repercussions on Feiner, who was expelled by the university and had his admissions to law schools revoked. According to his obituary in the *New York Times*, two New York State appellate courts upheld his conviction, as did the U.S. Supreme Court. The Court held that the possibility of civil unrest justified Feiner's arrest. Justice Hugo Black dissented, saying, "I understand that people in totalitarian countries must obey arbitrary orders. I had hoped that there was no such duty in the United States." As time passed, this decision, putting public order ahead of freedom of expression, was gradually superseded by other cases. Feiner eventually returned to Syracuse University, finishing his undergraduate degree in 1984. In 2007, the university invited him to lecture on the topic of free speech.[56]

SATURDAY, MARCH 19, 1949

William Patterson appeared on *CBS Views the Press*. He was allotted fifteen minutes and began by saying, "For more than a year, there has extended an almost complete blackout by the New York papers, and not for lack of its being called to their attention either. For all that has been going on only sixty miles from New York, it might as well be on the moon." He described the case of the Trenton Six as it had developed and their current circumstances and began to see results. Don Hollenbeck's *CBS Views the News* spent an entire broadcast on the case, pointing out, "It was a long time before the Sacco-Vanzetti case began to get news prominence back in the twenties; it is now an important chapter in the history of American jurisprudence. Off to a slow start, the press may in time discover that it has another such cause célèbre on its hands—and do something about it."[57]

On this day Bessie Mitchell sent a postcard to Jack MacKenzie: "Dear Jack, I only wish I knew why you did not take new lawyers, but I know under the circumstances you can't. *Keep your courage, we are all still fighting*."[58] Bessie spent much time speaking at CRC rallies held in New York and throughout New Jersey.

FRIDAY, MARCH 25, 1949

Mystery writer Dashiell Hammett, state chairman of the New York Civil Rights Congress, sent out letters accompanied by the "Lynching Northern Style" pamphlets, as well as petitions, explaining the Trenton Six case and asking to have the petitions returned as quickly as possible. Among those joining in the fight, Hammett listed playwright Arthur Miller.[59]

SATURDAY, MARCH 26, 1949

In an article titled "'Due Process' in New Jersey" in this week's issue of the *Nation*, Hugh Graham, a Princeton writer, set out to introduce more people to the Trenton Six:

> Readers of the *Daily Worker* are already familiar with the "Northern Scottsboro case," which has received enormous attention in that journal. Many Europeans are also familiar with it, for it has been fully and sensa-tionally reported in the British and French press and presumably, by now, in the press of Eastern Europe. The few non-Communist Americans who have heard of Trenton's "legal lynching," as the *Worker* calls it, are apt to dismiss the hullabaloo about it as just another piece of agi-prop [*sic*]. That would be a mistake. While it is true that the case has served the party well as a means of raising temperatures and dollars, it is equally true that any objective observer must regard the events which followed William Horner's murder in Trenton fourteen months ago with no less uneasiness than that expressed by the Communists, for it is quite apparent that six Trenton Negroes have been convicted for collaborating in a killing in which some or all of them may have had no part.

Graham then laid out the case in detail for the *Nation*'s readership. Princeton students formed a Committee to Free the Trenton Six, and Albert Einstein, on the faculty of the Institute of Advanced Study, also became active in the case.[60]

SATURDAY, APRIL 9, 1949

On this day Bessie Mitchell wrote a letter to Eleanor Roosevelt asking for help:

> My name is Bessie Mitchell, my brother and my brother-in-law and four other men are sentenced to the electric chair and are in the Death House.
> Maybe you heard or read of the Horner Murder Case or better known as the case of the Trenton 6, in Trenton, New Jersey.
> These men are innocent and the records show that.
> Since the time my brother was arrested I have been fighting for him and the other men.

They were arrested without warrants, held five days without a charge. I begged the police to let me see my brother and they would not let me.

Then I went to several organizations, newspapers, Veterans Administration, and even to the FBI. I also wrote to Governor Driscoll, Supreme Court and many rich people, they refuse me in a nice way.

Then I lost faith in the United States of America.

I had always believed before that the people found justice here when they couldn't anywhere else in the world. Then I learned about the Civil Rights Congress.

I begged them to help me. First they start to restore my faith in the American people.

Then gave me courage to keep fighting to win.

I remember you when I was a girl how interested you were in Negro People. Please help us now to restore peace.

My people can't stand these police brutalities much longer.

I remain Humbul, [sic] Bessie Mitchell

P.S. Please answer

Mrs. Roosevelt wrote to a friend, Geraldine Thompson, of Red Bank, New Jersey, asking if she knew anything about the case "that would lead this woman to have a basis for feeling that these people, who are evidently Negroes, are unfairly treated." She also wrote back to Bessie Mitchell, saying she had asked a "very influential person in welfare circles in New Jersey to communicate with the Governor" about the situation. Thompson replied to Mrs. Roosevelt that she had already inquired about the case to Judge Henry E. Ackerson, a member of the New Jersey Supreme Court, and written to the New Jersey attorney general, Theodore D. Parsons, and assured Mrs. Roosevelt that both men were "humane and liberal thinkers and men of impeccable character." Mr. Parsons, in turn, wrote to Mrs. Roosevelt, informing her that the Trenton Six would soon have their appeal before the New Jersey Supreme Court, in which he had great confidence.[61]

TUESDAY, APRIL 12, 1949

Buses arrived from New Jersey, New York, Pennsylvania, Connecticut, and Massachusetts, emptying their activists onto State Street near the New Jersey statehouse. Civil Rights Congress delegates had with them detailed instructions to march two abreast, with slogans provided by picket line captains, from noon until 3:00 P.M. The CRC provided a list of suggested eating places,

necessary to know because blacks would only be served in a few establish-
ments. A committee of twenty ministers, union leaders, and civic leaders attempted to see Governor Driscoll and Attorney General Parsons to give them
petitions signed by 50,000 Americans, asking Governor Driscoll to free the
Trenton Six. The 450 people picketing then spread out to street corners and
neighborhoods throughout the city, handing out thousands of leaflets to the
citizens of Trenton. William Patterson and Bessie Mitchell visited the Six in the
Death House before all the demonstrators joined together at a mass meeting
at the War Memorial. Late in the day, the governor, who had earlier claimed
to be too busy to meet with the CRC delegates, held a press conference and
pointed out that the CRC held a prime position on U.S. Attorney General
Tom Clark's list of Communist organizations. Five members did meet with
Attorney General Theodore Parsons, who listened carefully but declared that
any decisions would be made by New Jersey's Supreme Court.[62]

After this event and the media coverage that followed, Governor Driscoll
began to receive letters such as one beginning: "In Gods name, please investigate the case of the six negroes who are sentenced to death in your state.
The case stinks way out here!. . . . We would like to know what you are doing
about it? If nothing, why not? This is the United States of America where all
men are supposed to be created *equal*." Signed by several people living in Ann
Arbor, Michigan, the letter contained a P.S.: "We have white skins."[63]

Friday, April 29, 1949

The Civil Rights Congress asked the Human Rights Commission of the
United Nations, chaired by Eleanor Roosevelt, to look into the case of the
Trenton Six.[64]

Tuesday, May 10, 1949

In Manchester, England, Paul Robeson spoke and sang at a benefit rally for
the Committee to Free the Trenton Six. More than five thousand people attended.[65]

Friday, May 13, 1949–Thursday, May 19, 1949

The Civil Rights Congress sent Bessie Mitchell on a speaking tour across the
United States. In Phoenix a crowd of eight hundred people, black and white,
heard her tell the story of the Six in a local school auditorium, while hundreds

more waited outside. In Tucson two hundred people stood in the rain to hear Mitchell's talk after the local board of education canceled the CRC's permit to meet in a school. In Sullivan County, New York, hundreds heard Mitchell speak, despite a raging storm that caused the electricity to fail. Mitchell criss-crossed the country, speaking in union halls, churches, parks, and schools and drawing large audiences. Her supporters contributed money, letters, and petitions to the cause. From May 13 to May 19 alone, she gave sixteen talks at meetings with 25 to 150 in attendance.[66]

The Youth and Student Division of the CRC directed "additional communications in an effort to secure a large delegation of young people to see Mrs. Eleanor Roosevelt, as head of the Human Rights Commission, to appeal for an investigation of the case of the Trenton Six." This notation appears in Eleanor Roosevelt's FBI file.[67] Several hundred students from the New York City area successfully visited members of the commission on May 23.[68]

THE APPEAL

The Trenton Six arrived at their appeal with a multiplicity of lawyers and briefs. The Civil Rights Congress filed a 115-page brief, written by Solomon Golat and Clarence Talisman, on behalf of Collis English, Ralph Cooper, and James Thorpe. O. John Rogge argued their cases in court. Even before the appeal, the CRC lawyers took action regarding Judge Charles P. Hutchinson. The jury had found all six defendants guilty but did not specify whether in the first or second degree. However, the printed trial record mistakenly recorded the men as "guilty of murder in the first degree and so say they all." In a writ of error, Judge Hutchinson, prodded by the CRC attorneys, agreed to a return of the original wording.[69] The attorneys pointed out, early in their appeal brief, that Judge Hutchinson incorrectly sentenced the men to death, as they had not been sentenced to murder in the first degree. The lawyers then moved on to their major arguments. First, "The Trial Court erred in admitting into evidence the purported confessions of the Defendants-Appellants." Here the attorneys relied on the Fourteenth Amendment to the U.S. Constitution, claiming that the defendants had been deprived of "life, liberty, or property" without due process of law: the confessions were involuntarily made. The protracted questioning and the men's obvious fear indicated that the statements were coerced; in addition, the men were not made aware of their constitutional rights. Even if the confessions had been made voluntarily, their "use was unconstitutional in that they were obtained by illegal methods and unlawfully admitted into evidence." The confessions also violated New Jersey law in being obtained without the men having had a hearing before a judge within forty-eight hours of being confined.[70]

Point two of the CRC brief: "The verdicts and judgment of the trial court were unlawful and should be set aside." This argument referred to the legal impossibility of sentencing people to death unless the jury found them guilty of murder in the first degree. The CRC again contended that the confessions had been involuntarily made, claiming this of Collis English: "The evidence is persuasive that a poor, sick, economically dispossessed Negro surrendered his free will. The evidence compels the conclusion that Collis English mortgaged his life to achieve temporary peace. The record bears witness that the police of Trenton have coerced a confession."[71] In Cooper's case, his unknowing smoking of reefers [marijuana cigarettes or some other unknown drug] given him by Chief Detective Naples made his confession involuntary. Regarding Thorpe, who claimed innocence up to the moment of signing a confession: "There is no explanation for this kind of police callousness. One does not have to be imbued with lofty ideals to reject an offer to sign such a confession; one only has to have a simple sense of sportsmanship."[72] The CRC argued that the verdicts rendered by the jury deserved to be put aside because none of the defendant-appellants had been identified by witnesses. In addition, there had been no evidence that a robbery, or attempted robbery, ever took place, and each individual had reliable, reputable alibi witnesses. Their next major point referred to the quashing of the subpoena directing the supervisor of the New Jersey State Bureau of Identification to testify regarding fingerprint evidence. The brief included numerous case references to back up the contention that Judge Hutchinson had erred.

Defense lawyers Waldron, Turp, and Queen filed a fifty-eight-page brief on behalf of John MacKenzie and Horace Wilson. Their work covered much of the same ground as the CRC attorneys but brought up points particular to MacKenzie and Wilson. They focused on Judge Hutchinson's charge to the jury, which they claimed contained prejudicial error. First, "the question of recommendation of life imprisonment is left to the unrestricted discretion of the jury." However, Judge Hutchinson told the jury "to keep in mind your responsibility not only to do justice to the defendants, but also to remember your similar responsibility to the State in the administration of its criminal laws."[73] Thus, the defense lawyers claimed that Hutchinson tried to influence the jury improperly. They pointed out instances in his charge in which he misstated facts to the detriment of the defendants. About the verdict: "If the verdict is valid, it is, nevertheless, contrary to the weight of the evidence with regard to the defendant Wilson." The only evidence against Wilson came from the testimony of Mrs. Horner who claimed to have seen him once at her store. In contrast to her testimony, numerous reliable witnesses testified as to the actual whereabouts of Wilson on January 27, 1948.

For MacKenzie, the brief came to the same conclusions; if the verdict was legally valid it was contrary to the weight of evidence. MacKenzie had steadfastly maintained his innocence until given a pack of cigarettes. After smoking them, he began to see things and signed a confession of which he later had no memory. The only evidence against him presented by the state was in this confession. In contrast, he had abundant believable alibi witnesses. The question of the mug shots eventually admitted into evidence by Judge Hutchinson also came under scrutiny. Because the jury could clearly see all the men during the trial, these photographs were secondary evidence, unnecessary and prejudicial to MacKenzie and Wilson.

Frank Katzenbach, continuing to represent McKinley Forrest, produced a fifty-page brief on his behalf. He pointed out that Forrest's confession had been wrung out of him when he was in a disturbed physical condition, as numerous witnesses testified. Katzenbach argued that Judge Hutchinson erred in granting a motion allowing Prosecutor Volpe to suppress the subpoenas directed to Director of Public Safety Andrew J. Duch, Chief of Police William Dooling, and Captain E. Paul Sjostrum. As Katzenbach put it, "As this trial progressed it became increasingly apparent to the attorney for McKinley Forrest and counsel for the other defendants that the State in its presentation of the case against these defendants was reticent to explain many questions to which its proofs had given rise—reluctant to permit the examination or analysis of its case beyond the bare facts of a violent death and the narrow confines of the pages of paper offered as the confessions of those defendants."[74] He began with the missing fingerprint evidence but had a further list of items. According to the trial record, Prosecutor Volpe did not call witness Virginia Barclay to testify, implying that she was in very poor health. When she appeared in court at Katzenbach's request, it became obvious she was in good health, happy to testify for the defense, but in an "advanced state of pregnancy."[75] Among other items defense counsel hoped to learn was the whereabouts of Jerry Griswold.

The National Association for the Advancement of Colored People finally decided to enter the fray, filing an amicus curiae, or friend of the court brief, on behalf of the Trenton Six. The nineteen-page brief, written by Herbert H. Tate and Thurgood Marshall, requested that the convictions be reversed. They explained the interest of the NAACP in the case: obtaining confessions under duress had been an issue in which "the Association has played an active role for many years. The instant case presents that issue."[76] The brief argued, first, that the treatment received by the defendants violated the Fourteenth Amendment of the United States Constitution, which Congress created specifically to help "the poor, the ignorant, the helpless, the weak and outnumbered for whom constitutional protections stand as a shield against that exploitation which would otherwise be inevitable under any system of government." Tate and Marshall charged that Trenton police utilized two proscribed means of obtaining the confessions: persistent and protracted questioning and unlawful incommunicado detention.[77]

Finished with the Fourteenth Amendment, the brief moved on to a second point: "The verdict is against the weight of the evidence." Noting that the sixteen-volume record in the case is "a monument to confusion," Tate and Marshall wrote, "Throughout the record there shine two aspects of the trial—one that the Negro in Trenton was treated as he would have been in the South—and the other that the trial was perverted from a search for the truth into a search for support for the prestige of the police of Trenton."[78] The testimony of Elizabeth Horner was duly deconstructed, and the brief concluded, "That any person should lose his life in the electric chair by such flimsy evidence would strike a blow at the roots of justice. That six Negroes should die when only the most questionable identification connecting them with the crime has been made intensifies the injustice and heightens the danger to justice. It is therefore respectfully submitted that the conviction of these defendants in the Court below should be reversed."[79]

Prosecutor Volpe and Assistant Prosecutor Lawton submitted a ninety-one-page brief for the state. While the four briefs on behalf of the defendant-appellants considered the trial as a whole and then focused on smaller elements within it, the state brief applied itself specifically and in detail to rebut exact points brought out by the appellants. The first contention of the state concerned the sentencing done by Judge Hutchinson. Quoting New Jersey statutes, Volpe contended, "A killing in the commission or attempted commission of robbery shall be murder," and "such killing shall be murder in the first degree." Thus, Volpe claimed that Judge Hutchinson could correctly sentence the six men to death while not specifying the degree of murder of which they were guilty.[80] Volpe further maintained that Judge Hutchinson had not erred in his charge to the jury , the verdicts of Wilson, Forrest, and MacKenzie were not contrary to the weight of the evidence, and, in particular, the court properly allowed the confessions to be admitted as evidence:

During the time the defendants were at police headquarters, every possible precaution and safeguard was taken for the welfare and rights of these defendants. They were questioned in the captain's office. A doctor was sent for to examine Forrest to make certain that he was in proper mental and physical condition to make a statement. There were no long uninterrupted periods of questioning by relays of officers. They were not taken into the woods in the dead of night for questioning. None was deprived of sleep, rest, food, or cigarettes. There were no beatings, or threats of a "shellacking." There was no callous attitude on the part of the police toward the defendants. No friend, relative, or counsel was refused permission to see the defendants. Should the police at some point have termed the case insolvable and turned these defendants loose? If so, at what point? Even after the statements were reduced to writing, they were not signed until disinterested witnesses were present, and heard the defendants either read the statement aloud, or have it read to them aloud. Dr. Sullivan not only observed, he interviewed the defendants. . . . Where, in all this case, can anything be found to substantiate a claim that the confessions were not voluntary?[81]

Volpe went on: "It is a well established rule of law in this state that where there is a voluntary confession, full proof of the body of the crime is not required."[82]

The Civil Rights Congress, in the person of Solomon Golat, submitted a fifteen-page reply to the state's brief, commenting, "Upon analysis it appears that the Brief for the State is in default on the principal issues tendered on this appeal."[83] The CRC brief addressed what Golat felt to be errors in the state's brief and again asked for the judgment to be reversed and the convictions set aside. James Waldron, Robert Queen, and James Turp also responded with a short brief on behalf of MacKenzie and Wilson, pointing out errors in claims made in the state brief. Frank Katzenbach replied to the state's brief regarding McKinley Forrest, explaining why the Fourteenth Amendment applied to his case and why the state's contention that the court properly quashed the subpoenas for Duch, Dooling, and Delate was in error.

MONDAY, MAY 16, 1949

On a Monday at 10:00 A.M. sharp, the Supreme Court of New Jersey heard arguments in the appeal. At this point the Six had been in the Death House for ten months. State troopers surrounded the entire newly built New

Jersey State House annex, with all but the main entrance closed. Hundreds of people milled outside, hoping to get into the hearing, in stark contrast to the trial, when only relatives and friends of the men were interested. Troopers barred all but lawyers, reporters, and relatives of the Six from entering the court, patrolling the corridors, allowing no one to enter or leave once the hearing began (see figure 7). Seven black-robed justices filed into the courtroom, taking their places behind the long mahogany bar. All but one of the balding, gray-haired men was at least in his late sixties. The thickly carpeted, plush-draped room remained quiet throughout the two hours allotted for the original defense attorneys. Journalist William Reuben wrote that as he made the points in his brief, James S. Turp was "neatly dressed, of medium build and height, red-necked and balding, and looking like nothing in the world so much as a hardware salesman, . . .weak-voiced, trembling, stumbling, faltering, timid, and intimidated in addressing the seven justices of New Jersey's highest court. His entire demeanor was one of apology." Queen and Katzenbach then addressed the justices, whom Reuben described as looking bored.[84] The three original defense attorneys did not appear to be making much impression on members of the court.

When CRC attorney O. John Rogge began to speak the justices sat up and listened attentively. Unlike the previous three attorneys, Rogge carried with him no suggestion of deference. He thundered angrily, "I charge that the prosecutor's office cooperated with the police department to rape justice." When Chief Justice Vanderbilt admonished Rogge, reminding him that he was in a court of law, not addressing a hall full of people, Rogge retorted, "But I am outraged at this gross miscarriage of justice. I submit that the prosecutor didn't want to get at justice. I charge that the prosecutor suppressed evidence." Rogge continued, "I ask if it isn't a fact that some fingerprints were found on that bottle—the murder weapon—in the name of justice this prosecutor should answer. This case was as raw as any I've ever heard of except *Brown v. Mississippi*, where the defendant limped into the courtroom because of the beatings he had had at the hands of the local police."[85] In addition to the legal arguments made in the CRC brief, Rogge lambasted Volpe at length, tore into the way local newspapers goaded the police for a quick solution, described the callous actions of the police in rounding up suspects, stressed that the court needed to remember the background from which the men came, and concluded by emphasizing the worldwide importance of the case.

Prosecutor Mario Volpe then spoke, very softly, beginning by saying that the reason Rogge had attacked him so personally was that he had no other argument. He then defended holding the six men for lengthy periods without arraignment: "I say the time element as set out in this record is not an unreasonable delay." Justice Wachenfeld then inquired what kinds of restrictions the prosecutor thought should be placed on the police. Volpe answered, "The police can arrest people without a warrant, without charge—if they believe a crime has been committed." Wachenfeld responded, "So that in murder cases, if a man is suspected, there is no due process. Is that what you're saying?"[86] Volpe, apparently unable to provide a good answer, concluded by reiterating that the defendants had been treated well by the police, the actions of the trial judge had been wise, the jury intelligent, and "[t]he record is a monument to Jersey Justice—I'm not afraid to say it."[87]

A week after the hearing, while waiting for the court decision, William Reuben reflected on changes that had occurred as he worked on the case:

> It is almost six months since I first went to Trenton for the *Guardian*. Then I couldn't even see the defense lawyers, there were few people who would talk about the case. Mrs. English looked at me with bitterness and hatred in her eyes because my skin was white, and white-skinned men had taken her only son from her; the Thorpe family told me that they weren't going to do anything, that they were leaving their son's fate "in the hands of the Lord." Today Mrs. English stands on a street corner handing out CRC leaflets; I can walk into the lawyer's office, the police station, and even the Governor's office and be received kindly. Today millions of people know what has happened in Trenton and are signing petitions, talking about it, organizing meetings, and marching on picket lines to change it. When the Supreme Court rules on this case in a few weeks, they know they don't dare dismiss the appeal with some legal mumbo jumbo. And even Mr. Thorpe, traveling throughout the state to join picket lines, hold press conferences etc. has not lost his faith in God but has realized that he does better with some down-to-earth help.[88]

SUNDAY, JUNE 19, 1949

After returning from a trip to Europe, Paul Robeson spoke about his commitment to battling fascism and racism at a welcome home rally in Harlem: "The road has been long. The road has been hard. It began about as tough as I ever had it in Princeton, New Jersey, a college town of Southern aristocrats, who from Revolutionary time transferred Georgia to New Jersey. My brothers couldn't go to high school in Princeton. They had to go to Trenton, ten miles away. That's right—Trenton, of the 'Trenton Six.' My brothers or I could have been one of the 'Trenton Six.'"[89]

THURSDAY, JUNE 30, 1949

On the last day before summer recess, the Supreme Court of New Jersey met to announce its decision on the appeal. A dozen reporters from local and state papers and the wire services lounged together along the wall of expansive windows facing the Delaware River. In the rear of the room sat only five relatives of the six men: Bessie Mitchell, with James Thorpe's stepmother, father, grandfather, and uncle. Mrs. English had not come, saying she wouldn't have been able to control herself.[90] Justice J. Heher, author of the opinion, announced that based on four major points all seven justices voted for reversal, with one dissenting in part. First, "The judge did not have jurisdiction to pronounce the sentence of death." As Justice Heher pointed out, "One cannot be put to death for homicide unless there has been a verdict by a jury after trial of the issue in the constitutional mode, establishing in a specific term his guilt of murder in the first degree. This is a peremptory statutory direction."[91] Reason two: "The charge relating to the jury's function to determine the punishment upon a finding of murder in the first degree is assigned for error." Heher articulated that Judge Hutchinson's charge to the jury did not properly inform the jury that its consideration of the sentence must arise out of its consideration of the evidence in the specific case, instead of saying that they had to obey "no restrictions or limitations."[92] Point three regarded the quashing of the fingerprint evidence by Judge Hutchinson at the request of Prosecutor Volpe, saying that "this judicial action is also assigned for error." It should have been "admissible at the instance of the accused."[93]

Point four addressed the confessions. After recounting the manner in which Trenton police obtained them, Justice Heher noted: "Ours is the accusatorial as opposed to the inquisitorial system."[94] He referenced decisions by U.S. Supreme Court Justice Frankfurter in which "persistence of interrogation, failure to advise the petitioner of his rights, the absence of friends or disinterested persons," as well as a consideration of the circumstances of the defendant, all led to cases being overturned by the highest court. Those criteria, Heher advised, should be used to determine legal competency of the confessions under consideration. He clarified: "The meaning of the due process clause of the Federal Constitution is the exclusive province of the supreme federal judicial authority. Our function is to order a new trial when the judgment is tainted with error. We can do no more than to direct the application of the standards of the cited cases to the case made on the retrial. Confessions having the undoubted element of spontaneity are not within the compass of this case. We have no occasion to consider the probative quality of a volunteered confession while the confessor is in custody without arraignment. The judgment is reversed and a venire de novo is awarded."[95] Thus the trial result had been nullified and a new trial ordered.

William Reuben had to explain to Bessie Mitchell exactly what *venire de novo*, Latin for "to come anew," meant; when she understood the men would be retried, she buried her face in her hands and began to sob softly.[96] Bessie and William Patterson took the news to the men waiting in the Death House. "The six men looked wonderfully happy. They were very excited, naturally," Bessie told the *Daily Worker*. "While I talked with them, all kinds of things were happening. Men came in to measure them for suits, then along comes the doctor to check on their health; then along comes the minister who said 'Are you happy?' They could hardly talk but they were smiling ear to ear."[97]

The *Daily Worker's* headline exclaimed: "Trenton 6 Verdict Upset, N.J. Court Acts after Mass Protest." The article began: "The death sentences against the six framed Trenton Negro youth were reversed yesterday by the New Jersey Supreme Court in a decision that crowns a 10-month campaign by the Civil Rights Congress."[98] The paper ran a photograph of Bessie hugging her mother, Emma English, joy radiating from both.[99] The *National Guardian* featured a photo of Mrs. English, surrounded by celebrating neighbors and William Patterson.[100] The day's issue of the *Trenton Evening Times* sold out within minutes. City officials, unsurprisingly, refused all comment.[101]

Most coverage reflected a news article and editorial in the *New York Times* that gave credit for the appeal results to the "conscientious and well-functioning justice system" and discounted the efforts of the communists and the "self-serving propaganda of the extreme Left." The *Chicago Sun-Times* pointed out that the Civil Rights Congress was able to enter the case because a vacuum had been left by others who should have been fighting for the civil rights of the Trenton Six.[102]

Several days later police transferred the men from the Death House in the Trenton State Prison, where they had lived for forty-nine weeks, back to the Mercer County Jail. Waiting outside on the state prison steps, Mrs. English, Robert Forrest, and Jean Forrest (McKinley's twelve-year-old daughter) started toward the men when they appeared, but a deputy sheriff blocked their way.[103] They would not be able to visit the men until regular visiting time at the county jail.

Collis English wrote to William Reuben to thank him for his work on their case, as well as for the support of the *National Guardian*: "There are so much and so many people who are helping in this hear [*sic*] fight for our freedom and know that we are not guilty of this hear crime that we are charge with and we feel good to be out of the Death House and glad that the people believe in the truth what we told at the trial and we thank them one and all."[104]

A letter received by John MacKenzie from a *National Guardian* reader reflected the feelings of many at the time: "There are millions of people all over the world that have come to your defense and demanded a new trial for you. These people have offered money as well as prayers in your behalf. Your new trial is a victory for all of us. However we shall not be satisfied until you're completely free. Don't lose faith. We haven't and are still fighting. It has been hard for us as it has also been extremely hard for you. We are in this together. Your life represents our lives and the lives of our children."[105]

Friday, July 22, 1949

At a mass meeting in Trenton, Paul Robeson announced a campaign to immediately free the Trenton Six: "American Negroes must not be asked ever again to sacrifice on foreign shores. If we must sacrifice, let it be in Alabama and Mississippi where my race is persecuted. . . . The wealth of the USA was built on the backs of my people, yet we are made to crawl. We are loyal to the America of Lincoln and the abolitionists, but not to those who degrade my people. One percent of the American population gets 59 percent of the national income. I am a radical and I am going to stay one until my people get free to walk the earth."[106]

Also on this day, on a motion by Solomon Golat appearing before Judge Hutchinson, O. John Rogge, William L. Patterson, and Emanuel H. Bloch were admitted to practice before the court in order to represent Ralph Cooper, Collis English, and James Thorpe in their new trial. The CRC lawyers asked that their defendants be released on bail. One week later the judge denied this request.[107]

Tuesday, July 26, 1949

CRC attorneys had filed a Notice of Application for an Order to Inspect Finger Print Evidence, and the court served subpoenas on all state and court officials who could possibly have or know something about tests of the fingerprints

on the soda bottles in question. At a hearing on this day Rogge questioned
Lieutenant Alvin K. Sharp of the Identification Bureau. Sharp described his
work on the two soda bottles used as weapons in the Horner murder. He had
found no prints on the whole bottle and fragmentary ridges on the broken
bottle. He said he judged the partial prints to be worthless and wiped the
bottle clean.[108]

Friday, December 16, 1949

At a hearing before Judge Hutchinson, in the presence of all six defendants,
Frank Katzenbach asked to examine under oath Director of Public Safety
Andrew Duch, Police Chief William Dooling, and Lieutenant Andrew Delate,
as well as Detectives Toft and Stanley. He especially wanted to question Duch
about a dissenting report on the case apparently produced by Stanley and
Toft. O. John Rogge requested the address and official statement of Elizabeth
Horner, the descriptions of the murder suspects given out in police alarms,
and again asked that the defendants be allowed out on bail. He also wished
for Mr. Burchaell and Mr. Clark to have the opportunity to testify that they
saw Mrs. Horner shortly before the original trial started, when she told them
she could not identify any of the six defendants. The defense wished for her
to look at the six men in county jail but she told them, "Well, no, it would be
a waste of time, a waste of time, the store was dark and everything happened
so fast, I couldn't identify anybody. Anyhow, all colored people look alike."
Judge Hutchinson denied all motions but did provide the address of Elizabeth
Horner.[109]

Judge Hutchinson further announced that Frank Katzenbach would
be appointed to serve as counsel for McKinley Forrest, Robert Queen for
Horace Wilson, and James Waldron for John MacKenzie. Then, in a surprise
move, he declared that "of this moment he rescinded the order previously
made admitting Messrs. Rogge, Bloch and Patterson of the New York Bar
to practice in this court."[110] He charged that they had violated numerous
canons of professional ethics in their conduct: "All of your expressions, both
verbal and printed, have vehemently denounced the trial of these defendants
as unfair, biased and prejudiced in varying terms running from 'a travesty
of justice' through the gamut of 'an outrage,' 'a northern Scottsboro case,'
to a 'lynching.'" He accused them of using the case to raise funds for, and
awareness of, the Civil Rights Congress. He particularly objected to posters
"offering a reward leading to the arrest and conviction of the real murderer
of William Horner" and to the "enormous billboards situated at strategic

points on some of the main public highways of this State and in the State of New York—perhaps others. You have resorted to slanderous pamphlets, picketing the State Capital, slandering the judge and prosecutor, and the State's witnesses, and many other improper acts." He announced that other lawyers would be appointed for the three now without representation, and that the retrial would begin on January 9, 1950, at 10:00 A.M.[111] In response, Rogge, Patterson, and Bloch issued a statement saying that their clients wished to retain them for the second trial and "We are not unmindful of the fact that our clients were unlawfully sentenced by the same court which now seeks to deny them the constitutional right to counsel of their own choosing."[112]

MONDAY, DECEMBER 19, 1949

Judge Hutchinson requested the presence of six hundred possible jurors from which to convene the panel of jurors for the retrial.[113]

WEDNESDAY, DECEMBER 21, 1949

Having gotten Elizabeth Horner's address from defense attorneys, William Reuben attempted to interview her. He described her as a "thin, short, bird-like, fluttery woman; seems to have lost fifty pounds since the trial; impossible to recognize her from her pictures, she has changed so radically." He judged her manner to be odd and very nervous. When he asked her about the Trenton Six case she "shut up like a clam" and would answer no questions. She "lives like a hermit: shut off from the world, on an empty street, most of houses boarded up." When he later telephoned, she refused to speak with him.[114]

Also in preparation for the coming retrial, CRC investigators interviewed Boyd Johnson, a black window washer who took care of stores on North Broad Street. Both jeweler William Klein, next door to the Horner store, and shoemaker Frank Warren, across the street from Horner's store, told Johnson they had seen two light-skinned Negroes, or possibly two white men, emerge from the store right after the murder took place. Johnson had feared "trouble" ever since he publicly declared what the two store owners had told him, but he spoke up because he did not wish to see innocent men in prison. On January 24, 1950, Boyd's wife found him strangled to death in their home. Police charged his oldest son, Edward, with the murder.[115]

FRIDAY, DECEMBER 23, 1949

Ralph Cooper, Collis English, and James Thorpe filed an appeal in federal court to halt their second trial on the grounds that the trial judge had barred the counsel of their choice. Court papers filed by Solomon Golat stated that the attorneys had never been admonished for "improper, unethical, or incompetent conduct." Federal Judge Phillip Forman of the U.S. District Court for the District of New Jersey heard the men's appeal on January 16, 1950, saying he would weigh the rights of the accused under the Fourteenth Amendment against the state's right to decide who would practice before the bar of the state of New Jersey. Mrs. English, interviewed about Hutchinson's removal of her son's attorneys, put her feelings this way: "The devil comes up against you on every hand. You got to fight until you die." Protests in the form of letters and telegrams flooded Governor Driscoll's office.[116]

On this day Jean Forrest wrote to her father, "I think of you all the time, but it's worse around Christmas time. If you could only be home with us. There's nobody home but Nana and me to go to the table. When we sit down and we don't see your plates set out, we feel awful about it sometimes. When I come home from church or school I look for you to be standing on the stoop, but there's nobody home. . . . I hope next Christmas you will be with us. Your loving daughter, Jean."[117]

WEDNESDAY, MAY 24, 1950

A three-judge panel of the Court of Appeals for the Third Circuit in Philadelphia heard the question of whether a state court could refuse to permit attorneys from another state to represent defendants in capital trials. Rogge spoke for over an hour, presenting his case.[118] Others took note of the battle. The June 5 edition of the *Daily Worker* observed, "Scientist Albert Einstein and 14 other individuals denounced the court attempts to deprive the Trenton Six of defense by naming attorneys of their own choice and advocated that the public help in the struggle to preserve the Bill of Rights."

MONDAY, JUNE 19, 1950

Beginning on this day, Collis English spent several days in the hospital for treatment of his severe heart condition.[119]

SUNDAY, JULY 9, 1950

Warden Michael J. Bajek of the Mercer County Jail declared that the Six could receive no mail from outsiders expressing their support, no black periodicals, and no books. The men had been receiving mail from around the globe, as well as books on American history featuring blacks, all sent by supporters. English and MacKenzie would read these to the others.[120]

FRIDAY, JULY 21, 1950

The Third Circuit Court of Appeals ruled that Judge Hutchinson had erred in barring CRC lawyers from defending their three Trenton Six clients. However, the judges refused to order the restoration of CRC counsel, stating, "[W]e have little doubt that the New Jersey courts, if not the defendant [Judge Hutchinson] will rectify this deprivation of constitutional rights once the situation is brought to their attention."[121]

TUESDAY, AUGUST 8, 1950

The *Trenton Evening Times* reported that Prosecutor Mario Volpe requested a hearing before Judge Hutchinson on why "the Court should not refuse to permit O. John Rogge, William Patterson, and Emanuel Bloch to appear and act as counsel" for the three men.

TUESDAY, SEPTEMBER 19, 1950

Mrs. Emma English and her daughter Bessie Mitchell met with New Jersey Attorney General Parsons to present him with ten thousand signatures gathered by the CRC, demanding justice for the Trenton Six. Parsons insisted that he could do nothing as long as the case remained in the courts.[122]

WEDNESDAY, NOVEMBER 8, 1950

The hearing requested in August and delayed by the absence of one or another of the major players finally occurred before Judge Ralph J. Smalley, assignment judge for Mercer and two other counties, who assigned himself all further involvement with the Trenton Six, thus removing Judge Hutchinson from the picture. Born in North Plainfield, New Jersey, where he continued to reside, Smalley had attended Cornell University and New Jersey Law School. In 1935 he was appointed a district court judge in Somerset County, and four years later he was elevated to the New Jersey Court of Common Pleas. After six years, Governor Walter Edge named him judge on the state's circuit court. Governor Alfred E. Driscoll then appointed him to a seven-year term on the superior court. Before his judicial service, Smalley worked as city counsel of Plainfield and was the Republican Party chairman of Union County.[123] Present in court were all of the defendants, Prosecutor Volpe, Assistant Prosecutor Lawton, and representatives of the state. O. John Rogge made a motion to withdraw as counsel for Cooper, English, and Thorpe, the Civil Rights Congress having decided to withdraw from the case. Judge Smalley granted the motion.

WEDNESDAY, NOVEMBER 29, 1950

Before Judge Smalley, Emanuel Bloch moved to withdraw as counsel, and Ralph Boe, appearing on behalf of William Patterson, made a similar motion. Judge Smalley agreed, thus ending the involvement of the Civil Rights Congress and the Communist Party USA in the case of the Trenton Six. In their final statement about the Six, CRC counsel indicated that their assistance was no longer necessary, as other well-known lawyers from respected organizations had now indicated a willingness to join the fray. They did not say, but it was true, that the fight over representation now coming to a close had cost each of the Six a year of their lives in time spent in the Mercer County Jail. They did say, and it was also true, that they had made the words "Trenton Six" known around the world. All six men, not just the three represented by CRC lawyers, felt that the mass campaign "broke down prejudice to give us a fair trial." McKinley Forrest summarized: "I think they did the right thing in bringing the case to the people."[124]

In a book about the history of the *National Guardian* newspaper, one of the founders, Cedric Belfrage, commented "Some day, perhaps, a historian will give Communists their due credit for defending black fellow citizens, not always wisely but with great courage."[125] Consider it done.

CHAPTER 5

SECOND TRIAL, PROSECUTION

The withdrawal of the Civil Rights Congress left a vacuum soon filled by Thurgood Marshall, chief counsel for the National Association for the Advancement of Colored People (NAACP) and future U.S. Supreme Court justice. On December 15, 1950, he appeared before Judge Ralph J. Smalley, asking to represent John MacKenzie and Horace Wilson. Several weeks later the Princeton Committee to Free the Trenton Six, a group of Princeton professors and clergy, brought in Arthur Garfield Hays, legal counsel for the American Civil Liberties Union (ACLU) and a highly regarded civil rights attorney, to represent Ralph Cooper, Collis English, and James Thorpe (see figure 10). Hays was nearing the end of a storied career. He had grown rich defending corporations and became famous defending civil liberties. Among his previous clients were Nikola Sacco and Bartolomeo Vanzetti, Italian anarchists executed in 1927 for a murder they denied having committed; the Scottsboro Boys; and John Thomas Scopes of the Tennessee "monkey" trial. He received his law degree from Columbia and formed his own practice, profiting greatly from defending Wall Street firms. In 1912 he became general counsel for the ACLU and remained active with that organization for the rest of his life.[1]

Joining the ACLU's Hays, who remained in New York City and commuted, was Trenton lawyer George Pellettieri for Cooper, English, and Thorpe. Pellettieri had an unusual career. In his youth he sang in churches, in concerts, and for the radio. He studied voice and instrumental music in Trenton and in New York City. He then turned to law, graduating from New Jersey Law School in Newark in 1929, opening his own law firm in Trenton that year, but still singing opera "at the drop of a hat." He served as judge of the Trenton District Court for a five-year term, appointed by Governor Moore. He grew to be a powerful force in the Mercer County and New Jersey Democratic Party politics. Five years before the creation of the Social Security Administration, he campaigned for a government program to aid the elderly poor. A champion of liberal causes, Pellettieri was regarded as one of Trenton's foremost criminal and labor lawyers.[2] Frank Katzenbach III remained as counsel for McKinley Forrest.

In January 1951, Thurgood Marshall brought in black lawyer Raymond Pace Alexander to work in his place for MacKenzie and Wilson; Marshall's role was to make sure defendants had good counsel rather than doing the job himself. Alexander had graduated from Harvard Law School in 1924. After settling in Philadelphia, he successfully represented plaintiffs in some of the earliest school desegregation cases in the United States, opening up a number of previously all-white schools and districts. In 1951 he won a seat on the Philadelphia City Council. He also worked for desegregation in public accommodation in Philadelphia and throughout Pennsylvania. He served as counsel to the NAACP Legal Defense and Educational Fund, which is why Marshall brought him into the Trenton Six case.[3] Local black NAACP lawyers Clifford H. Moore and J. Mercer Burrell assisted him. Moore had served with distinction as an artillery officer in Italy in World War II, receiving a Purple Heart and Bronze Star. In 1948 Federal Judge of the U.S. District Court for the District of New Jersey, Phillip Forman, named him a law clerk while he was in his last year at Temple University Law School.[4] In total, the Six went from four lawyers in their first trial to six this time, and three of the lawyers were black. The NAACP's involvement extended beyond the direct work of its lawyers; its Legal Defense and Educational Fund created "The Fantastic Case of the Trenton Six," a widely circulated eight-page pamphlet that explained their situation and asked for donations.

Although all the attorneys regarded the continuing protests of the Civil Rights Congress as unhelpful, the group contained a mixture of personalities and styles. Pellettieri and Hays argued forcefully and forthrightly, willing to challenge conventional thinking, legal and otherwise. Alexander and Katzenbach were more circumspect, kept a lower profile in court, and deferred more to authority. Alexander, unique in the group, incorporated quotations from poetry and otherwise used flowery rhetoric when it suited him.[5] In spite of their differences, the men worked well together, pitching in to aid each other when necessary.

MONDAY, FEBRUARY 5, 1951

Court began amid heightened security, arranged by Sheriff Thomas Brennan, with one policeman assigned to guard each defendant, four other officers in the courtroom at large, two at the door, and two more in the corridor. The allotment of 75 spectators filled the courtroom half an hour before the opening at 10:00 A.M., with 125 more waiting to get in. Sheriff Brennan banned photographers from the courtroom and all forms of demonstration from the entire building. Court would be in session daily from 10:00 A.M. to 1:00 P.M. and from 2:00 P.M. to 4:00 P.M. The focus of this day was jury selection, with one juror seated by day's end and twenty having been rejected by the prosecution or the defense. John Muste of Trenton, the only juror acceptable to both sides, said he had come in contact with Negro fliers in World War II and found them to be "excellent."[6]

George Pellettieri asked Judge Smalley to instruct the prosecution to turn over police blotters, teletype descriptions of the defendants, and other material repeatedly promised before the trial began but never delivered. Pellettieri requested an item for the first time, a report allegedly written by Detective Lieutenant William Stanley and Detective Donald Toft asking to be permitted to withdraw from the case because they felt four of the prisoners were innocent of the murder charge. When Volpe argued against this, Arthur Hays commented, "I am grievously disappointed that government secrets become more important than human lives."[7]

TUESDAY, FEBRUARY 6, 1951

Assistant Prosecutor Lawton announced that Prosecutor Volpe had been hospitalized for an emergency appendectomy, causing Judge Smalley to announce a mistrial, setting a new trial date of March 5. The CIO began a fund-raising campaign for the defense of the Six, and the *New York Times* began extensive coverage of the case.[8]

FRIDAY, FEBRUARY 16, 1951

A pretrial hearing began (see figure 11), with Judge Ralph Smalley, fifty-six years of age, balding and ruddy, presiding. Defense counsel had subpoenaed a number of Trenton officials and police officers and were still attempting to see documents previously withheld. First on the stand was Director of

Public Safety Andrew Duch. Katzenbach and Pellettieri particularly wished to question him about a report by Detectives Toft and Stanley. Duch clarified that he had heard of a report by the two men investigating the alibis of the Trenton Six. He testified that he then "made a statement as to the duty of a police officer to arrest a person charged with a crime, and that it was his duty not only to prosecute the guilty but it was also his duty at the same time to make every effort if a man is innocent to see that he is proven innocent. I sort of sent out what I felt the responsibilities of a police officer were." Pellettieri asked why he had taken this action. Duch responded, "Because it had been brought to my attention that there was an alibi in this case, and I called the attention of the Police Department to the fact that they should pursue every remedy to check the alibi in an effort to determine whether there was any proof in it or not. And that's why I made the public statement that I did." Pellettieri then asked, "And if there was truth in the alibi what further did you say?" Duch answered, "I said they should follow it through because I didn't want any innocent people convicted, but I wanted the guilty prosecuted to the limit. But I did not want to see an innocent man prosecuted."[9] Over numerous objections from Assistant Prosecutor Lawton, Pellettieri learned that Duch took this action after a conversation with Detective Lieutenant Stanley.

Chief of Police Dooling stated that he had no records of the Horner murder case, that all had been given to the prosecutor's office. This caused Pellettieri to complain vociferously to Judge Smalley that Volpe had previously stated in court that he only had copies and that the originals remained with the police. Lieutenant Andrew Delate stated that all records remained with the prosecutor. Chief Detective Frank Naples did not answer his subpoena; he was in Florida and supposedly in ill health. Detective Stanley also did not appear in court, as he was recovering from knee surgery. From the vigorous questions asked by the defense attorneys, it seems clear they felt they were being given a runaround by the Trenton police and the prosecutor's office. Police Clerk Henry Miller, who had participated in questioning the Six after their arrest and then typed their statements in place of the usual typist, had been promoted after the first trial and was now serving as special investigator for Prosecutor Volpe. Defense counsel George Pellettieri wished to question Miller about "a lurid account of the Horner case which appeared in the *Detective Story Magazine* with photographs of the place and Volpe and the electric chair. Trenton was swamped with copies of this story long before the normal release of the magazine but immediately before the previous trial. Now we are trying to establish the identity of the author. . . . That was the sole article that was published for gain. Aside from its inflammatory language there is a variance with the subsequent proof." Assistant Prosecutor Lawton objected and Judge Smalley did not allow Pellettieri to question Miller along these lines.[10] Pellettieri clearly suspected that Miller had authored the article, which had served to stir up the community against the defendants.

Monday, February 19, 1951

Defense counsel continued efforts to find reports made by Detectives Toft and Stanley. Toft indicated they would have been sent to Police Clerk Edward Kelley. After many precise questions, Pellettieri learned that Toft had written a statement of the case at the request of Deputy Police Chief DiLouie.[11]

Tuesday, February 20, 1951

Chief of Police William Dooling revealed, after much interrogation, that he had received a request by Director of Public Safety Duch on April 22, 1948, to investigate the handling of the Horner murder case. Duch told him "Someone is not telling the truth and whoever it is should be punished." Dooling asked Captain of Detectives James DiLouie to undertake an investigation, which he did. He reported back to Dooling, who then gave the report to Duch on May 17, 1948. Judge Smalley ruled that under the guidelines of *State v. Bunk*, which he followed in his court, the defense did not have the right to see this material. At the request of defense counsel, it was impounded by the court. The *Daily Worker* noted that Duch himself had made no mention of this report when he testified on February 16.[12] Numerous policemen subpoenaed to appear with their records appeared in court empty-handed, denying any knowledge of the files. Finally, Judge Smalley met with Assistant Prosecutor Lawton in his chambers. Courthouse gossip disclosed that the judge ordered Lawton to produce the requested records in court.[13]

Monday, March 5, 1951

Spectators jammed the courthouse, some waiting two hours to get a place. The relatives of the Six were given priority seating. Approximately twenty newspapers were covering the trial.[14] On this day the process of voir dire, or jury selection, began again. The first question each prospective juror faced was: "If found guilty of murder in the first degree would you have any scruples against a verdict which calls for the death penalty for these defendants?" Almost half of the potential jurors were excused because they expressed an inability to bring in a guilty verdict that would result in a death sentence. (It is still true that anyone who expresses opposition to capital punishment cannot sit on a jury in which a death sentence is demanded.) Two of the excused were blacks: one had a "favorable opinion" of the defendants and was acquainted with James Thorpe, while the other did not believe in capital punishment. Some of those excused admitted to racial prejudice and/or prior opinions of the guilt or innocence of the accused gained from media during the initial trial. At one point when questioning a prospective juror, Volpe used the term "brutal crime" and was quickly challenged by defense attorneys Pellettieri and Alexander, causing the judge to warn the prosecution against using such biased language. Judge Smalley gave the defense sixty peremptory challenges, while the state had thirty-six, giving the defense ten for each defendant and the state six. A peremptory challenge could be used to dismiss a juror without having to establish any particular cause. Only two prospective jurors survived questioning by defense and state on this day: Mrs. Alyce F. Spellman, the widow of a serviceman killed in World War II, and Robert J. Nolan, an assistant engineer for the state highway department. This evening the Civil Rights Congress held a rally in Trenton attended by three hundred, roundly denounced by defense counsel as unhelpful to their cause.[15]

TUESDAY, MARCH 6, 1951

Two more jurors made it through the selection process: Miss Eleanor V. Weld of Princeton, a Princeton University librarian and former Navy WAVE (Women Accepted for Volunteer Emergency Service in the U.S. Navy) in World War II, and Mrs. Beatrice A. Doran, a Trenton housewife and grandmother.[16] The only black person to be examined was peremptorily challenged and removed by Assistant Prosecutor Lawton, drawing muffled groans from spectators. During a short recess, defense attorney Pellettieri told the reporter for the *Trenton Evening Times*: "Remember you're not the hangman yet. . . . I remember your editorial three years ago, titled the 'Idle Electric Chair.'" Pellettieri referred to an article that had appeared in the January 29, 1948, *Trenton Evening Times*, two days after William Horner's murder, calling for more use of the electric chair as a way to reduce crime. A short time later Pellettieri drew the admission from a prospective juror that such stories had biased him against the defendants. Twice, one of the defendants requested their counsel to more thoroughly examine a prospective juror before coming to a decision. Albert Feole, operator of a grocery store in Trenton, with a wife and six children, was asked by defense counsel if he could leave them for as long as six or eight weeks. His quick reply "I sure can"—caused chuckles in the courtroom. However, he was not selected. [17]

MARCH 7, 1951, AND MARCH 8, 1951

Only one juror per day was found acceptable by both prosecution and defense. Edward B. Kerr, a twenty-eight-year-old Trenton postal clerk and World War II veteran, and Horace Stevenson, a salesman for the Delaware Valley Company, father of four and grandfather of seven, joined the lineup. The Princeton Committee to Free the Trenton Six announced a $25,000 fund-raising campaign to cover defense costs. Sheriff Thomas A. Brennan warned the Civil Rights Congress to stop distributing leaflets in the courtroom. Lewis M. Moroze had been handing out a mimeographed statement describing the Trenton Six case as a "frightful miscarriage of justice."[18]

FRIDAY, MARCH 9, 1951

Jury selection proceeded so slowly that Judge Smalley announced that next week the proceedings would begin at 9:15 A.M. In the afternoon James Thorpe told his attorney, Pellettieri, that his arm stump was causing extreme pain. Judge Smalley arranged for two doctors to assess Thorpe's condition; they assured the judge that they could treat Thorpe as the trial continued, and Thorpe agreed that he wished the trial to proceed. Court ended for the week with six jurors selected. The *Philadelphia Afro-American* pointed out that Mrs. Florence Adams, a Negro, was in charge of the care of women jurors for the trial, quite unusual at the time.[19] Her job was to make sure they were healthy and happy, in keeping with the court-imposed restrictions on their free-time activities.

MONDAY, MARCH 12, 1951

The Monday morning session proved fruitful, adding three members to the jury: Ida Cagan, a Trenton housewife married to a grocery salesman; Henry Schmidt, a sixty-year-old Ewing Township farmer; and Anna Toth, wife of a Roebling employee. Lawton used his tenth peremptory challenge to remove a juror satisfactory to all defendants. Pellettieri used James Thorpe's first such challenge and Ralph Cooper's third. Thorpe's was issued for Joseph Distefano, who expressed the belief that no one could be submitted to such pressure that he would admit to something he did not do. Judge Smalley, always conscious of passing time, ordered that court would run until 5:00 P.M. in order to accomplish more each day.[20]

TUESDAY, MARCH 13, 1951

Cora E. Biesecker, a Trenton carpenter's widow, sixty-four years of age, the mother of two and grandmother of two, became juror number ten. Irene Case, a Canadian-born housewife married to a mechanic and the mother of a five-year-old, became number eleven, and Ruth Boss, a middle-aged housewife whose husband was a painter and decorator, was juror number twelve. Women with several small children as well as expectant fathers were excused. The defense rejected three: Alex Mackey, who stated that he would favor police testimony over that of the defendants; Mrs. Marie D. Stanley, who, when asked if she could take the juror's oath without bias, replied, "I couldn't take an oath because I am prejudiced"; and Mrs. Helen Slake who stated, "I think they had a fair trial before and I think that's the way it should stand." One hundred ninety-eight jurors had been questioned, the state had used ten of its thirty-six peremptory challenges and the defense eight of its sixty. Of the total prospective jurors, eight were black, and all were rejected, mainly by the state.[21]

WEDNESDAY, MARCH 14, 1951

Judge Smalley deemed two extra jurors necessary to avoid a mistrial in case of illness or family emergency. The two additions were John J. Kelly, a foreman at the Trenton Post Office and father of two World War II veterans, and Hubert J. Kelch, a bookkeeper at Cold Springs Bleachery and father of a five-month-old. Kelch told the court, "I'd rather not serve, but if I'm otherwise qualified it is my duty and I will serve." Two blacks interviewed were subject to Volpe's peremptory challenges, resulting in an all-white jury. All the jurors stated they were willing to sentence the six men to death if they found such a course of action warranted. All also stated they felt no animus against blacks and thought it possible that individuals could be coerced into confessing guilt to actions they had not committed.[22]

Saturday, March 17, 1951

In an unusual Saturday session, the second trial of the Trenton Six began. Defense counsel Pellettieri requested that the defendants be seated alphabetically in order to make individual identification easier for the jury, and this was done. Prosecutor Volpe spoke briefly, giving the opening on behalf of the state. He read the indictment and explained, "The State contends that this murder was committed in perpetrating or attempting to perpetrate the crime of robbery, and therefore it is murder in the first degree." Furthermore, if found guilty of murder in the first degree, the defendants shall be sentenced to death, unless "hard labor for life" is recommended. He then delved into the heart of the case, the confessions: "The State maintains and will prove that the confessions were spontaneous and were voluntary." After Volpe finished his brief opening statement, Pellettieri rose to request a mistrial, not liking the manner in which Volpe described the disputed confessions, but Judge Smalley disagreed and denied Pellettieri's request. Pellettieri remained dynamic close to the point of belligerency throughout the trial.[23]

Defense attorney Raymond Pace Alexander rose to deliver the opening on behalf of John MacKenzie and Horace Wilson. He began with a basic contention of the defense that no robbery occurred, given that William Horner died having large sums of cash in three different pockets, all still neatly folded. He went on to point out the tiny dimensions and crowded condition in the Horner store, so that Elizabeth McGuire, called Horner, clearly would have known how many individuals were present and what they looked like. He moved on to descriptions provided by both cigar salesman Frank Eldracher and neighbor Virginia Barclay that the murderers were young and light-complexioned, while five of the Trenton Six were quite dark-skinned. At this point Alexander turned dramatically to the seated defendants and shouted, "Stand up, Thorpe!" He asked Thorpe to raise his arms and pointed out that no witnesses mentioned a one-armed man. He referred to the fact that among themselves, blacks called policemen "the law," an entity seen as overwhelming and fear-inducing. Introducing two points not brought up at the first trial, Alexander noted that when interviewed at the hospital, Mrs. Horner told police that she had bitten the finger of the man who attacked her, and Alexander noted that none of the Six had a lacerated finger at the time. In addition, because of a photograph not seen at the first trial of the damage inflicted upon Mrs. Horner, police thought brass knuckles had been used as the assault weapon. Alexander told jurors some of the details that he would focus on in his defense of MacKenzie and Wilson and indicated that he would "Tell you why not only these six men are on trial but New Jersey justice, American justice, in this great drama that is being unfolded before you, and a drama it is."[24] Throughout the trial Alexander himself was a source of great drama, using theatrical gestures and eloquent, sometimes florid, rhetoric.

Katzenbach, beginning for McKinley Forrest, described the course of the trial: "We don't have a chance to bring out our evidence until the State is all completed; and I just ask you carefully just because some State's witness says something up there, don't just accept that that is proved; but wait, because we have got an answer for it." As an example, he brought up Mrs. Horner and a fact they had recently learned: the prosecution "brought her into Court during the last trial and had her sit in the Courtroom during the time we were examining jurors, and none of us knew she was there; but she had quite a little time to rehearse this thing. We will prove to you that is just exactly what happened." Katzenbach had Forrest stand up for the jurors and stated, "As for my defense, it is pure and simple. He is absolutely innocent; he had no part in the crime, neither in its planning nor in its execution. . . . The first evidence I am going to offer is the man himself." Approaching forty years of age, Forrest had never been arrested until he appeared in the First Precinct police station at his mother-in-law's request. He held two jobs, was married and a father, and his character was well known in the community. "He just isn't the kind of a person who could commit a crime of this sort . . . he is going to be my number one Exhibit, and you will find him quiet, and kindly."[25]

Next, Pellettieri gave his opening for defendants Cooper, English, and Thorpe. He began by saying pointedly, "We intend to prove to you that Mr. Volpe did not give them a fair trial the first time," which caused Assistant Prosecutor Lawton to rise and object. Judge Smalley ruled that as a result of questions raised during voir dire, all the jurors were well aware of a previous trial and told Pellettieri he could proceed. He did so: "We are going to prove there was evidence in that file [pointing to a file sitting on the table before Prosecutor Volpe], at the first trial that would have completely exonerated these men, and they would not have had to spend three years in jail." He further mentioned that during World War II Prosecutor Volpe had been in the Office of Strategic Services, which became the Central Intelligence Agency after the war, and that sodium amytol, a hypnotic drug, "was used on prisoners of war, and that sodium amytol was used in this case." He then laid out the main points of the case he would be making.[26]

MONDAY, MARCH 19, 1951

Prosecutor Volpe began the presentation of the state's case. He proceeded almost exactly as in the first trial, with the same witnesses in approximately the same order, in spite of the fact that the New Jersey Supreme Court had overthrown the first trial result. Events diverged quickly from the first trial, however, as the defense objected to the prosecution's first witness, a policeman who brought the maps he had made of the Horner store. Katzenbach explained: "We are opposing this map in showing the physical condition of the store which we contend is one which any person standing in the store can be seen or can see everybody there; but this particular map here shows none of the mass of furniture in there, but just a rough outline and naming things, and it looks like an orderly place; and it is entirely misleading." Judge Smalley agreed, and the jury did not see the map. The second witness brought in photographs of the interior of the Horner store, and the defense objected to these, as many had been cropped and then enlarged in a way that eliminated the ceiling or a wall, destroying the perspective of the dimensions of the room. Judge Smalley agreed that the original negatives would be used to create photos for the jury to examine.[27]

The prosecution brought in Lieutenant Elvin K. Sharpe of the Identification Bureau as its third witness. Sharpe explained that on both the broken bottle top and the unbroken bottle he found numerous fragmentary ridges but no fingerprints he considered good enough to serve as evidence to photograph or make any other permanent record. Pellettieri asked, "If you had preserved those fragmentary ridges, not that they would have identified the culprit or the person who committed the crime, but they would have been and would have had some characteristics within those ridges which, after you had taken the fingerprints of each of these men, could at least have eliminated some if not all of these defendants?" Lieutenant Sharpe answered, "We do not invite elimination with fragmentary ridges." Lieutenant Sharpe wiped both bottles clean and returned them, along with a verbal report of no fingerprints obtained, to Detective Lieutenant Stanley. Sharpe also tested a letter and a receipt, finding no usable prints on either.[28]

Doctor David Eckstein, who had performed the autopsy on William Horner, agreed that the damage inflicted on Horner's skull could have been inflicted by brass knuckles as well as by the bottle in evidence.[29] And from Mrs. Laura Anderson, William Horner's daughter, it became clear that Horner had deserted his wife and children in 1916.[30]

TUESDAY, MARCH 20, 1951

On this day Volpe produced his key witness, Mrs. Horner. Volpe led her through her testimony fairly quickly, but she spent most of the day on the witness stand being peppered with questions by defense lawyers. Volpe established that William Horner did not keep his money in a bank but instead always carried large sums of cash on his person. Then he asked Mrs. Horner to step down from the witness stand to identify the men involved in Horner's murder. First she stood and placed her hand on Ralph Cooper's shoulder, saying she had seen him about 5:30 P.M. on January 16, 1948, Cooper having come into the store to look at a mattress. Next she indicated McKinley Forrest and Collis English, commenting that she had seen them both in the store the afternoon of January 20, 1948, as they looked for a mattress. Forrest went into the back room with Horner while English stayed by the heating stove, since it was a very cold day. Forrest paid a two-dollar deposit on the mattress, and Mrs. Horner handed him a receipt. On January 26 the two men returned to the store, bringing the mattress, saying they wanted their money back because it had a hole in it. Mrs. Horner gave him two dollars and the receipt, which Forrest signed. At 10:30 A.M. the next day, January 27, three men, Forrest, English, and Horace Wilson, who said he was not with the first two, entered the store. Forrest told Mrs. Horner, "We came after the mattress. We couldn't find a mattress all over town." Wilson asked to see a heating stove and "I had to stoop down because the stove was a little low and as I did stoop down like that a terrible crash came down my head and I naturally went to take my head up and I felt another awfully hard blow alongside the face." After that "I didn't know anything until I was hanging out the front door, lying out the front door over the transom, calling for help."[31] Mrs. Horner required thirteen stitches in her head and suffered a fractured cheekbone and two fractured ribs.

Volpe had Mrs. Horner tell of the various men and photographs of men that were brought to her to identify. Detective Toft brought several men, as well as photos, to her in the hospital and she recognized none of them. Then, on February 7, 1948: "I tried to identify those colored men. I was taken to a small room [at the police station] and I was looking through a piece of glass like smoked glass, you know, square, about so long, and I had a black shawl over my head and looked through." She examined four or five men and could identify none. Katzenbach questioned how she knew the defendants names this time, when she had not at the first trial. She revealed that Volpe had recently brought her into the station to go over photos and her testimony from the previous trial, in fact lending her a copy of her previous testimony to study. Pellettieri asked how she eventually picked out these particular men: "Why, I just saw those men's pictures in the Prosecutor's office, and I picked them out." Pellettieri asked: "You could tell better from pictures than you could from the men themselves, is that right?" "Yes."[32]

She described Forrest as wearing a blue Melton cloth coat the day she was attacked and English in a "tan outfit with a peaked cap, with a peak, you know, board, like the jockeys wear." Katzenbach asked what Forrest talked like, was his voice "high and squeaky or low and deep?" She answered, "It was ordinary." She also insisted that Forrest signed the receipt. Katzenbach pointed out that Forrest never owned a blue Melton cloth coat, spoke with a pronounced stutter, and could not write. Mrs. Horner's response: "Well, he was the man, I am positively sure." This engendered loud murmuring in the court, causing Judge Smalley to interject: "I would like to say to the spectators that I am delighted to have you, but you will have to remain very quiet during the very serious taking of testimony, or I will be obliged to clear the Court room. Now, it all depends on you people."[33] Katzenbach also asked Mrs. Horner about Jerry Griswold, who had been in Baltimore trying to obtain a driver's license at the time of the attack. Mrs. Horner was furious at Griswold for not being there to help defend Mr. Horner and herself.

Defense attorney Pellettieri asked repetitive, detailed questions about her nonidentification of men in the hospital: "And you had no trouble with your eyes then?" "They were close, right to the bed, and I could see them." "Yes, and you could see all the time, could you not?" "Yes." And then, just to be sure, "Well, there was nothing wrong with your eyes, you could see, correct?" "Yes." Pellettieri pointed out that she stated at the first trial that she could not identify the men at the police station because of her swollen and puffy eyes. Mrs. Horner's response: "Well, when I was up there [at the hospital] I had trouble with my eyes." Pellettieri then asked, "Did you tell the police you were struck with brass knuckles?" "I imagined that because the crack was so hard." "And you told them that you bit the finger of one of them?" "I imagine I did."[34]

Pellettieri moved on to information gained from a report by the defense investigator, Mr. Burtchaell, of his conversation with Mrs. Bowker, who rented a room above the Horner store. Pellettieri asked, "After coming back from the police station, didn't you tell Mrs. Bowker that they were not the men, that you couldn't identify them?" "I told her I wasn't sure." Pellettieri and Mrs. Horner had this exchange: "You told her you didn't identify them because you weren't sure they were the men?" "I wanted to be sure, I didn't say yes or I didn't say no." "And then subsequently it came to you, did it not, that they were the men?" "But I wasn't sure." "But it came to you?" "In a way." "In what way?" "Well, faintly, it went through my mind." "Did you have a dream, or a vision?" "No." "When did it come on you that these are the men?" "Just imagination." At this point groans filled the crowded courtroom. Pellettieri: "Just imagination?" Horner: "Yes." Regarding the individuals she looked through smoked glass to see at the Chancery Lane police station: "And you are certain they were not the men?" Horner: "Yes." Pellettieri: "And I am asking you again." Horner: "No, I am certain they were not the men." Pellettieri: "You realize what you are saying?" Horner: "They were not the men. I didn't recognize them." The men she had viewed through the smoked glass were the first five arrested, that is, all but John MacKenzie.[35]

During Raymond Pace Alexander's cross-examination of Mrs. Horner, he brought up a statement regarding identification she made to Burtchaell one week before the first trial: "Well, it would be a waste of time, a waste of time, the store was dark and everything happened so fast I couldn't identify anybody. Colored men—they all look alike to me." Now Mrs. Horner denied making any such statement. Alexander pointed out to the jury that Mrs. Horner had been brought four times from her home in Ocean Grove, New Jersey, to speak with Volpe, Lawton, and Naples about her testimony for this second trial.[36]

WEDNESDAY, MARCH 21, 1951

Cigar salesman Frank Eldracher took the stand, stating as he had before that he could not identify the two men he saw leaving the Horner store the morning of January 27, 1948, as he had not paid much attention to them. He described the men as light-complexioned Negroes between twenty and thirty years of age, one taller than the other. In response to cross-examination by Katzenbach he agreed that the prosecutors had never asked him to look at the six men being held at the Mercer County Jail. He agreed with Katzenbach that

Forrest looked older than the men he had seen and agreed with Alexander that Wilson looked too old as well.[37]

The defense used the testimony of Police Officer Stirling J. Pettit to illustrate how little light penetrated the gloom of the Horner store. They also used the testimony of a new state witness, ophthalmologist Ervin Sacks-Wilner, to show that Mrs. Horner's vision was essentially normal when she left the hospital. From police dispatcher Francis T. Parr the defense finally obtained the descriptions broadcast over the wires to surrounding states in the aftermath of the murder. At 11:00 A.M. the day of the murder the following went out: "Two colored men, one age thirty-five, 140 pounds, wearing a cap and a tan short coat; No. 2, five feet six inches, age 25, medium dark skin, wearing a short coat." At 11:51 A.M. information about another man was sent: "Five feet, eleven inches, wearing double-breasted overcoat, had a pencil mustache, weight, 165 to 170 pounds, one of the men wore eyeglasses, all cleanly dressed. Brass knuckles were used in this assault." Then at 3:32 P.M. the same day: "Occupants of a 1936–1937 Plymouth sedan, four-door bluish-green, dull finish, trunk on rear, New Jersey registration plates, registration unknown. 3–4 colored men in same. Driver wearing dark green overcoat. Same believed to be implicated in general alarm 69." One further alarm added: "One of these men is very young. Looks like a boy. Wearing silver-rimmed glasses. Tan overcoat, tan slouch hat, rear trunk has a hump on same, and driver wearing a light green coat." These descriptions emanated from Detectives Toft and Stanley, who got the last information from Mrs. Virginia Barclay. All of the police alarms were for assault and battery, changed to murder when Horner died, but not one mentioned a robbery.[38]

When defense attorney Pellettieri, exhibiting his vigorous temperament, argued a point regarding these records with Judge Smalley, Smalley expostulated, "Please do not shake your finger at me all the time." Pellettieri responded, "I am not being disrespectful when I do that, it is a habit of mine, the same as when your Honor brushes his nose and mustache; I know it is not because you disbelieve what I say, but it is a habit. That is a habit I have acquired over many years. If it annoys your Honor, I will apologize, but it may happen again." Judge Smalley responded, "I am never annoyed."[39]

Cross-examination of Patrolman Edward Kelly revealed descriptions that had never been heard in the first trial. Mrs. Horner had characterized the two men who went into the back room with Mr. Horner: "[H]eight about 5 foot 11 and 190 pounds; male, color—black; age 20 to 23; color of hair—black; complexion—dark; wearing a dark blue double-breasted overcoat. The second man was height about 5 feet 6 inches; weight, heavy;

male, color—black; age 20 to 23; color of hair—black; complexion—dark, wearing an army cap and jacket, with dark glasses." Kelly further testified that Mrs. Horner told him about the mattress receipt, which he then retrieved, signed by a man named Eppsom.[40] In an effort to speed up the trial, Judge Smalley proposed that court be adjourned for Good Friday but meet on Saturday. While the jury was willing, the defense attorneys did not agree with the idea; they needed the days off to prepare for court.

THURSDAY, MARCH 22, 1951

The defense recalled Mrs. Elizabeth Horner to the witness stand for additional testimony. Under Pellettieri's questions, Mrs. Horner revealed that she took her money out of a bank during the Great Depression and from then on kept her money in her stockings. At the hospital, when a nurse helped her undress, Mrs. Horner removed her life savings of nine hundred dollars, of which she had not been robbed. During the assault, nothing had been taken from the store, and she never complained to the police that she or Mr. Horner had been robbed, as asserted by the prosecutor. During the selection of jury members for the first trial, Sergeant Creeden did take her into the courtroom. She could only vaguely remember telling a policeman about the receipt with the name of Eppsom.[41]

Louis F. Neese brought copies of the police teletypes for the court; Katzenbach pointed out that Neese's information had been suppressed at the first trial, a remark to which Volpe strongly objected. Pellettieri responded, "Mr. Volpe is very stuffy and finicky about the remark of counsel that was made, and he said that it was made for the benefit of the jury, and I don't think that is a gentlemanly thing to say, and I resent it, and it should be stricken from the record." Volpe answered, "Counsel may resent it, but it is my feeling." Judge Smalley stepped in: "Now, gentlemen, now, gentlemen. You have got a long way to go before this is over, and these things will only increase your blood pressure and make you a worse risk for your insurance company. You might remember that, both of you, or all of you. Now let's get along."[42]

Patrolman Arthur Dennis, one of the first on the murder scene, testified that he observed glass bottle fragments in the front room of the Horner store, but they were not contained in a sock and he never saw a sock on the premises.[43] At the end of the day several Catholic members of the jury took an opportunity to express concern to Judge Smalley that they would not be able to attend mass on Easter. The judge contacted Bishop George W. Ahr, who excused jury members from their obligation to attend mass for the duration of the trial. Sheriff Brennan took jurors to the seaside resort of Asbury Park for the long weekend.[44]

Monday, March 26, 1951

Detective Donald Toft revealed the sources of the teletype descriptions sent over the wires. He did a "composite teletype based on information from Mr. Eldracher, Mrs. Barclay, and Mrs. Horner."[45] Mrs. Horner told him that the person who signed the mattress receipt was named Jessom or Jessup.[46] When Pellettieri questioned Toft, he repeatedly expressed anger at Toft's facial expression, particularly when Volpe objected to questions and the judge sustained the objections. Finally, Pellettieri admonished, "Now, please, Officer, don't smirk, don't—" Volpe interrupted, "Now, if your Honor please, I want to be fair, but these remarks certainly ought to be stricken from the record. The man is trying to do his best here, and to be badgered—" Judge Smalley: "I will let the remark and the record stand. The jury is looking and listening and observing."[47] John P. Brady, state police chemist and toxicologist, stated that the bottle top already examined by Lieutenant Sharpe had not been wiped clean of fingerprints and contained several animal hairs, as well as a white hair that could have come from Mrs. Horner.[48]

At this point in the proceedings, the prosecution planned to call witnesses in relation to Collis English's statement. All counsel agreed that the jury should not be present for this testimony. Judge Smalley told the jurors that he had a legal problem to resolve; the jurors left at 2:08 p.m. He excused them "for a little while, it may be longer than a little while." The jury did not return until Monday, April 16, 1951, three weeks after they left the courtroom. The testimony for these three weeks focused on whether the statements made by the defendants were voluntary or not. In the sections of this chapter that follow, only material new to this second trial will be discussed for the period without the jury.

Tuesday, March 27, 1951

Attempting to show that the confessions had not been voluntarily made, Pellettieri questioned Patrolman Nicholas Lichtfuhs, pointing out the size of Collis English, about five feet four inches tall and of a slight build, and the policemen, typically five feet ten or more, weighing 180 or so pounds. Alexander, feeling able to do so without the jury, pointed out to the audience that now mattered, Judge Smalley, that all of the policemen involved were white.[49] Alexander asked how many blacks had been arrested for the Horner murder, but Volpe objected. Pellettieri brought up the machine-gun-toting special squad, but Judge Smalley would not listen. Arthur Hays of the New York ACLU, now joining the trial on a more regular basis, spoke up: "If there was a general reign of terror here, that would have an effect on a young colored boy in the hands of the police; and I think we should be entitled to show what the general situation was, because from that you can get some idea of the attitude of mind which we claim would lead this boy to say anything the police wanted, rather than oppose the police." At one point Hays asked Lichtfuhs: "You wouldn't call the questioning of a person for 19 hours without a chance to rest or sleep putting pressure on him?" Smalley sustained Volpe's objections, and material regarding events in the larger community was not permitted.[50]

In questioning Patrolman Louis Amman it became clear why going into Klein's jewelry store turned up in Collis English's statement. The original wire report listed the assault and battery at Klein's jewelry instead of the Horner store.[51] Pellettieri brought up the defense desire to question Detective Lieutenant Stanley; Volpe responded that he could not appear in court for medical reasons. After much back and forth, Pellettieri exclaimed, with tears in his eyes, "He forgets his duties, Mr. Volpe does, to protect the innocent as well as to convict the guilty. And our job is to protect the innocent, as well as convict the guilty." At this moment a black woman appeared in the courtroom door shouting, "Glory be to God! I'm here! I'm here! Those boys are not guilty!" Sheriff's deputies were hustling her away even as she shouted, "Those boys are not guilty." In reaction, a woman spectator in the crowd burst into tears and had to leave court to regain her composure. Judge Smalley recessed the proceedings for ten minutes so all involved could collect their thoughts. The "intruder" turned out to be Sister Pauline Hamilton of the Brooklyn House of Prayer for All Nations. She told a court attendant, "The Lord sent me here to save the boys." Before entering the courtroom she had preached a brief sermon in the first floor corridor against the sin of authorities in prosecuting six innocent men.[52]

In questioning Sergeant James Creeden, Hays again attempted to show the bigger picture: "The attitude of the Police Department was to get somebody, whether the thing was sound or not, and as soon as they got confessions from these boys they quit looking for anybody else. I claim it shows a desire to get victims." Judge Smalley continued to uphold Volpe's objections and allowed no further questions along these lines.[53]

Figure 1. The Trenton Six during their second trial. Left to right: James Thorpe, Ralph Cooper, Collis English, McKinley Forrest, John MacKenzie, and Horace Wilson. Courtesy of the Photographs and Prints Division, Schomburg Center for Research in Black Culture, The New York Public Library, Astor, Lenox and Tilden Foundations.

Figure 2. Interior of William Horner's secondhand store in downtown Trenton, New Jersey. Courtesy of the Trenton Police Department, Police Director Irving Bradley Jr.

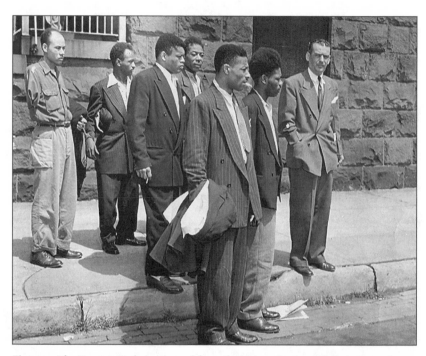

Figure 3. The Trenton Six being moved from the Mercer County Jail to their new home in the Death House of the Trenton State Prison on August 6, 1948. Handcuffed in pairs, from left to right are James Thorpe, Collis English, John MacKenzie, Horace Wilson, McKinley Forrest, and Ralph Cooper. AP photo. Courtesy of the Newark Public Library, New Jersey Photo Collection, Charles F. Cummings New Jersey Information Center, Newark, New Jersey.

Figure 4. William Patterson, executive secretary of the Civil Rights Congress, which stepped in to aid the Trenton Six in their appeal. Photograph by Julius Lazarus. Courtesy of the Photographs and Prints Division, Schomburg Center for Research in Black Culture, The New York Public Library, Astor, Lenox and Tilden Foundations.

Figure 5. Picketing the New Jersey statehouse, February 14, 1949. At left on steps: Bessie Mitchell and William Patterson, executive secretary of the Civil Rights Congress. Keystone USA. Courtesy of the Photographs and Prints Division, Schomburg Center for Research in Black Culture, The New York Public Library, Astor, Lenox and Tilden Foundations.

Figure 6. Cover of the Civil Rights Congress pamphlet "Lynching Northern Style," by "had." On the final page readers were urged to "Cut the Lynch Rope—Clip the Coupon" to make a contribution to the Committee to Free the Trenton Six, Paul Robeson, Chairman. Courtesy of the Labadie Collection, Special Collections Library, University of Michigan, Ann Arbor.

Figure 7. Some members of the public turned away from the New Jersey Supreme Court hearing, May 16, 1949. Courtesy of Photographs and Prints Division, Schomburg Center for Research in Black Culture, The New York Public Library, Astor, Lenox and Tilden Foundations.

Figure 8. Bessie Mitchell, front right, distributing flyers and posters in Trenton, November 1949, before the second trial. Courtesy of the Photographs and Prints Division, Schomburg Center for Research in Black Culture, The New York Public Library, Astor, Lenox and Tilden Foundations.

Figure 9. Mrs. Emma English declared Mother of the Year by the New Jersey Civil Rights Congress, Mother's Day, May 14, 1950. Receiving gifts from Mr. Joseph Collins, community leader, Trenton, and Mrs. Remel Roberson, church leader and newspaperwoman. Courtesy of the Photographs and Prints Division, Schomburg Center for Research in Black Culture, The New York Public Library, Astor, Lenox and Tilden Foundations.

Figure 10. Defense lawyers for the second trial, from left to right: Raymond Pace Alexander, J. Mercer Burrell, Frank S. Katzenbach, Arthur Garfield Hays, George Pellettieri, and Clifford R. Moore. Courtesy of the Photographs and Prints Division, Schomburg Center for Research in Black Culture, The New York Public Library, Astor, Lenox and Tilden Foundations.

Figure 11. Leaving the courtroom after a pretrial hearing prior to the second trial, February 16, 1951. Top row, left to right: Ralph Cooper, McKinley Forrest, and John MacKenzie. Bottom row, left to right: Court attendant George Penkoske, Collis English, James Thorpe, Horace Wilson, and court attendant Charles H. Mulford. Courtesy of the Photographs and Prints Division, Schomburg Center for Research in Black Culture, the New York Public Library, Astor, Lenox and Tilden Foundations.

Figure 12. Horace Wilson at NAACP National Headquarters, 20 West 40th Street, New York City, after his acquittal. Courtesy of the Photographs and Prints Division, Schomburg Center for the Study of Black Culture, The New York Public Library, Astor, Lenox and Tilden Foundations.

Figure 13. John MacKenzie
and McKinley Forrest at
Robert Forrest's home
in Newark, admiring the
Newark newspaper head-
lining their acquittal.
Courtesy of the Newark
Public Library, New Jersey
Photo Collection, Charles
F. Cummings New Jersey
Information Center,
Newark, New Jersey.

WEDNESDAY, MARCH 28, 1951

Lieutenant Charles Dawson of the Detective Bureau expressed his doubts that Collis English actually knew anything about the crime. He admitted, "This was the first phase of the investigation. I was glad to get something that was in the Horner case, because up until that time we hadn't gotten anything and this man was volunteering information."[54]

THURSDAY, MARCH 29, 1951

Lieutenant Andrew Delate (in this second trial he was generally referred to by that rank rather than as acting captain as in the first trial) spent the entire day on the witness stand, interrupted only by the sheriff informing Judge Smalley that one of the sequestered jurors, Alyce F. Spellman, was ill and needed a physician. All attorneys agreed on a doctor to call, and he was later sworn in as a deputy. John J. Connell was also sworn in as a deputy, to serve as barber to the jury.[55]

Pellettieri and Volpe, each with a combustible nature, appeared likely to drive each other to distraction, with an unhappy Judge Smalley along for the ride. When Pellettieri questioned Delate about differences in details between current testimony and that in the first trial, Volpe insisted he read the record verbatim: "There is a dash in there." Pellettieri: "Oh." Volpe: "You read all the dashes before." Judge Smalley: "All right." Pellettieri: "All right, I will read all the commas and all the periods, then." Volpe: "It might be well to do so."[56]

FRIDAY, MARCH 30, 1951

During their cross-examination of Lieutenant Delate, defense counsel again attempted to bring up the community environment existing when police arrested the Six, during what defense counsel described as a "reign of terror." Alexander introduced the editorial "The Idle Electric Chair" of February 3, 1948, as well as an article published two days later titled "What Is the Trouble with the Trenton Police Force?"[57] Katzenbach brought up the special machine-gun-toting squad, dubbed the Crime Crushers. Then Hays and Pellettieri cited cases in which judges had ruled in favor of the inclusion of communal feelings and atmosphere as an important consideration. Volpe shot back, "Now, we are trying to inject into a retrial of this case an element which never existed in this case, and that is the question of the color of the defendants. . . . Are we going to try the State of New Jersey on this racial question, or are we going to try the community of Trenton on a racial question, or are we going to determine the innocence or guilt of the defendants?" Hays responded, "He says we are trying to bring color into this case. You can't keep color out of this case, your Honor." Hays insisted that in many aspects conditions in New Jersey were the same as in courtrooms in the South. Katzenbach persisted, pointing out: "They are holding a machine gun on the front page, they appear as a machine gun squad with orders to shoot to kill." Furthermore, those conditions existing four days before the apprehension of the Six "would indicate that this witness [Delate] had a particular deep-seated interest in solving this crime by any method. . . . The tendency would be to consider evidence pointing to the guilt and to disregard any evidence pointing to the innocence of these or any other accused who had been taken into custody at that time."[58] Judge Smalley refused to allow any questioning of Lieutenant Delate beyond the specific scope of his actions regarding the defendants. Katzenbach asked Delate if any people had been in to see McKinley Forrest. When Delate denied that Forrest had visitors, Katzenbach asked if Mrs. Mitchell and Mrs. Forrest were in court. They both rose and came to the front of the spectator section. Delate denied having ever seen them or hearing that they had asked to see Forrest, even though they had spoken to him on Sunday, February 8, 1948, at the police station, requesting a visit with Forrest.[59] Pellettieri did get Delate to admit that on the day after his arrest, Ralph Cooper did not know Wilson, Forrest, and Thorpe, even though the prosecution charged him with being part of a plot with these men.[60]

APRIL 2 AND 3, 1951

Pellettieri questioned Henry Miller, the police clerk who had typed up the men's statements and then read them aloud at the first trial. He had been a police clerk for eighteen years and estimated he took down 200 statements a year, approximately 3,600 over his lifetime. Pellettieri asked, "Now, at any other time on any other occasion had any strangers to the defendant and to the police and the law enforcement agencies been invited in to witness or to attend the signing procedure?" After Lawton objected and Smalley allowed it, Miller answered, "Not to my recollection, no." When Pellettieri asked why it was done in this case, and Lawton objected and Smalley allowed it, Miller replied, "I wouldn't know that, because I wasn't in any authority to send for anyone." Miller had begun working for the prosecutor after the first trial, so Pellettieri wanted to know: "Were you appointed or did you take an examination?" Lawton objected, and Smalley upheld the objection.[61]

WEDNESDAY, APRIL 4, 1951

Peyton "Scrappy" Manning, a "tall, bespectacled Negro" who had accompanied Dr. Sullivan for the middle-of-the-night signing session, told the court that Collis English appeared sick to him, while Forrest "seemed to me to be in a daze." Pellettieri applied to Judge Smalley for permission to have a psychiatrist examine the six men in the Mercer County Jail. He gave his reasoning thus: "We want this psychiatrist to go in there and advise us as to whether or not these men are the type of men that the psychological impact which we allege they suffered was such to cause them by reason of their environmental background, their limited education, their aspects on life, could be placed in a position where they could be subjected to psychological duress and fear." Lawton objected and requested that a psychiatrist for the state be allowed to see the men also. Judge Smalley took the matter under advisement.[62]

THURSDAY, APRIL 5, 1951

Dr. James Minor Sullivan III testified again about the physical state of the six men when he examined them at the middle-of-the-night confession session. When Pellettieri asked him about the effects of drugs, he indicated that they could make an individual more suggestible, more fatigued, excitable, irritable, and confused. As to Cooper, Dr. Sullivan agreed that marijuana could have been given the defendants without their knowledge; the condition of Cooper's eyes "could have been due to reefers." Sullivan said Forrest appeared "in a state of excitement, shaking all over as he tried to take his clothes off" for the physical exam, while Cooper was drowsy.[63]

In its coverage of the day's testimony, the National Guardian reminded its readers that one week after Sullivan examined the men, the city of Trenton appointed him to a $2,500-a-year job. Shortly before the second trial was to begin, Sullivan had been given a $4,000-a-year post with Mercer County.[64]

During the noon recess Dr. Frank Nunziato and Dr. Edgar Fiestal were summoned to examine Collis English specifically because of concerns about his heart. During the morning session he had been observed slumping in his chair and sweating. Dr. Nunziato stated that English was suffering from an "enlarged, leaky heart, originating from rheumatic fever suffered during his World War II service, exacerbated by the courtroom testimony." The physicians provided a sedative and court adjourned for the day.[65]

FRIDAY, APRIL 6, 1951

Doctors found Collis English improved this morning, so the trial continued. Judge Smalley ordered the appointment of three heart specialists to examine Collis over the weekend and report their findings, including the results of an electrocardiogram and X-rays.[66]

Dr. Sullivan resumed the witness stand, with defense counsel Alexander focusing his questions on MacKenzie in his "nervous and excitable state" and the possibility that he had been given drugs, specifically sodium amytol, a barbiturate that could cause a nervous, excited state, with loss of memory. Sullivan stated that psychiatrists sometimes used it in order to suggest things to their patients; it was known as "truth serum." He agreed that in his opinion this drug could have been used on MacKenzie. He also agreed that violence could be inflicted on an individual in ways that would not leave physical evidence. When questioned by Pellettieri about Thorpe's signing his statement even while insisting he was innocent, thus inferring that he had been told he "would only get a few days or a month," Dr. Sullivan expressed the opinion that Thorpe must have been promised something. These responses were too much for Volpe; he began questioning the doctor about the differences in his answers at this trial versus the first one. Pellettieri then protested that the state was improperly attempting to impeach the testimony of its own witness in an effort to demonstrate Dr. Sullivan's lack of credibility.[67]

MONDAY, APRIL 9, 1951

Dr. John A. Kinczel reported to Judge Smalley that Collis English could probably complete the trial if he were checked regularly and given adequate rest. The *Trenton Evening Times* reporter commented: "The defendant appeared more at ease today as he sat in the courtroom."[68] Judge Smalley agreed with defense counsel that the defendants could be examined by psychiatrists of the defense's choosing in the Mercer County Jail.[69]

TUESDAY, APRIL 10, 1951

In preparation for his decision regarding whether the confessions could be used during the trial, Judge Smalley heard the defense argument on motions to exclude confessions. Arthur Hays began with the Fourteenth Amendment and the Fifth Amendment. He pointed out that although he knew New Jersey law differed from federal law, the aggregate of the Six's situation made the statements inadmissible. New Jersey law indicated that material taken by the police under physical or moral pressure was to be viewed with suspicion. He described in detail the constant pressure that English had been under for twenty-two hours straight after being arrested. He indicated that where federal and state law differed, when the case was appealed to federal court, federal law would prevail, reversing state judgments.

Next Raymond Alexander dealt specifically with New Jersey cases he thought would provide guidance for Judge Smalley. He began with Judge Heher's opinion overthrowing the initial trial results. Judge Heher mentioned twenty criteria that might indicate invalid confessions. Alexander listed those factors present in this case: arrest without a warrant, incommunicado confinement, interrupted rest, poor-quality meals, poor sleeping accommodation, primitive facilities for personal needs, lack of lighting, prolonged interrogation, interrogation in a limited space, coercion, fraud and duress, interrogation by a prosecutor and assistant, no immediate arraignment, blacks from a southern background, police officers afraid to testify honestly because of potential job reprisal, illiterate defendants, intelligence of defendants, and the health of defendants. Next Alexander brought up the influence of Trenton newspapers, quoting U.S. Supreme Court Justice Robert H. Jackson: "Newspapers in the enjoyment of their constitutional rights, may not deprive accused persons of their right to a fair trial."[70]

Pellettieri, for his three clients (English, Cooper, and Thorpe), pointed out: "There is far more testimony, in this case, your Honor, at the present time than there was at the first trial, that those men, that their constitutional rights had not been acquainted to them . . . I say to your Honor without reservation that this case is stronger today in this posture than it was at the first trial." He also indicated where testimony of various police officers conflicted.[71]

Katzenbach had just begun making his case for Forrest when Judge Smalley interjected, "May I interrupt you for a moment Judge, I don't like to." Collis English had suddenly slumped over in his seat. Bessie Mitchell then cried out, "Oh my God!" Judge Smalley demanded "Quiet!" but Bessie continued, "It is a shame before God. Why don't you stop killing innocent people." Bessie Mitchell and her mother left the courtroom sobbing as attendants carried Collis English from the room. Judge Smalley spoke again: "Sit still, ladies and gentlemen." He then called for a short recess as the other defendants and jury tried to regain their composure. At 3:20 P.M. he suspended court for the day; Collis English clearly required medical attention.[72]

WEDNESDAY, APRIL 11, 1951

Judge Smalley convened court by making a statement: "I am aware that one defendant is suffering from a heart condition, which, however, all medical advice that we have had including thorough and careful hospital examinations, X-rays, and so forth reveal that the situation is serious but not acute. It will undoubtedly be uncomfortable at times for the defendant and every known treatment is being given and the individual is under the constant care of very reliable and trustworthy physicians who have authorized and stated to this Court these proceedings are in no wise contributing to a more serious acute condition." After assuring that all consideration would be given to the defendant, he went on: "But that doesn't give any spectators the right to indulge in actions which this Court will not tolerate. And a repeating of the performance of yesterday by those in the audience will mean either the clearing of the courtroom or these particular people will be barred."[73]

Frank Katzenbach then resumed his argument that McKinley Forrest's statement should not be admitted into evidence. Katzenbach focused on the fact that Forrest's actions stemmed from fear induced by psychological coercion, and he provided numerous details. Volpe then rose to explain precisely why all of the statements, oral and written, should be allowed. He reiterated long-familiar testimony and was interrupted at times by questions from the bench. Judge Smalley asked, "What about your testimony of Doctor Sullivan?" He referred to the doctor's testimony that several of the men appeared to be influenced by drugs. Volpe answered, "At times he had a very difficult time to recollect his previous testimony. He dealt in conjecture." Judge Smalley: "My recollection is, however, Mr. Prosecutor, that Doctor Sullivan said that MacKenzie was in some sort of a controlled condition." Volpe: "He was unable to state what could have produced it or whether it was produced by anything. . . . It goes without saying that considerable pressure has been borne upon, and I don't mean by defense counsel, but by the community generally upon a witness such as Doctor Sullivan [who was black] to have him change his testimony, the sense of feeling within himself compelled him to go far beyond what he did at the first trial." Judge Smalley: "Are you not bound by what he has testified to?"[74]

Judge Smalley also questioned Volpe about Thorpe's refusal to sign his statement and his ultimate capitulation. Volpe, in return, pointed out that defense counsel had made much of the fact that the defendants had little if any education; however Collis English, with his tenth-grade education, provided the police with almost all of their information while Horace Wilson, with perhaps the least education, insisted on his innocence throughout.[75] Judge Smalley brought up the matter of Ralph Cooper unknowingly smoking "reefers." Volpe answered that Judge Smalley could "either accept the testimony of Doctor Sullivan in all respects and discount all the police officers, or the Court will have to accept the testimony of the others in conflicting matters and not accept that of Doctor Sullivan. I see no other choice for this Court at this time."[76]

In a Machiavellian move, when Volpe turned his focus to McKinley Forrest and his lawyer, Frank Katzenbach, he brought up a court statement by Katzenbach's own father. The senior Katzenbach had been a New Jersey Supreme Court justice, and Volpe quoted him as saying, "The sense of guilt usually weighs heavily upon the accused if guilty of committing the crime. It produces wakefulness, loss of appetite, fear and despondency, until the mind is so tortured that the accused to relieve his mind from the strain confesses." Volpe added, "I say, your Honor, those very same words are very applicable in this case." And if coercion had been used against the defendants, Volpe asked, why didn't Wilson confess?[77]

When Volpe finished, Pellettieri rose to rebut. He argued that since the police rather than detectives had headed the case investigation, "this whole thing smells of amateurism and I say that without hesitation." As to Dr. Sullivan: "Well, probably he wasn't probed and probably he wasn't questioned with the skill of my associates on cross-examination as he was in this trial. . . . We aren't seeking the blood or the reputation or to injure anyone. We are seeking justice."[78] Then the defense team called witnesses to buttress the points they had made in their arguments. Pellettieri produced articles from Trenton newspapers showing the pressure police were under to solve the Horner murder, including a February 9, 1948, article quoting Volpe as saying that confessions had been signed in the case several days before the middle-of-the-night confession session occurred. Judge Smalley upheld Volpe's objection to entering the newspapers in the record.[79] The defense called Director of Public Safety Andrew Duch, Chief of Police William Dooling, and Ferdinand Pilger, head of the Crime Crusher squad, to the stand, but Judge Smalley agreed with Volpe's objections, and none had to testify about the squad and its operations.[80]

THURSDAY, APRIL 12, 1951

The defense team continued its effort to illustrate the broader circumstances affecting the defendants. Alexander put Horace Wilson on the stand to testify about the conditions the men lived in while being interrogated in the Chancery Lane First Precinct police station. He described life in the cells as one of constant noise, amazing filth, inedible food, and only a simple board for sleeping.[81] Susanna Thorpe, James's grandmother, testified that he could not speak plainly and had never been able to pronounce words properly, thus making it difficult for him to defend himself.[82]

FRIDAY, APRIL 13, 1951

On Friday the thirteenth, the state called witnesses to rebut the defense witnesses just heard from. Ernest Sands was a surprise to the defense; a short man, with glasses and a small mustache, he ran a business selling used clothing and general merchandise in Trenton, and he stated that he had seen three of the six men in his store several days before the Horner murder. He left the stand to indicate Ralph Cooper, McKinley Forrest, and Horace Wilson; his point was that Wilson did know the other two before the murder. When he saw in the newspapers that the case was being retried, he came forward to see that justice was done. Wilson denied ever having seen Sands or being in his store.[83]

After more arguments from both sides, Judge Smalley retired briefly, then reappeared to announce his decisions on the admissibility of the confessions. He agreed with defense counsel that the oral statement by Ralph Cooper would not be admitted but ruled that the one Cooper wrote himself in longhand would be. Judge Smalley told the packed, tense, and silent audience that the typewritten and signed statements of James Thorpe and John MacKenzie would also not be admitted but that those of Collis English and McKinley Forrest would be. He evidently relied on the testimony of Dr. Sullivan, who stated that Cooper and MacKenzie appeared to have been drugged and Thorpe had apparently been promised a short sentence in return for his statement. Judge Smalley also stated, "I am going to tell this jury that notwithstanding those alleged confessions that have been admitted by me that it is for them, under my instructions, to determine whether or not they are voluntary. And if they don't find they are voluntary then they disregard them entirely."[84] At 3:59 P.M. the judge had the jury back in his courtroom and repeated his statement. He also emphasized that "a confession or admission is binding only upon the person who is said to have made it. Any reference, therefore, which the confession or admission makes to any other person or defendant is not binding upon that other person or defendant." Judge Smalley told the jury he would see them Monday morning at 10:00 A.M.[85]

APRIL 16, 1951, AND APRIL 17, 1951

The state laid out its case, calling policemen who repeated their stories of the questioning of Collis English. With the jury back in place, objections by both sides flew fast and furiously, considerably slowing progress. Ike Williams, a native Trentonian and world lightweight boxing champion, appeared in the courtroom to show his support for the Trenton Six.[86]

WEDNESDAY, APRIL 18, 1951

Lieutenant Andrew Delate took the stand; his testimony did not conclude until the following Monday. Delate spent most of the time being cross-examined by Alexander, Pellettieri, and Katzenbach. He spoke softly, constantly having to be reminded to keep his voice up so the lawyers, judge, jury, and court reporter could hear.[87]

THURSDAY, APRIL 19, 1951

Judge Smalley repeatedly excused the jury so the lawyers could battle over the issue of what testimony could be presented to jurors up to the point of making the statements that Judge Smalley had excluded. Lieutenant Delate, clearly unhappy at his treatment by Pellettieri, inquired plaintively at one point, "Stop this man from bulldozing me, won't you, Judge?" Judge Smalley responded, "I suggest to all of you including Counsel and the witness that we handle this thing in a quiet, fair way, and without emotions and get to the facts. And please answer them in the same frame of mind. Just take it easy." Pellettieri continued to press Delate about every detail of the questioning of English and Cooper; Volpe objected frequently, which resulted in little forward progress being made. Pellettieri aimed to show the jury Delate's lack of credibility, essentially saying that Delate had made up a story of what happened and then told it to English and Cooper; Delate admitted this, to a point.[88] However, Pellettieri could easily have been perceived by the jury as bullying the witness.

When Pellettieri questioned Delate regarding the current whereabouts of the money found in Horner's pockets, Volpe revealed that it had been turned over to the administrator of the Horner estate. At this point Pellettieri announced that the defense moved for a mistrial, as the state charged that a robbery/murder had taken place yet had not kept the evidence. Alexander added, "The character of the bills would give us other information; were there bloodstains on the bills, for example; were the bills in such condition to give evidence for or against and in this instance we believe evidence that would buttress the defendants' defense of innocence." Judge Smalley denied the motion for mistrial or a direction of acquittal but said the defense could renew its motion at the end of the state's case. At the end of the day, after excusing the jury, Judge Smalley reminded counsel: "This jury has been sequestered since March 5th. They are the people that are going to decide this case. In the interest of all, I ask Counsel to make an effort that this case move along as reasonably even and with all possible speed, taking into consideration, of course, the right of the defendants, but I am asking that I might have the cooperation of Counsel in moving this case along."[89]

FRIDAY, APRIL 20, 1951

Delate continued on the stand, questioned by Pellettieri, who asked if there was any evidence other than the confessions against the men. Delate's answer: "The only thing the Detective Bureau, Lieutenant Stanley had [was] that bottle. Outside of that there was nothing." Pellettieri: "There were no fingerprints of Collis English on that bottle?" Delate: "I was never informed so." Delate agreed that outside of the statements, he had no direct evidence tying English, Cooper, or Thorpe to the crime. The *New York Times* article on this day was headlined: "Trenton 6 Win Point, Police Officer Admits Lack of Evidence Against 3 Men."[90]

When Alexander took his turn questioning Delate, he focused on the description he got from Collis English about Buddy Wilson: "A light-skinned boy, around five foot seven; he didn't know him very well." Alexander had Horace Wilson stand up, pointing out that he had been thirty-seven years old at the time, and obviously had very dark skin. Alexander made a motion that Delate's testimony about taking MacKenzie's and Thorpe's confessions be stricken, as Judge Smalley had thrown out the confessions themselves. The judge stated that he would rule on Monday.[91]

Monday, April 23, 1951

Judge Smalley began by denying the motions regarding Delate's testimony of MacKenzie and Thorpe before they made their confessions. He said he would rule on other such circumstances as they arose.[92] Henry Miller, former clerk typist and now special investigator for Prosecutor Volpe, spent this Monday and part of Tuesday on the witness stand. Judge Smalley ruled that the jury needed to hear in detail about the manner in which police obtained the confessions that he had allowed into the trial, before the confessions themselves could be read to the jury. Smalley repeated, as he had done previously, that he was doing his very best to be absolutely fair both to the state and the defense.[93]

Tuesday, April 24, 1951

Following Judge Smalley's instructions, Volpe called back to the stand state witnesses who had been involved with the defendants at the time they signed their confessions. This gave the defense the opportunity to bring out details not made clear before. Henry Miller, after a long series of questions by Pellettieri, agreed that Cooper only knew the other men as Chancey, Red, and Shorty, but not by their actual names until told their names by the police. The same was true for Collis English, who had provided the police with names, which the police later assigned to the defendants. Peyton Manning testified that McKinley Forrest appeared fearful, was shaking, and incoherent right before initialing his confession.[94] When Dr. Sullivan returned for additional questioning, Katzenbach asked him closely about Forrest. Sullivan agreed with Manning's description and said he had not been told that a doctor had been called to see the moaning and sobbing Forrest only seven hours before he signed the statement and that the doctor had left a capsule, possibly sodium amytol, to calm Forrest. Forrest shook so badly that Drs. Corio and Sullivan had to help him remove his clothing for the physical exam. Sullivan agreed that a drug could have caused the symptoms Forrest showed. He described Forrest as being "in a daze, who did not face his questioners but stared straight ahead as if he didn't know what was going on, exhibiting nervousness to the point of hysteria." Judge Smalley did not let Volpe read Cooper's handwritten confession, the one that he had ruled into evidence, until the jury heard testimony regarding its voluntariness.[95]

WEDNESDAY, APRIL 25, 1951

Dr. Sullivan spent the entire day on the witness stand. When Pellettieri asked him about Collis English's condition, the answer was: "He had a psychoneurosis associated with a cardiac condition brought on by stress, mental stress and strain of the heart." Under more questioning he added, "Cardiac patients have one outstanding symptom; they would like to keep anything from making their heart worse, so they will go along and testify to anything you suggest." He expanded on this: "Under mental pressure he would not be acting of his own free will." This was too much for Prosecutor Volpe, who announced that he would have to plead surprise, meaning he wished to neutralize the testimony of his own witness. Volpe spent the rest of the day attacking Sullivan on apparent changes in his testimony about the conditions of Forrest and English, while the defense countered that Sullivan was merely expanding on his previous answers. In order to compare them, Volpe brought up statements that Sullivan had given to Detective Dore before the first trial, testimony from the first trial, and his testimony at this trial in the absence of the jury. Defense counsel objected to almost every question Volpe put to Sullivan. Finally Judge Smalley told them all: "Now, gentlemen, you have been here a good many weeks, and I guess we are going to be here many more. Let me give you all a little advice, this is bad for your blood pressure. Now let's move along." Four o'clock and adjournment arrived to end the heated discussion.[96]

THURSDAY, APRIL 26, 1951

Both sides arrived in court armed with citations and motions. Clearly, all the attorneys spent hours each evening reading the previous day's record and researching arguments for the next day. In the jury's absence, Volpe made a motion that in view of the doctor's changing testimony, Judge Smalley should reconsider eliminating the three disallowed statements and now admit them. Smalley expressed his surprise and denied the motion.[97] The jury returned and heard the evidence of Dr. William James Moore, who had been called to the Chancery Lane First Precinct police station on Tuesday, February 10, 1948, to attend to McKinley Forrest. When Moore first observed Forrest, he was sitting with his hands covering his face, peering through his fingers; he then announced that he was going to die. Lieutenant Delate told Dr. Moore that Forrest had said something about jumping out the window. Moore then gave Chief Detective Naples a capsule of sodium amytol to give to Forrest, if needed, to prevent him "from becoming excited and try to hurt himself."

Naples asked Moore what effect the capsule would have, asking if it would interfere with Forrest's thinking. Moore answered that it would, so, Naples claimed, he destroyed the pill.[98]

FRIDAY, APRIL 27, 1951

Over the vehement objections of George Pellettieri, Volpe entered into evidence a peaked cap and leggings belonging to Collis English, allegedly what he wore when committing the murder.[99] Chief Detective Naples spent the day on the stand, first questioned by Pellettieri, who delighted in probing contrasts between Naples's current and former testimony. Naples insisted that he had been seeking "Horace Wilson" all along, not a mythical Buddy Wilson. When questioned by Alexander, Naples adamantly stated that he had been told by English to look for a one-armed man, not a man "with one shoulder higher than the other," as described at the first trial.[100] When Pellettieri asked about the signing of the confessions, Naples volunteered that Dr. Sullivan asked English, "Are you guilty of murder?" and English answered yes. There had previously been no such testimony; it caused Pellettieri to get so angry and frustrated that he told Judge Smalley, "I am sorry, your Honor. I am all worked up. If you give me a second I will calm myself." Naples then expanded his comments, saying Dr. Sullivan asked each defendant the question and they all answered positively. At 4:00 P.M. Judge Smalley dismissed the jury and told all counsel, "We have wasted a lot of time. . . . This jury has been here a long time, and you can look at them yourself and see the lines in their faces and the strain that they are under. We are all under somewhat of a strain, but be that as it may, we are all officers of this Court, you are just as much as I am. . . . Let's conduct ourselves as officers of this Court to the end there shall be a fair trial. See you Monday morning."[101]

MONDAY, APRIL 30, 1951

Frank Naples resumed his place on the witness stand, questioned by Pellettieri. Judge Smalley interrupted Pellettieri and Naples several times, admonishing both that their bickering was unhelpful: "I'm not interested in any of these side remarks and I don't think the jury is either."[102] Pellettieri evidently rattled Naples, as the chief of detectives now claimed that there were three trips to Robbinsville, instead of the two testified to by everyone else. Naples stated he never made any notes on the case and commented that he knew English "started to tell the truth when he implicated himself."

Regarding the questioning of the men: "We woke them up whenever we wanted them to come in for questioning or identification, not at the normal hour." English had given Naples a description of Buddy Wilson as thirty-two years of age and five feet eleven inches tall. Defense attorney Alexander had Wilson stand up in court to illustrate that he was forty years old and only five feet five inches tall.[103]

TUESDAY, MAY 1, 1951

Frank Naples again took his place on the witness stand, interrogated by Katzenbach. Naples admitted that Forrest had been locked up without being told why and without ever being questioned, and that police were more interested in getting admissions from him than checking his alibi. Forrest had continued to deny all participation in the crime, a denial Naples ignored.[104]

Prosecutor Volpe now brought forth a surprise, and very surprising witness: George English, father of Collis. He told the following story: On January 9, 1948, he came home from work at 8:00 P.M. He went into his basement because his boiler was going out, and while there he heard Melrose Diggs come in; Melrose was the daughter of his wife, Rubie English, by a relationship she had before she married George. Ralph Cooper then entered the house and told Melrose he wanted to use George English's car to carry out a robbery on Broad Street, at a secondhand furniture store. Cooper also asked Melrose to say that her stepfather, George English, hit or slapped her, in order for Cooper to get George into trouble. George confronted him and Cooper left. While George prepared dinner for Rubie and her little girl, Myrtis, he discovered they had no bread in the house; he sent Myrtis to get some. Because she took three-quarters of an hour doing this, and with permission from Rubie, George "gave her a licking." This caused Myrtis to go to Cooper's house for help, saying she had been abused. What occurred according to everyone else: Melrose Diggs sought Cooper's help in the middle of the night when Rubie found her husband molesting Myrtis. Policeman Frank Murphy subsequently booked George English on a rape charge; he was freed on bail on February 6, 1948. George English continued his story: when painting his house in March 1948, he found in his shed a short coat of his own and a coat belonging to Ralph Cooper. In Ralph Cooper's coat he found a bottle in a sock. These he put in his basement. From April 1948 to August 1950, he served a prison term for molesting a minor. Upon his return home he found the two coats upstairs in a closet and the bottle in the basement. He told this story to his lawyer, Irving Lewis, who then told the prosecutor. Volpe, along with photographers, went to the English home at 12 Behm Street to see the evidence.[105]

Next George English told the court that he knew Horace Wilson, John MacKenzie, McKinley Forrest, and James Thorpe. While this in itself was not significant, he revealed that he had seen Wilson, Cooper, and Thorpe together more than once in December 1947. When Volpe finished questioning George English, Alexander rose to make a motion to strike his testimony from the record because it was "highly speculative and too irrelevant and immaterial to the issue we are now trying, to permit a jury to weigh any part of it for any efficacy it might have. It is unworthy of belief." Volpe responded, "As to the weight and the credibility to be given to it, that is a matter for the jury to determine." Judge Smalley denied Alexander's motion. It is worth noting that when authorities released George English from prison in August 1950, it was two years before he should have been eligible for parole.[106]

Pellettieri, having obtained a copy of George English's criminal record, questioned him about it. On April 8, 1926, he had been convicted for "carnal abuse" of his ten-year-old stepdaughter, Bessie Mitchell, and served one year. Explaining that Bessie Mitchell was not his daughter, George English stated, "A gang of women carries my name, a gang of them, sir." He claimed that he was not married to Rubie. Later he asserted, "So far as I'm concerned, I don't know whether I got any child or not, only just what the women say." On March 21, 1940, George had been sentenced to the workhouse for three charges of "atrocious assault and battery with a pistol" during which one man was wounded. On the January 1948 issue of rape, George claimed that Ralph Cooper had framed him. During this questioning Judge Smalley interrupted Pellettieri to say, "I have no objection when you vigorously cross-examine any witness, but I do not expect you to indulge in such shouting and pounding in my Court, and I ask you not to do it." Pellettieri responded: "I humbly apologize to your Honor and apologize to the jury if I have offended someone. Unfortunately it is my temperament, and I will try to control it." George English continued to claim that Wilson, Thorpe, and Cooper had known each other before the Horner murder, but when questioned by Pellettieri he became extremely vague about dates and places, as he also was when discussing when and to whom he told the story of overhearing Ralph Cooper and Melrose Diggs scheming.[107]

On this day a Communist-inspired May Day parade took place in New York City; a number of parade floats and banners demanded justice for the Trenton Six. Writer Howard Fast, in an article on the demands made, wrote,

"The Hitler-like murders of the Negro people must stop! John Derrick and the seven Martinsville martyrs already dead—the Trenton six and Willie McGee to die—the bloodbath must end!"[108]

WEDNESDAY, MAY 2, 1951

Pellettieri took George English in minute detail through the conversation he had allegedly overheard while in his basement, including having him draw up a rough map of his basement and the location of the heating vent. Today English included the information that Cooper planned a murder as well as a robbery. Judge Smalley allowed two members of the defense team, Mr. Hays and Mr. Moore, to visit George English's house to see the basement and layout of the home for themselves.[109] After the lunch recess, they reported to the court that it was "impossible for two people to be in a position for this man, as he stated he saw Cooper and the Diggs woman, from where he was standing he could not see that which he testified." Moore meant that from where George English said he was positioned in the basement it would not be possible to see two people in the living room. Pellettieri asked that the jury be permitted to see the site, but Judge Smalley denied permission. The previous day, George had denied being married to Emma English, his first wife, so Pellettieri produced a family Bible showing the marriage date and children's names and birth dates. George English denied that it was his Bible, or his handwriting, saying it belonged to his cousin, also named George English.[110]

Late in the day, Alexander took his turn questioning George English, asking him about Horace Wilson. English insisted that in his work as a contractor for farm labor, he had hired Wilson in 1947. However, he could produce no records or any other evidence to verify this. Volpe marked the two coats found in the basement as evidence, and Judge Smalley agreed to their admittance. Pellettieri objected: "There is no specific direct proof that this coat or any of them belonged to Ralph Cooper."[111] Then Volpe wished to have Cooper's oral statement, the one allowed by Judge Smalley, read to the jury. Over objections from Pellettieri, Assistant Prosecutor Lawton read it. In his statement Cooper mentioned a bottle in a sock as the murder weapon.[112]

THURSDAY, MAY 3, 1951

Volpe wished to admit into evidence the bottle found in the pocket of the green coat that George English described as being Ralph Cooper's coat.

Clearly, Volpe meant the jury to infer that Cooper had worn this coat on the day of the crime, with the bottle being the murder weapon. Pellettieri asserted, "The proffered evidence has in no way been connected either directly or inferentially with the defendant Cooper or with the crime in question. It is incompetent, irrelevant, too remote, and is not admissible in evidence." He then reminded the judge that Mrs. Horner told the court that she saw Ralph Cooper only once, on January 16, 1948, when he came into the store to see a mattress, and she did not place him on the premises on the day of the murder. Judge Smalley admitted into evidence not only the bottle but also photographs taken of George English's furnace, pipes, with the bottle tucked into a ceiling joist. Defense attorney Hays objected mightily to the introduction of the pictures, saying that no proper foundation had been laid to show that the evidence actually had anything to do with Ralph Cooper.[113] The state then called John B. Brady of the State Identification Bureau to tell of his testing of the dust found on the sock and in the adjacent cellar area. Brady made clear that he had found no fingerprints on the bottle itself and the dust was probably unsettled for "at least a year." Hays objected to this evidence, saying it was "remote from any question at issue here, and not being connected it is immaterial."[114] Arthur Hays made an eloquent plea to have Lieutenant Detective Stanley testify, saying that the state bore the burden of protecting the innocent as well as finding the guilty; Judge Smalley denied the request. The defense team objected to the reading of the statements of Collis English and McKinley Forrest; Judge Smalley overruled the objections. Henry Miller, former police clerk and now special investigator for the prosecutor, read both confessions aloud in court.[115]

Friday, May 4, 1951

Against Volpe's wishes, Judge Smalley refused to allow into evidence the mug shots taken of the defendants.[116] The state rested its case. Judge Smalley heard lengthy arguments on motions by Alexander to throw out testimony surrounding the giving of Thorpe and MacKenzie's statements, as Judge Smalley had not allowed the statements themselves into evidence.[117]

Monday, May 7, 1951

Judge Smalley denied Alexander's motion on Thorpe and MacKenzie as well as Pellettieri's argument that the state had never proven that a robbery took place.

TUESDAY, MAY 8, 1951

In the absence of the jury, Pellettieri and Alexander spent the day arguing for a directed verdict of acquittal for all six defendants, providing reasons that the state had never proved its case. Pellettieri called the original trial "[a] grave injustice resulting from the unscrupulous actions of the police." He further commented, "No man is safe if the police power in this community is to be abused with impunity as it was in this case."[118]

WEDNESDAY, MAY 9, 1951

After hearing a response to the defense motions from Prosecutor Volpe, Judge Smalley summed up the issues the defense wished him to consider: a directed verdict of acquittal for all defendants, based on the theory that insufficient evidence had been given for the proof of robbery "and that the evidence is too confused and beset with fatal contradictions to a degree that the jury should not be permitted to speculate on the evidence so far adduced." Judge Smalley ruled that there was sufficient legal evidence that the jury should be permitted to see, and he denied all motions.[119] Now, after seven and a half weeks of the second trial, the defense's turn would come again.

CHAPTER 6

SECOND TRIAL, DEFENSE

WEDNESDAY, MAY 9, 1951

Two years and ten months after presenting their defense the first time, the Trenton Six began to do so again. Raymond Alexander began by calling Horace Wilson to the witness stand. First, Alexander made clear to Wilson that if he did not understand any question, he was to say so, telling the lawyer or the judge. Then Wilson, with great composure and dignity, told the story of his arrest and his confrontations in the police station with the other defendants, arranged by Acting Captain Delate: Delate brought Cooper into his room, pointed his finger at Wilson and asked, "Is this the man?" Cooper answered, "Yes, that is him." Wilson responded, "You're crazy, boy, you don't know what you are talking about." This sequence was then repeated with both Cooper and English present, both identifying Wilson as "the one." Wilson objected, stressed his complete innocence, and said he could prove he was working on Koppel's farm under the supervision of Mr. Murphy at the time of the murder. Wilson told Delate, "I wish you would call Mr. Murphy or Mr. Koppel; they will tell you the same thing as I am telling you." Delate left and came back in a few minutes with a paper "and he said he called the people up and they, these people said they don't know anything about you." Before court adjourned for the day, Judge Smalley signed an order for Collis English's examination by a cardiologist of the defense's choosing.[1]

THURSDAY, MAY 10, 1951

Judge Smalley granted George Pellettieri's request to have a psychiatrist examine Ralph Cooper, Collis English, and McKinley Forrest. Horace Wilson spent the day on the witness stand, where Alexander had him elaborate on his responses to Captain Delate. Wilson had asked Delate to take him to see his employers so he could prove his innocence; this was not done. On the Monday evening after Wilson's arrest, Chief Detective Naples provided a pack of cigarettes to Cooper, Thorpe, McKinley, and English but said that Wilson "was not worth a pack." At this point, Pellettieri interrupted proceedings to object to the "grimaces by these officers back here, particularly Sergeant Creeden," referring to officers observing the proceedings, presumably attempting to cast doubt on Wilson's testimony. Smalley remarked that the jury would disregard any such mannerisms and asked, as he did frequently, that they "move along."

On the same Monday evening after his arrest, Wilson said Chief Naples stopped outside his cell, where Wilson was lying on the board which served as a bed, with his coat serving as a pillow against the bars, and asked if he was ready to tell the truth. Wilson answered, "You want the truth and I told you the truth, and now you want me to tell you a lie?" In response, Naples kicked his feet against the bars toward Wilson's head and then complained, "You done caused me to hurt my feet." Later Naples brought Wilson a sandwich, which Wilson did not eat: "Well, after he kicked at my head in the cell then come back and tried to give me a sandwich, then I just wouldn't accept the sandwich. That's all." Pellettieri took this opportunity to point out, "The one man who did not partake of food, drink, or cigarettes produced by Chief Naples did not make a confession. We allege the men who signed the confessions were drugged, were not acting properly, were in a controlled state." Such allegations seem fantastic now, but do match the facts at the time.

After luncheon recess, Alexander asked Wilson about the recent testimony of George English. Wilson stated that he had never seen George English before he appeared in court and had never worked for him. Further, when George English identified Wilson in court, Wilson said, "He looked to me as if he was crazy. He didn't look as if he had good sense. I thought he was crazy sure enough," referring to the "silly grin" on English's face.[2]

FRIDAY, MAY 11, 1951

George Pellettieri brought George English back to the witness stand to question him further about where and when he purchased his coat, but received only evasive responses. Then Pellettieri, stage-managing events, had a court attendant bring in Rubie English, who had been found with great difficulty by an investigator in the backwoods of Georgia. George English denied that

Rubie was his wife. Rubie English then testified; she had brought with her the marriage license from her wedding to George on July 5, 1944, in Cecil County, Maryland, as well as a certificate of marriage signed by the Reverend A. C. Austin. This caused Pellettieri to ask, "At this time, your Honor, I move that George English be cited for contempt, for a contempt committed in the presence of the Court, and that this Honorable Court sit as a Committing Magistrate and hold him for perjury for action of the Grand Jury." Judge Smalley deferred action on this request.[3]

Next Pellettieri elicited the fact that, according to Rubie English, it was not possible to look from the basement through the register into her living room. She had never seen the pipes separated in the manner shown in photographs previously introduced into evidence. Ralph Cooper never lived with her and George at 12 Behm Street, and she had never seen either of the two coats her husband claimed he found, first in his shed and then in his basement. While her husband had been in prison, she had spread the entire basement with lime twice and had never seen the coats. She emphatically stated that George could not have fit into the jacket he said was his, a size thirty-six, as he weighed over two hundred pounds at the time he said he wore the coat.

Pellettieri led her through the events of January 9, 1948. Neither her daughter Melrose Diggs nor Ralph Cooper were in her home that day. She did not send her daughter Myrtis Fields out to get bread. After she put Myrtis to bed for the night, Rubie went to look in on an ill neighbor. Soon she heard a commotion outside and saw George chasing Myrtis down the street. She came out, urging them to return home, whereupon George began beating both Myrtis and herself. Myrtis broke free and ran to the nearby home of Frank Murphy, a local police officer, with Rubie running behind. Mrs. English then charged George with abuse of her daughter.[4]

MONDAY, MAY 14, 1951

Under cross-examination by Volpe, Rubie English made clear that she had her older daughter, Melrose Diggs, by a man named Tom Whitfield, and her younger daughter, Myrtis Fields, by Oliver Fields, both before she married George English. Mrs. Melrose Diggs, heavily pregnant, then testified, confirming her mother's version of events. She added that when police released George English on February 6, 1948, she and Myrtis both moved out of the house on Behm Street until George began his prison sentence, when they moved back.[5] In the evening, only hours after testifying,

Mrs. Diggs gave birth to twins at a Trenton hospital. Newsmen following the trial sent a gift for the babies.[6]

TUESDAY, MAY 15, 1951

Collis English took the stand, appearing nervous and on edge; he again declared his innocence, saying that at the time of the murder he was helping his mother with laundry and cashing his disability check. Sitting among court spectators was Dr. John Kinczel, the physician caring for Collis, who checked him during recesses. Regarding his father, George, Collis related that while his father was in the county jail, at his request he went to Fort Dix to get George's paycheck, took his stepmother Rubie to church, and got groceries and coal for George's house, all using his father's black Ford.[7] Pellettieri questioned Collis in detail about his interrogation by police, which had been done mainly by Chief Detective Naples and Acting Captain Delate. Collis English related being sick and scared: "I got thinking about what happened, how they treated a lot of people, colored people. How they could go in and drag them out of houses and all that; how they bring them out and beat them and all that. . . . I heard the radio and read in the paper how they had a machine gun squad, all that, that got me all the more scared. They were trying to put in my mind that I did something that I didn't do." After several rounds of police questioning, he said, "Chief Naples took me in the back room in the Captain's private office back there, and he told me, 'I am going to show you some things, and I want you to say exactly as I say them, and as I say them you say them right behind me. If you don't say it, you won't get away. And if you do say it the way I say it, you can go.'" Naples showed him photos of where things happened, where he stood, and where he went through Horner's pockets. English kept pleading for someone to get his medicine from his mother, but Delate told him, "You don't need nothing."[8] Pellettieri asked English how they spoke to him: "Captain Delate and Chief Naples, they were talking out loud and beating the desk and saying 'You know you did it. You know you did it. You know you did it.' Chief Naples kept on beating the desk the same way. They had pistols, guns, and blackjacks sometimes on the table in front of me, sometimes they had pistols and blackjacks waving in my face or waving around and walking around with them in their hands." Naples told him they were going to bring in Thorpe and instructed English to call him Red: "'I want you to come on and say that he was there or else you ain't going back.' He brought me back there. There was nothing else for me to do with them Policemen down there all around me." Pellettieri asked, "So what did you say?" English replied, "All I could say was just that was Red. That's all. Because Captain Delate, Chief Naples done told me that."[9]

WEDNESDAY, MAY 16, 1951

Judge Smalley, concerned at the toll of the lengthy trial on the jury, announced that starting on May 21 court would sit daily from 9:30 a.m. to 4:30 p.m. and on Tuesday and Thursday evenings from 7:30 p.m. until 9:30 p.m. A third court reporter would be added.[10] Collis English, again nervous, agitated, and breathing quickly, spent the day in cross-examination by Volpe, covering well-trodden ground yet again. The *Baltimore Afro-American* ran an article titled "Must Six More Die?" asking readers to contact Governor Driscoll.[11]

THURSDAY, MAY 17, 1951

English finished his testimony, recollecting that he saw Dr. Corio give McKinley Forrest a pill, described as a "truth pill," dissolved in a paper cup of water.[12] Next, Ralph Cooper took the stand, speaking in a resonant baritone voice as he responded to questions from Pellettieri. He reiterated his story of spending the morning of the murder at the home of George English, with Melrose Diggs. He explained being nervous and scared about being locked up, as he did not know why he was being held. Cooper testified, as English had before him, that Chief Detective Naples "told me they had the goods on me, and why don't I tell the truth. And I said I didn't know anything about it, and they kept telling me the story over and over again. . . . I was scared and nervous because I know when a colored man gets into the hands of the white police they don't have any chance, they would have to do what they said or they would take them out and beat them." Eventually, Cooper agreed to write a statement, had a sandwich, coffee, and a cigarette and remembered nothing more until he came to himself in the Mercer County Jail on Friday. The statement he wrote by hand, which Cooper claimed was word for word as dictated by Chief Naples, at least until he blacked out, was the one admitted into evidence by Judge Smalley. Cooper denied being in George English's home on January 9, 1948, denied having any conversation with Melrose Diggs about a murder and robbery, and denied that the coat entered into evidence ever belonged to him.[13]

FRIDAY, MAY 18, 1951

Cooper resumed his place on the witness stand, to be cross-examined by Volpe. In spite of Volpe's apparent incredulity, Cooper insisted that after he finished a sandwich, drank coffee, and had a cigarette, all furnished by Chief Naples, he remembered nothing for the next five days. Cooper stated Clerk Miller told him that James Thorpe was nicknamed Red and that "Chancy" referred to McKinley Forrest. He agreed with Volpe that on February 20, 1942, he had been convicted of larceny in Reedsville, Georgia, and sentenced to eight months. He was also convicted of forgery on May 17, 1943, in Brunswick, Georgia, and sentenced to two to three years in prison. Pellettieri then sought to show that at the time he began his statement, Cooper had within him a reasonable fear "with the long knowledge of the history of his race, the long years of suffering they had at the hands of Police in certain circumstances from the sections of the country from which this man stems, we have the right to show the psychological factors, the history of the race and the knowledge of other incidents which occurred to colored persons in the South." Assistant Prosecutor Lawton's objection was upheld by Judge Smalley, so Pellettieri could not continue in this vein.[14]

Next it was McKinley Forrest's turn to testify; he was questioned by Frank Katzenbach. He told of his work at Katzeff and Wiener's butcher shop the morning of the murder. He cleaned calves' feet and went to the bank for Mr. Katzeff. After offering details of his arrest, when he brought keys for George English's car to the station at his mother-in-law's request, he explained that Acting Captain Delate had told him, "Look, we are going to tell you the story, not you tell us." Forrest told Delate, "I don't know nothing about no murder on North Broad Street, I was at 22 Union Street. If you don't believe it, you can call up Mr. Katzeff down here," and he gave Delate the telephone number. He then told of going down on his knees to swear that he was telling the truth, and Chief Detective Naples ordered, "Get up off your knees, because you know you are going to swear to a damn lie." Then Forrest asked Delate for a cup of water. "He brought me back a paper cup of water. So, I drink the water. Then I turned the water up to drink it, I took it down there and just by looking in the cup I see like it were white, something like aspirin, a powder." Subsequently, Naples informed Forrest that he had admitted to "hitting the old man over the head with the bottle." Forrest said this made him feel "sick and nervous and I felt my eyes blinking and everything going dark and seeing stars like that." Forrest claimed he had surely never owned a dark navy blue coat as witnesses described one of the murderers wearing.

On the day of the murder he was wearing his working clothes, black trousers, an army jacket, and a brown hat, all entered as exhibits. When Alexander took a turn questioning Forrest, he and Volpe got into a side argument. This provoked Judge Smalley to remark, "Come on, gentlemen. It is getting near 4 o'clock. It is Friday afternoon, late. My nerves are getting a little bit taut, so let's be a little bit easy for the next 15 or 17 minutes. Then, after that you gentlemen can go out in the hall and settle it."[15] The end of the court day and week arrived without further incident.

MONDAY, MAY 21, 1951

James Thorpe, prematurely balding, took the witness stand to testify on his own behalf. He related that he was unable to work, having a newly amputated arm, so throughout the morning of January 27, 1948, he kept his grandfather company while the older man was working on a car parked in front of the house, in full view of the neighbors. In the afternoon he went to the movies. Under questioning by Volpe he said that Chief Naples told Collis English to refer to him as Shorty. Naples then told Thorpe, "If I would come on to say I was Shorty, he would let me off easy and I would get a few days." When Volpe questioned his veracity, Thorpe practically shouted, "I'm up here to tell the truth and I'm telling it." When questioned by Pellettieri, Thorpe described Cooper as having red eyes and Forrest as "shaking like a leaf on a limb" during the nocturnal confession session. Thorpe's questioning took time, as he had to answer very slowly and carefully because of his speech impediment. However, the questioning was shortened by the fact that Judge Smalley had not allowed Thorpe's statement into evidence.[16]

In the afternoon, John MacKenzie took the stand on his own behalf, seated in a poised manner, hands laced over his knee. Questioned by Alexander, he recounted seeing the five photos of his fellow defendants in the Trenton newspaper with the headline "Five Confess to Horner Killing," and reading each day about the case. Then, on Wednesday, February 11, 1948, two policemen appeared at 247 Church Street, asking if his name was Kelly or Martin. MacKenzie answered no and showed them his military discharge papers. The policemen took him in anyway, refusing to tell him why he was wanted, but they assured him, "It won't be long. You will be right back." On the evening of Thursday, February 12, in a cell at the Chancery Lane First Precinct police station, a police officer brought him a pack of cigarettes. After smoking a cigarette, MacKenzie remembered nothing until a week later, February 20, when he came to himself in a segregation cell in the Mercer

County Jail. Before he "came to himself" he had hallucinations, saying he heard men "hollering and shooting off guns." He firmly stated he never served as a "lookout man" for a robbery and had nothing to do with the Horner murder. Judge Smalley had not allowed his confession into evidence, so he could not be questioned on it.[17]

TUESDAY, MAY 22, 1951

In the effort to finish the trial more quickly, the session continued after dinner from 7:30 p.m. to 9:30 p.m., making it a very long day for all involved. Katzenbach questioned John MacKenzie about the behavior of his uncle, McKinley Forrest, while in the police station. When his uncle was brought out of the cells for arraignment, MacKenzie watched him walk right into a wall and had to guide him to the courtroom and lead him back to the cell block. When he questioned MacKenzie, Volpe asked, "Isn't it a fact that some of you men, and I am referring now to your co-defendants, got together and said that you were going to act crazy like?" MacKenzie denied this, as well as any knowledge of or participation in the crime. At the end of the day, when Pellettieri objected to perceived sarcasm on the part of Volpe, Judge Smalley remarked, "I hadn't noted any sarcasm, Judge. I think maybe we are all a little bit tired. The fact is, I am amazed that you have all behaved as well as you have, as many weeks as we have had to look at each other. That even includes this Judge."[18]

WEDNESDAY, MAY 23, 1951

The first of more than fifty alibi and character witnesses began to appear, giving the same testimony as in the first trial. Collis English's mother, Emma, backed up her son's alibi. A tiny woman who had attended every single court session, she spoke in an almost inaudible voice. Counsel for both sides pulled their seats close to the witness stand, and Judge Smalley moved his chair forward and leaned over in order to hear. Pellettieri called two witnesses to refute testimony given by George English. Louis Marshall, George's probation officer, said he had no memory of George's telling him about a plot by Ralph Cooper to rob and murder someone on Broad Street. Robert McQueen, defense lawyer in the first trial, testified that George English told him in April 1948, that he knew nothing about the Horner murder case. Judge Smalley convinced the attorneys that it would be good to work on Decoration Day (now known as Memorial Day) in order to finish more quickly.[19]

THURSDAY, MAY 24, 1951

Friends, neighbors, relatives, employers, almost all of whom had testified at the first trial, continued to appear as witnesses for the defendants. There were some were new witnesses, such as Holmes Perrine, of the Edward Dilatush Company, who made it clear that Horace Wilson worked from 8:00 A.M. to noon on January 27, 1948.[20] Another witness testifying for the first time was LeGrand Brown of Robbinsville. He clearly remembered February 7, 1948, because of the four police cars searching the tiny community of shacks. Plainclothes police knocked on his door at 6:30 A.M. and when he opened the door they walked in, saying, "Oh, it's nice and warm in here." Then they asked about a "little, short guy" but told him no name. They had no warrant but left when Collis English, who was in the car, told the police that Brown "looked something like the guy they were looking for." Brown told the officers that he did not know English. As to how English looked: "He was awful frightened, the same as I was." When Assistant Prosecutor Lawton questioned Brown about how he remembered English so clearly, having just seen him once, many years ago, Brown answered, "When he said that I looked something like the guy they were looking for, I looked him right dead in the eyes, and said 'No, sir, not me.'"[21]

Pellettieri had obtained Collis English's medical record of his hospitalization at Fort Dix hospital in 1947, which he read into the court record. Leanna Turner told again of the police arrival at Wilson's cinderblock home in Robbinsville on February 7, 1948. The police told Wilson to get up and get dressed; Turner quoted Chief Detective Naples as saying, "Get up, you black son-of-a-bitch, you."[22]

Mercer County Sheriff Thomas Brennan gave an Associated Press reporter a glimpse into the lives of the jury. Their morale was "very good." Every weekend officers took them on excursions around the state. They would eat at public restaurants but in private rooms arranged in advance. Every Wednesday evening they had a picnic, often featuring grilled steak, at local parks. Their favorite food seemed to be steak for dinner and corned beef sandwiches at lunch. One juror, a farmer, reported feeling ill at the beginning of this month. Judge Smalley thought he might be missing his farm in springtime. Sheriff Brennan suggested he might feel better if he could "[r]un around on some ground in his bare feet." That evening, during the usual Wednesday picnic, the juror took off his shoes and socks and walked around barefoot. Brennan reported, "It did the trick." In their evenings at the hotel, jurors read, played cards, and listened to radio programs. The sheriff censored their newspapers, magazines, and radio listening so they would not receive news of crime of any kind, not just of the Trenton Six trial. Jurors remained content, except for missing their families, something Sheriff Brennan could not rectify.[23]

Friday, May 25, 1951

Defense witnesses continued to testify regarding the defendants' alibis. Then Pellettieri brought in Roy Eisenhart, foreman of the Royal Crown Bottling Company of Allentown, Pennsylvania. He explained that the bottle in the sock brought in by George English had been made by the Owens-Illinois Company in 1947 and received by his company at the beginning of August of that year. However, his plant had too many bottles on hand then, so the first time that particular bottle could have been used was in June 1950, well after Horner's murder on January 27, 1948. Mr. Hays stepped forward to make a request: "I ask your Honor to hold George English for perjury and at this time it is perfectly clear that there is no truth in his testimony in view of what the last witness testified to." Judge Smalley denied his motion. Hays then asked that Prosecutor Volpe withdraw both the bottle and the stocking from evidence; Volpe indignantly declined to do so. Hays continued on the attack: "I think there ought to be an investigation of the District Attorney's office, who, without investigating the source of a bottle or when it was first distributed, will endeavor to put it in evidence as a part of a scheme, as part of evidence to convict men of murder." This caused Judge Smalley to ask, "Mr. Hays, you are from New York State?" Hays agreed that he was, and the judge inquired, "Are you really serious with such a statement?" Hays responded that he was: "The District Attorney's duty is to protect the innocent as well as to present evidence against the guilty, and it was his duty to investigate the source of that bottle." Volpe answered that he did investigate and found the bottle had been manufactured in 1947; Judge Smalley denied Mr. Hays's request.[24]

Monday, May 28, 1951

On this Monday morning Judge Smalley delayed the trial for one day because of James Thorpe's hospitalization. Over the weekend Thorpe had developed an acute abscess, causing him severe pain in the stump of his amputated arm. On Sunday afternoon Dr. Herman Cohen removed the abscess and thought that Thorpe would be able to return to court on Tuesday.[25]

TUESDAY, MAY 29, 1951

Character and alibi witnesses continued to appear. McKinley Forrest and Horace Wilson seemed exceptionally well thought of by their employers. Ralph Cooper, so newly arrived in Trenton and without relatives, was the only one with few such witnesses. Handwriting expert J. Howard Haring of New York City testified, as he had in the first trial, that the signature on the mattress receipt provided by Mrs. Horner "never could have come from the mind and muscle of McKinley Forrest."[26]

WEDNESDAY, MAY 30, 1951, DECORATION DAY

Judge Smalley held court today in spite of the holiday, in order to shorten the trial, now in its eleventh week. Most of the day was consumed by Dr. Frederick Wertham, an eminent specialist in neuropsychiatry in New York City, described as "a graying bespectacled man with an athletic bearing." Pellettieri established Dr. Wertham's credentials as a specialist by having him describe his accomplishments as senior psychiatrist in the Department of Hospitals in New York: he was a textbook author, editor of the *American Journal of Psychotherapy*, and researcher into the effects of drugs on the mental states of normal individuals. Pellettieri then read Wertham a lengthy hypothetical question containing Collis English's background, his arrest, and questioning. He also showed Wertham a copy of English's confession, and asked, "Doctor, in signing this statement, was Collis English acting of his own free will with considered choice and as a free agent?" Wertham did not have an opportunity to answer this question, as Volpe objected. Judge Smalley ruled that Volpe should have the time to read Pellettieri's summary statement regarding English before Dr. Wertham answered. This process was then repeated with Katzenbach asking the same question regarding McKinley Forrest after reading a summary about his client. Judge Smalley ruled that Volpe should also have the opportunity to read Katzenbach's remarks about Forrest, before he ruled on whether either man could receive an answer from Dr. Wertham.[27]

THURSDAY, MAY 31, 1951

Dr. Wertham spent the entire day, including the after-dinner session, on the stand, Judge Smalley having ruled that he could answer questions about the voluntariness of English's and Forrest's confessions. He concluded that

Collis English did not act of his own free will in signing his confession due to his heart disease, which would create anxiety in the best of circumstances and cause him to do almost anything to avoid further anxiety. He would have spiraled into a mental state of turmoil "practically at the very moment when he was arrested and he was told that this was a serious arrest." Wertham went on to comment about the difference in race between Collis English and all of the police officers, detectives, and jury. As soon as he brought up the color of the jury, Volpe objected and was sustained by Judge Smalley. Wertham recounted the situation that English found himself in during questioning, and concluded, "It is my opinion that this man was scared out of his wits in a literal sense so that he couldn't use them anymore." He further mentioned the effects of lack of sleep, having the confession session in the middle of the night, and having to strip naked for the physical in front of complete strangers as contributing factors. Regarding the confessions in the middle of the night, he quoted Shakespeare: "Tis now the very witching time of night, When churchyards yawn and hell itself breathes out Contagion to this world." Continuing with more factual matters, Wertham pointed out that of the sixty-six questions in English's confession, fifty-seven contained incriminating statements and were not actually questions at all. English then took the line of least resistance to end his immediate torment, not perceiving the consequences of doing so. Wertham described the statement as "induced fiction."[28]

Mr. Katzenbach examined Wertham on McKinley Forrest's confession. Wertham felt that Forrest did not sign his confession "acting of his own free will as a free agent exercising a choice of his own. This man was born in very, very poor circumstances; that his whole childhood and early life was lived in segregation and discrimination in the deep South, in Georgia; that he was exposed to child labor as a cotton picker when he was very young, that he was illiterate, so could not read what he was signing, had a severe speech defect and was singled out by his schoolmates and teased, and then is thought to be 'Chancy,' mistaken for somebody else, I think I would deduce that it is occasion for terror." Further, "Out of fifty-six questions, forty-six are suggestive, leading, directing. Whatever he said, he had to say something that was already suggested in the question itself." Wertham noted as further evidence that Forrest had become so agitated that even the police felt the need to call a doctor. Whether or not Forrest received a pill in a drink of water he requested, Wertham stated that his conclusion about Forrest's extremely disturbed mental state would be the same.[29]

FRIDAY, JUNE 1, 1951

Virginia Barclay testified for the defense, as she had at the first trial. She told of seeing a blue green four-door 1936 Plymouth parked in front of her apartment building, just down the street from the Horner store. She described three men approaching the car at about 10:30 on the morning of January 27, 1949. Two got in the back seat and one in front next to the driver, with the car pulling away from the curb so quickly that it left with the right rear door still open. The three men were light or medium-complexioned blacks in their late teens. One, who looked "like a kid," wore metal-rimmed glasses. When asked to look at the six defendants to see if any looked like the men she had seen, she said they did not.[30] After this final witness, the defense team rested its case. Examining all counsel about their expected timing and wishes, Judge Smalley agreed to conclude the day at 1:00 P.M. so the state could prepare for its rebuttal witnesses. He then remarked: "I don't believe I have ever said this to any jury at this stage of the proceedings, but we can now begin to see the end of this trial, and for your extraordinary patience and attention you have my greatest respect and admiration." The court stenographer reported that some 2,500,000 words had been recorded in testimony, arguments, and court rulings. On this day the daily transcript total reached the ten-thousandth page.[31]

MONDAY, JUNE 4, 1951

After sparring with defense counsel over several motions, Prosecutor Volpe called rebuttal witnesses to the stand, mainly policemen, who repeated their claims of never mistreating the defendants in any way.[32]

TUESDAY, JUNE 5, 1951

With the court's permission, the defense brought in one more witness, a man named John Bethea, whose nickname was Long John. He had known a man named Chancy Birch, who was now dead. Bethea wore silver-rimmed glasses and had a mustache, high cheekbones, and slanted-looking eyes, thus resembling the description Mrs. Horner originally gave of one of the two men who entered the Horner store on the day of the murder. In producing this witness, Pellettieri presumably wished the jury to question identifications made by Mrs. Horner of the Six. The rest of the day consisted of Chief Naples, Captain Delate, and others insisting they treated the defendants well at all times.[33]

WEDNESDAY, JUNE 6, 1951

State rebuttal witness and Robbinsville farmer J. Herbert Brown took the stand. Before he gave up farming in 1947 he had a man in his employ named Willie Anthony, commonly known as Jack Kelly, another name bandied about when the Six were arrested. Brown testified that Horace Wilson worked for him in both 1946 and 1947 and at that time Brown saw him in the company of Collis English and James Thorpe. Pellettieri became increasingly upset by Brown's claiming to remember seeing two individuals he did not know, on the road in Robbinsville, and being able to identify them four years later in court. At one point Pellettieri shouted, "How much are you being paid for coming to court?" Brown bristled, and Volpe and Lawton leaped to their feet to object, while Judge Smalley reached for his gavel. Smalley told Pellettieri, "Just calm down, and ask your questions." Brown had no proof that Wilson ever worked for him as he had burned all his records when he quit farming. Pellettieri eventually got Brown to admit that Detective Dennis Dore had visited him recently and then brought him to Assistant Prosecutor Lawton's office where he had been shown photographs of the Six.[34]

Next Lawton called Ernest Sands to the stand. He had testified previously, but during the period when the jury was out of the courtroom. Mr. Sands ran a used clothing store down the street from Mr. Horner's store. He claimed to have seen Ralph Cooper, McKinley Forrest, and Horace Wilson together in his store during the early part of January 1948, thus shortly before the Horner murder. When questioned by Pellettieri, Sands declared that he recognized the men from their pictures in the newspaper after their arrest. He did not go to the police, however, until he learned that the men's guilty verdicts had been tossed out and that they would be tried again. He explained, "I had a civic duty when I went to the Police." He had been shown photographs of the men shortly before his testimony.[35]

Now Volpe called, as a further rebuttal witness, Dr. James B. Spradley, a psychiatrist recently retired as superintendent of the Trenton State Hospital. His past experience included work for the U.S. State Department, doing psychiatric examinations of 105 Nazi officers convicted at the Nuremberg trials in Germany after World War II. He had been present in court for the testimony of Dr. Wertham, the defense psychiatrist. Regarding Collis English's statement he declared, "I don't believe that the answers to these questions, with the detailed information which they contain, were supplied to this defendant by the Police Officers." Indeed, he would "question, based upon my experience with the police over a period of years, that they would attempt to get a confession from someone who was innocent." Further, regarding the use of pressure to obtain confessions: "I don't think they could do that. It is of considerable doubt that anybody could do it and certainly no one has ever claimed to do it in this short period of time which elapsed here from the time of the arrest to the time of the confession." He thought that "the Police took more than the usual care in protecting the rights of this individual" by having called in "two trained observers, two physicians to examine these men at the time they were in this state of mind, whatever it was. But here two physicians were called in. Both of these physicians are competent physicians. They are trained observers." Under questioning by Volpe he clarified his belief that an individual is competent to sign a confession as long as he is legally sane and is thus responsible for his acts. He felt all of this to be true of McKinley Forrest's statement also, that the police had taken good care of Forrest, who was undoubtedly legally sane and thus responsible for his statement. Questioned by Volpe about the use of sodium amytol, he explained, "It is a sedative and it is used by the Doctors to prompt relaxation, physical and mental relaxation and to produce sleep, depending on the size of the dose and what the Doctor is attempting to gain from the drug." He felt that Forrest had not been drugged and that English's heart condition would not make him more "suggestible" than anyone else.

In cross-examination, Arthur Hays pointed out that Spradley had sat at the prosecutor's table when listening to Dr. Wertham, and that in the past he had testified twice as often for the prosecution as for the defense in cases. Getting to the heart of his questions, Hays asked, "Don't you know that human beings often do things because of pressure even though they are quite competent?" Answer: "No, I don't know that." Hays persevered: "You don't know that as a psychiatrist?" "I don't know that as a psychiatrist or as a physician or as an individual, that a person who is mentally free of disease, who is not insane, can be forced by what you call psychical suggestion . . . I don't believe that normal people will give and sign statements confessing to participation in a crime unless it is a fact." Hays asked him: "Do you know in the Scottsboro case that every one of the defendants confessed?" Volpe objected, and Judge Smalley ruled that Spradley did not have to answer the question.[36]

THURSDAY, JUNE 7, 1951

Dr. Spradley appeared for the entire morning of questioning, but Arthur Hays could not make a dent in his belief: "You mean a sane man is always in the position where he can exercise free choice?" "That's right." "And the only people who don't exercise free choice in a situation are people insane?" "That is correct." After the defense questioning of Dr. Spradley was completed, the state rested its case.[37]

The defense produced its final rebuttal witnesses. Defense attorney Burrell examined farmer Elmer R. H. Hutchinson, who testified that Horace Wilson had worked for him in the summer months of 1946 and 1947 and lived on his farm while doing so, contradicting what farmer Brown previously stated.[38] Defendant James Thorpe then took the stand, questioned by Pellettieri. During the summer months of 1946 and 1947 he had worked as a truck driver for A. Scheideler Company and had never walked down a street in Robbinsville with Horace Wilson or anyone else. Ralph Cooper then testified that he had never been in a used clothing store run by Mr. Sands and had never laid eyes on Mr. Sands before he testified in court. Horace Wilson explained that in 1946 he had worked on Brown's farm in the spring, planting potatoes, but after that worked for farmer Elmer Hutchinson, operating his combine. He did not know Collis English until the afternoon of January 27, 1948, when English and Cooper drove through Robbinsville and stopped at his house. Furthermore, he had never seen Mr. Sands, or been in the Sands store: "I don't buy clothes very often, and when I buy I don't buy second-hand clothes at no time, not in any second-hand store." Lastly Pellettieri questioned Wilson regarding farmer Brown's story that he knew James Thorpe. Wilson asserted he had never seen Thorpe in his life until they were locked up together in the Chancery Lane First Precinct police station. Pellettieri questioned defendant Collis English, who asserted that he never visited Robbinsville in 1946 or 1947 and did not know Horace Wilson at that time. Then Katzenbach asked McKinley Forrest to take the stand. Forrest testified that he had never been in Mr. Sands's store and did not know Ralph Cooper or Horace Wilson until all three found themselves in jail. Having now rebutted the testimony of Brown and Sands, the defense rested its case.[39]

FRIDAY, JUNE 8, 1951

The defense wished to present a number of motions; Judge Smalley excused the jury for the day, and thus the weekend, saying, "Well, now, you won't be too impatient, will you, ladies and gentlemen? You have been so very nice. We are in the home stretch now. Next week we ought to conclude this case, so bear with us a few more days, won't you?"[40]

Katzenbach moved for a judgment of dismissal for all six defendants, saying, "the State's proofs are in such an order that it presents an impossible task to the jury." He gave examples of the many inconsistencies among the confessions, and how these applied to his client, McKinley Forrest. He also moved to have Forrest's confession dismissed from evidence that would go to the jury. Alexander then spoke on behalf of MacKenzie and Thorpe, saying that the only evidence tying them to the crime at all was their confessions, which Judge Smalley had disallowed. He also pointed out that Horace Wilson's employers testified that he was elsewhere at the time of the crime and he had never signed a confession. Pellettieri then spoke regarding Ralph Cooper, whose handwritten confession stated that he was there at the crime scene, but did not take part, while Mrs. Horner did not place him in the store. He also pointed out that none of the state witnesses ever mentioned a one-armed man, such as Thorpe, being involved. Pellettieri reminded Judge Smalley of the earlier New Jersey Supreme Court decision by Justice Heher that the rights of the Six could not be ignored and that it would be a great shame if the results of the current trial had to be appealed to the U.S. Supreme Court, which would perhaps throw out this trial and they would have to start all over again. He mentioned the questionable caliber of the testimony by George English, farmer LeGrand Brown, and storekeeper Ernest Sands, all new in this second trial. Pellettieri then repeated arguments he had made when the state originally rested its case, which he summarized this way: "I feel that the evidence, your Honor, as produced here creates a mere suspicion of guilt and at best it raises a conjecture or suspicion unfavorable to all the defendants, and that the proof here has failed and fallen below the standard of rebutting the presumption of innocence and of proving guilt beyond a reasonable doubt." The defense contended that the state's case proved so weak that it should not even be given to the jury; it asked for a directed verdict of acquittal. Prosecutor Volpe, in his turn, indicated that all of these motions had been previously argued, which was true, and that the state had convincingly presented its case. Judge Smalley denied all defense motions, and court ended for the week.[41] The lawyers spent the weekend preparing their summations, while Judge Smalley worked on his charge to the jury.

MONDAY, JUNE 11, 1951

Defense summations for the jury took the entire day, including an evening session running until 11:00 P.M. Katzenbach spent the morning giving his conclusions regarding the innocence of McKinley Forrest, whom he had represented throughout both trials. He began by speaking to the jury about its responsibilities. They had been closely questioned to find any hidden racial prejudice, so necessary to do in this case. After all, he said, "Prejudice doesn't walk in with a placard." He had personally been impacted, he told them: "I have been out in public and I have had to meet these little things that are said, these misunderstanding that people have." He had to reason with his own friends about the case, "gradually getting a convert here and there." The trial involved "a minority group who, since the inception of this country have not had the advantages that members of the white race had had. We are dealing with a dangerous thing. That is why I say I am so happy that we did take the trouble and the care we did to make sure that we had jurors that would not have any prejudices in their minds, that would realize that this country has always fought against prejudices." Then he reminded them that the burden of the state was to prove the defendants "guilty beyond a reasonable doubt.... We would rather see a hundred guilty men go off than see one innocent man convicted of something that he did not do."

Now Katzenbach turned to specifics. He brought up the testimony of Dr. Spradley, the psychiatrist for the state, who "was of the opinion that if a person is legally sane, you can't get him to sign something that incriminates themselves. That just simply isn't human experience." For a confession to be admissible, legally, it must be freely given and not behind closed doors, by an isolated individual who "has no help, no counsel, no friends.... Our Supreme Court of the United States has said that there is torture of mind as well as body.... They want to know was there psychological pressure upon him of such a sort that he took the easy way out?" Forrest eventually said: "All right, I hit the old man over the head." After this Forrest "stood up and walked towards the window, then tried to go right through the window. Then it was that he thought he heard his daughter outside." Delate testified that "[h]e kept on sobbing and moaning and saying he was going to die.... It is a pitiful thing to think that men would go ahead and try to take an incriminating statement from a man who was in this deplorable, deplorable condition."

Katzenbach went over Dr. Sullivan's testimony that Forrest, at the time he initialed his confession, was in a state of "medical excitement." He reminded the jury of the episode when Forrest's brother Robert, plus two lawyers, visited McKinley in jail, and McKinley did not recognize his own sibling. Eventually, Acting Captain Delate's concern for Forrest grew to the point of calling in a doctor; having him give a statement a few hours later "is going too far." Katzenbach discussed the soda bottle said to be the murder weapon with which Forrest hit Mr. Horner over the head; he pointed out that the police wiped the bottle clean of its partial prints: "It is absolutely tragic. . . . Gone forever." He then came to the testimony of Elizabeth Horner, who had looked at four men through a one-way glass and declared that she did not recognize any of them, then turned around at the trial and indicated Forrest as having been the one in the store who talked with her and signed a receipt. This proved her identification to be in error since Forrest could not write and spoke with a pronounced stutter, which she did not mention, even when asked, in her testimony. The state insisted that Forrest had worn a long, navy blue double-breasted coat at the time of the murder, but they never produced any such clothing. However, Katzenbach had brought in, and now held up for the jury to see, the work clothes that numerous witnesses agreed Forrest had worn on January 27, 1948. Cigar salesman Eldracher told the court that Forrest looked too old, at thirty-five years of age, to have been one of the men he saw leaving the Horner store. And police had initially used Virginia Barclay's identification of the getaway car, broadcasting it to surrounding states, not mentioning George English's black Ford. Katzenbach ended where he began in his opening statement, saying that his best exhibit was McKinley Forrest himself, who had never been in trouble with the law, was a widower, a breadwinner working two jobs and "nothing in this case has ever occurred which would cause me to be shaken in one small bit in my faith and confidence in McKinley Forrest. And McKinley Forrest, I do believe in you." He concluded by "urging to you the innocence of McKinley Forrest and in pleading with you that you will find him not guilty of the charge made by the State of New Jersey."[42]

The summation of each defense lawyer clearly revealed his style. While Katzenbach hewed closely to the facts of the case in a simple but eloquent manner, Alexander, up next, created complex rhetorical flights, providing the basic facts in between.

Alexander observed to the jury that he rose to perform a serious duty and that this was perhaps "one of the most serious moments in your own lives. We have now been looking at each other and appearing before each other for one hundred and one days. That is a record in this State and one of the records in the trials of criminal courts in the history of America." He continued, "I am certain you recognize it as one of the greatest responsibilities in your own lives, which has taken place, when the fourteen of you were called and placed in the jury box." Alexander then praised Judge Smalley for his patience and fairness. In considering prosecutors Volpe and Lawton, he remarked, "I have never been engaged in a trial of a case which makes me shudder more and makes me wonder why and how could fine gentlemen of the class and quality of these two fine men become so engaged themselves in a trial of a case which I consider one of the most monstrous, completely erroneous, prosecutions that I have ever read or heard about, as affecting these defendants."

Bringing in the racial issue, Alexander, one of three black attorneys in the case, reminded the jury that "all of us stem from one God, irrespective of what may be the color or complexion. . . . There is no difference except color between the image of your face and the image of mine and these poor fellows whom I represent." He quoted a James Weldon Johnson poem, "Go Down Death," when reminding the jurors that these innocent men would have been put to death if the sentence of the first trial had been carried out. The authorities could have been "taking six dead bodies out on a slab and putting them on to a wagon and hauling them off. That is the seriousness of this case, my friends." He then turned to a topic not previously addressed at length, the "alibi" witnesses. "The word *alibi* suggests something fictitious, but in law it is fundamental, the defense having the opportunity to point out their truth."

Alexander laid out the elements in the case that showed the men had not received their due process as guaranteed by the Fourteenth Amendment to the Constitution: arrest without a warrant, not being advised of the cause of arrest, incommunicado confinement, long periods of questioning, interrupted rest, poor food, poor sleeping accommodations, primitive hygiene facilities, interrogation in a small space, questioners wearing arms, no timely arraignment before a magistrate, no advice as to their constitutional right to remain silent, to have legal assistance, and see friends, power of suggestion by repeated emphasis of police on material points in the case, and the condition of health or weakness of the defendants.

Getting down to specifics, Alexander noted that Chief Detective Naples and Detective Miller, in their testimony, revealed that more than three policemen could hardly fit into the Horner store. Yet the prosecution demanded in its case that five of the defendants, plus Mr. and Mrs. Horner, were all in the store at the same time. He went again through the circumstances of MacKenzie's arrest, when police had no warrant and no charges against him. Alexander pointed out that this did not happen "behind the Iron Curtain or the satellite countries where they don't regard law or anything else." (At the time of this trial, in 1951, the behavior of Eastern European Communists was of extreme concern to many.) Alexander laid out the case against the men to make clear for the jury that MacKenzie was never mentioned by the prosecution or other defendants until the very end, when Collis English identified him as the lookout man. And English's identification was the total case against John MacKenzie.

Turning to Wilson, Alexander described him as "[o]ne of the most honest, decent, fine, hardworking citizens in our community." Cigar salesman Eldracher had stated in court that Wilson looked much older than the two men he saw leaving the Horner store. After giving details of both cases, Alexander turned to something never mentioned before, the issue of motive. What motive could MacKenzie and Wilson possibly have for murdering Horner? Both men were hardworking, had jobs, had never been in trouble with the law. They both had excellent reputations in the community. He quoted Shakespeare's Iago: "He that filches from me my good name robs me of that which not enriches him, and makes me poor indeed." He went on, in his own words, "What good is it that one lives a straightforward life and walks the narrow path, after leading a carefully planned, honest life unless some credit accrues to that individual?"

Now Alexander, for the first time, brought in a personal experience. In July 1950, when he had no connection of any kind with the Trenton Six, he was working for the U.S. State Department visiting army camps in France, England, Germany, and Belgium to check on the "status and positions of colored soldiers in our Armed Forces." In Paris he saw a newspaper article with photographs of the Six, then found articles about them in each country he visited. He commented, "Folks, this is one great opportunity that you have to set at rest the malicious propaganda which had spread not through New Jersey, not through America, but the whole world, that America does not treat its minorities right, fair and equal." Referring again to Communists, he added, "Subversive interests would be served by an improper verdict, and I mean every word." After eloquently asking for a verdict of not guilty, he concluded by noting, "Now, my duty is at an end. It has been a real pleasure to be with you. . . . From now on I shall always think of you and will never forget your expressions and will never forget the cordiality extended to me during these many months. Thank you for the privilege and the pleasure."[43]

Since Alexander took the entire afternoon session to make his remarks, and both jury and judge wished to conclude the summations this day, all agreed to come back for a night session, beginning at 8:15 P.M. with Pellettieri. His manner and style had been pugnacious and brash, but earnest, throughout the trial, and remained so until the end. As both Katzenbach and Alexander had before him, he addressed the jury regarding itself: "I know that you are free from prejudice and you are going to decide this case as honest men and women, and that is all that anyone can ask at the hands of a jury. The only thing you don't have in common with the six innocent victims, is color, but after questioning you as we did, we feel certain that that is not going to enter one bit in your deliberations, because each one of you has said that you concede equal rights to all." He then moved on to a discussion of Prosecutor Volpe: "I disagree violently with the Prosecutor's proposition that my interests and your interests and the interests of all of our fellow citizens require that these defendants, or any one defendant, be deprived of their lives on the strength of such evidence as has been produced here."

Pellettieri then laid out what he described as nine different versions of the murder. The first, from police reports the day of the murder, had two men in the store, then three, then four men all together, with Mrs. Horner describing the weapon used on her as brass knuckles. The blue-green Plymouth served as the getaway car. The second version, by Collis English, had Cooper and Wilson in the store several days before the crime, Wilson signing a receipt, English and Forrest in the back room with Horner, and three others in the front of the store with Mrs. Horner. A black Ford was the getaway car. The third version, that of McKinley Forrest, made no mention of planning the crime beforehand, placed four men in the store, identified a soda bottle as the weapon, and never mentioned John MacKenzie. In the fourth version, Mrs. Horner claimed that Forrest signed the receipts, that Wilson struck her, and English and Forrest assaulted her husband. She made no claim of robbery. Cigar salesman Frank Eldracher gave the fifth version, in which he saw two light-skinned men leave the store. The sixth version, by Ralph Cooper, used a bottle enclosed in a sock as the murder weapon. The seventh version was what Prosecutor Volpe provided in his opening statement, in which the murder weapon was a full Step-Up soda bottle. The eighth version was given by Volpe and occurred near the end of the questioning of witnesses, when Pellettieri claimed Volpe told the court that he did not know what the murder weapon was. George English gave the ninth variation by producing the bottle in the sock that came from his basement. Given all these descriptions of the most basic element, the crime itself, Pellettieri asked: "How can you, when the State offers nine versions of a crime of murder, find any one of these defendants guilty?"

Pellettieri then reminded the jury of a persistent question, the missing testimony of Lieutenant Detective Stanley, the highest-ranking person at the crime scene. Volpe had brought in for testimony the patrolman who pulled the alarm box, turnkeys who simply escorted the defendants to and from their cells, but never Stanley. Why not? Pellettieri then moved on to George English: "A man who has not even the first inkling of decency." Recounting George English's testimony, he held up to the jury the coat brought from the basement that supposedly belonged to English, and reminded them of English's size, apparently much too big to fit into the coat. Pellettieri, going back to basics, moved on to ask, "Why was not the Horner store dusted for fingerprints?" After all, Eldracher had seen one of the men close the door by placing his hand on the knob. He then repeated much of the material he had used in his motion to dismiss and finally focused on the initial questioning of Collis English. Without any apparent reason, Patrolman Lichtfuhs had suddenly begun asking about the murder on North Broad Street: "By virtue of what rights or privilege did this police officer feel free to pick up a young negro man on a minor Motor Vehicle violation and to undertake to question him on charges wholly unrelated thereto? It indicates a police practice that must be branded as reprehensible, a practice which feels free to pick up young negro men on minor charges or on no charge at all and then proceed to question them concerning every unsolved crime which the police may have on their books." At this point it was 11:00 P.M. and Pellettieri had not finished his summation. Judge Smalley decided to call it quits for the day.[44]

TUESDAY, JUNE 12, 1951

Pellettieri once again took the floor to finish his summation: "Last night in my summation I was, to the best of my ability, attempting to be the cold legal analyst of these facts. This morning I have thrown away my notes. I want to speak to you as a human being, the same as yourself. I am not asking for sympathy. I am asking for justice." He went on, "I fervently differ with the methods used in this case. I say that the actions of some of the police were reprehensible, but I say that if you acquit these men you are not indicting the Police Department. If you convict these men, you are not giving the Police Department a clean bill of health." He then focused on Chief Detective Naples and Captain Delate, citing testimony that showed they told the men what to say in their confessions. He stated that Naples had a "Machiavellian mind." Only the confessions, nothing scientific, had been produced against the defendants. He concluded that "the State has failed miserably to prove its case." Pointing out the bigger picture, he noted, "In England and France and India . . . in every country where people of color reside—this case is receiving as much newspaper coverage and publicity as it is here in Trenton."

Pellettieri had frequently shouted in exasperation during the trial, but he remained comparatively calm and mild as he urged the jury to free the six men.[45]

Now Prosecutor Volpe had his turn; he took the rest of the day, presenting his summation in a manner very different from defense counsel. But first, as the others had, he praised the jury members for the exemplary manner in which they had maintained their attention and patience. He stated, "In the course of my summation I shall make no reference to poetry. I have no touching passages to give you or to recite." He went over the case, defendant by defendant, laying out the state's case against each one, in mind-numbing detail. He began with James Thorpe, explaining what Thorpe admitted other than in his confession, which Judge Smalley had thrown out. He pointed out that Thorpe's alibi witnesses were all relatives, who would obviously say anything to protect a family member, and noted that when released from the hospital, Thorpe must have had his arm in a sling, and with a coat over it he would look like a man with one shoulder higher than the other, the description of the person they were seeking.[46] However, as Thorpe's counsel Pellettieri would have pointed out, Thorpe did not have enough of an arm left to put in a sling.

Moving on to John MacKenzie, Volpe indicated that he would not bring up racial issues, but somehow worked in his own participation in the Battle of the Bulge in World War II, during which all men wearing the same uniform were brothers. He referred to MacKenzie's "state of unconsciousness and blankness or amnesia, whatever it might be," in an effort to show how unbelievable MacKenzie's defense was. His alibi witnesses were relatives who would "[n]aturally tend to do anything within their power to be of assistance to this particular defendant."

Moving on to McKinley Forrest, he pointed out what perhaps would be seen as a point in favor of his innocence: at the request of his mother-in-law, he voluntarily brought the keys of George English's car to the police station, where he was then arrested. Volpe asked, "Would a man who had participated in a robbery proceed to the Police Station with a set of keys? Have you ever heard that a criminal almost always returned to the scene of the crime? The idea was to get Collis English out of the First District Police Station before anything was ever said by him concerning any Horner robbery. That is the reason McKinley Forrest went there voluntarily." He pointedly questioned Forrest's state of blankness for six days. He referred to statements about Forrest given by the other men, which the jury had been told over and over could not be applied to anyone other than the individual making the statement. Regarding Forrest's alibi of being at work at Katzeff and Wiener's,

Volpe maintained that the "alibi witnesses support the contention of the State" in that the crucial time period of the murder could not be solidly accounted for. As to the testimony of the handwriting expert, J. Howard Haring, who said McKinley Forrest could not have initialed the bottle and his confession, he commented, "There is no question that McKinley Forrest was a nervous person from his early days. That was reflected in his confession and reflected in his handwriting on the Exhibits," and his stuttering confirmed this nervous condition.

Next Volpe considered the case of Horace Wilson. Wilson had moved into the cement-block house in January 1948, and thus needed furniture, which could be found at William Horner's store. Then, discussing Wilson's questioning, Volpe used a statement that worked well for him in the first trial: "It would have been the word of all the Police Department or personnel present in that room as against the word of Horace Wilson, but no, the officers do not want that word on their conscience. They are men who have dedicated years of service to the Police Department." Therefore, the jury should believe what the police said, rather than any words of Horace Wilson. After claiming that "[a]ll of these men knew from the very first moment they walked into the First District as to the reasons why they were there," he asked, "Now, aren't Police Officers telling you the truth as to what happened?" Regarding Wilson's alibi, he pointed to the erasure on the work record, as well as the fact that January 27, 1948, was an unusually cold day and the bosses did not spend all their time outside supervising the workers. Thus, Wilson could easily have slipped away to commit murder and return unnoticed. "When Horace Wilson came back on January 27th to the Dilatush farm and realized that he was never missed from work, he knew then that he had a perfect alibi, one that couldn't be destroyed, and therefore he was the only one who throughout the investigation persistently stated that he had no participation in the crime."

After the lunch break, Volpe focused on Ralph Cooper, who spent much time at 12 Behm Street visiting his girlfriend, Melrose Diggs; while there he not only ran errands for Mrs. Rubie English but frequently went to the basement to fix the boiler. Thus, everything that George English testified to regarding Ralph Cooper plotting against him could easily have been true.

About Collis English, who said he was at home helping his mother with laundry at the time of the murder, Volpe remarked, "Well, this was the day when the pipes were frozen down on Union Street; the day when the blocks were frozen in automobiles, and yet Collis English was putting out the wash that particular day. I don't know anything about laundry, ladies and gentlemen, but it seems to me that you don't hang up clothes on a day which is a freezing proposition. I may be wrong. But it doesn't make sense to me." The eight women jurors could have pointed out that women frequently had to hang their laundry inside. Relating English's reported fear of the police and the way they treated blacks in Trenton, Volpe remarked, "Charged with murder, the men received roast beef sandwiches and cigarettes and here is a man who received candy. That is the kind of treatment they received at the hands of the Police." Regarding English's main alibi witness, his mother, Volpe said of his own mother: "She would swear that the sun was shining at midnight if it meant my life. I would expect Emma English to do likewise." He turned to the testimony of the defense psychiatrist, Dr. Wertham, who described the confessions as "forced responsiveness." Volpe countered: "It is not a mental disease. . . . If those men were under any mental deficiency of any kind in February when they signed those confessions, they would be hopelessly insane today."

Looking at the case of the Six as a whole for the first time in his summation, Volpe considered that the confusion of the case, the fact that stories did not add up, that disorder existed, proved that the state did not create it, that it was, in fact, real. After all, "Don't you think the Police would have done a much better job in conforming one confession to the other?" He summarized: "I do and can say that from the evidence here presented I say that the State has carried its burden. Compare the testimony of the Police Officers with the testimony as given by men charged with murder, their lives at stake, and look at the type of witnesses, the type of testimony here presented. Are not Police Officers men of conscience?" He then went through the entire case as it unfolded, laying out the successful work of the prosecution.

In an effort to rebut any parts of the defense that he felt might have been effective, he brought up the blue-green getaway car seen by Mrs. Virginia Barclay. After reviewing the timing, he concluded that the car she saw was half an hour too late to be the car used in the murder. Regarding the motive, he pointed out, "It is very, very, coincidental to me, Cooper was out of a job. Just got laid off. Collis English not working. Thorpe out of work. Rather coincidental I should say." He addressed the defense criticism of English having been brought to the police station for questioning about using his father's car, which then moved quickly to the murder of William Horner: "Why certainly, everyone who is apprehended for crime is interrogated because the police know from experience that nine times out of ten when a man is brought in you will find that there has been a series, and if there isn't the man will say 'No.' He will give an account of himself so that he couldn't have possibly been at that particular place at the time of crime." Tying up another loose end, that of Mrs. Horner's saying that only three men were in the store when the murder occurred, that just proved the honesty of the police not having her change her testimony "for the sake of putting the rap on some individuals whom the State did not feel that there was evidence against."[47]

About 5:00 P.M., after presenting his summation fairly calmly to that point, Volpe gradually worked himself into a frenzy, arms flailing, shouting that became screeching, as he roared that the confessions offered into evidence were true and had been given voluntarily. The men "were accorded good treatment while in the hands of the Police." Calling the murder of William Horner "[o]ne of the most brutal crimes ever perpetrated in this country," he concluded that the state met the burden of proving that the defendants perpetrated the crime and added at the last: "The Police Department is deserving of the respect of this County and the respect should be reflected in your verdict." Then, as to what he wished the jury to do: "I do not want to avenge the death of William Horner. That is not my function here, but the State demands the death penalty in this case so that in the future those who take upon themselves the right to take the life of others will know that they cannot get away with it. If you want the State of New Jersey to support these six men for the rest of their days, that is your privilege; but if you want to set an example, if you want to stop this type of crime, if you want to prevent a recurrence, if you want to show others that we in Mercer County do not tolerate stick-up men, highway men, murderers, then I ask you in the name of the State of New Jersey, that you return a verdict of guilty of murder in the first degree. Support your authorities in protecting society from this type of men. Thank you."[48]

Also on this day, the Trenton Negro Citizens Committee of 100 held a vigil for the Trenton Six organized by Mrs. Lizzie Brister. Her brother, Clarence Hill, was widely viewed as the innocent victim of a frame-up conducted in 1944 by Prosecutor Volpe and Chief Detective Naples.[49]

WEDNESDAY, JUNE 13, 1951

Judge Smalley spent the morning giving his charge to the jury. The defense team thought his message a model of clarity and evenhandedness. He began by reading the indictment, which he told the jurors they would have with them in the jury room; he emphasized that being indicted in itself provided no proof of guilt. Judge Smalley pointed out that the jury must operate under the rules of law that he would state. The jury would be "the sole judges of the facts, the weight of the testimony, the credibility of the witnesses, the inferences to be drawn from the facts and the ultimate conclusions to be reached on all of the facts." Next followed the basis of the law: "Now the State has made the charge against these defendants and under our law it must bear the burden of establishing their guilt of the offense charged in the indictment and each of its elements beyond a reasonable doubt . . . for these defendants are presumed innocent." He gave examples of what "a reasonable doubt" would entail. Then he informed the jury of New Jersey law, explaining that murder committed with robbery would be murder in the first degree. If convicted of murder in the first degree, the sentence would be death unless the jury recommended imprisonment at hard labor for life. "A consideration for you is whether these defendants were engaged in robbery or an attempted robbery at the time the alleged killing of William Horner took place." He then laid out testimony regarding the robbery-murder as the state explained it. He sifted carefully through each defendant's description of his experience in the Chancery Lane police station, noting, "The testimony of the State's witnesses and the testimony of the defendants as to what transpired in the Chancery Lane Police Station is as far apart as the Poles."[50]

Judge Smalley moved on to sum up the testimony of expert witnesses such as Dr. Wertham, who testified for Collis English and McKinley Forrest, and Dr. Spradley, who testified for the state, opposing everything Dr. Wertham presented. He also included the handwriting expert, Mr. Haring. He moved on to testimony in which the state clearly had one version and the defendants another, such as that by George English, LeGrand Brown, and Ernest Sands, saying to the jury that they should not consider the evidence of any witness they did not believe.

Regarding the statements of the defendants, the judge reminded the jury that he had declined to admit into evidence the typewritten confessions of Cooper, Thorpe, and MacKenzie, "holding that the State had failed to show beyond a reasonable doubt that those alleged confessions were given freely, voluntarily and understandingly, and consequently were not competent and admissible." Of the remaining statements, "Before you may give these alleged oral admissions any consideration, you must first decide whether they were in fact made by the defendant to whom the witnesses attribute them, and whether they were made in the form and manner as testified." Furthermore, "if you find in your deliberations that these alleged written confessions or oral admissions, which are in evidence, were not voluntarily given, then you must discard them and give them no consideration whatever."[51]

Now came an element that defense counsel had made much of: the defendants had not been advised of their right to remain silent and their right to counsel, and they were arrested without warrant. Judge Smalley informed the jury of New Jersey law, which held that a person could be arrested by a policeman without a warrant when the police were "acting in good faith," and that cautionary instructions "are not an essential step in the establishment of the fact that a confession or admission is voluntary." Thus, New Jersey law had not necessarily been violated. And if the jury decided the remaining confessions were voluntary, he told its members, "then you will pass to a determination of their truth."[52] The jury needed to sort out the difference between the state testimony that the defendants received good treatment from the police, including the care of Dr. Sullivan and Dr. Corio, and the treatment described by the Six in their testimony.

After a brief recess, Judge Smalley moved on to the defendants' alibi witnesses, summing the evidence as given by, and on behalf of, each. Regarding those who testified, "You may take into consideration the interest any of the persons who testified have in the outcome of the trial, their motives, biases, prejudices, if you find any, their means of obtaining knowledge of the facts, their power of discernment, memory and description, their candor or their evasion, if you saw either; and you will apply your knowledge and observation of human actions, motives and conduct in your search for the truth." He added that in the jury's search for the truth, "It is proper for you to take into account his education or lack of education, and his or her apparent mental or physical condition as you observed it, and the fact that the witness may be a police officer is no reason why greater weight should be given to his testimony than if the witness was not a police officer." He concluded by thanking the jury for "your patience and for your attention during these many long weeks of trial. This Court stands in salute. You have set a standard of performance superior to any experience of mine." He reminded the members, "You must not allow passion, prejudice or partiality to enter into your deliberations."[53]

Tensions began to rise; it was now time for the clerk to take fourteen slips of paper, each bearing a juror's name, put them into a box, and draw them out one at a time. Whoever was first became foreman or forelady, the next eleven would be jurors, and the final two would be excused, their services no longer needed. As the clerk of the court proceeded, evidently being quite nervous, he missed a number and called out one juror's name twice. Judge

Smalley told him: "Just take your time now, Mr. Clerk." Edward B. Kerr became foreman, and Ida Cagan and Cora Biesecker were excused. The defense team of Pellettieri, Alexander, and Hays all praised Judge Smalley; Alexander said, "It was an excellently prepared charge, magnificently delivered so it could not be misinterpreted or misunderstood." The jury stepped into the jury room, Judge Smalley swore in court officers to attend them, all exhibits were checked and placed in the jury room; the jury left court at 12:46 P.M.[54] The jury requested a late lunch, and sandwiches and coffee at 10:00 P.M. and again at 3:00 A.M. It took eighteen hours and forty minutes to reach its decision. County jail warden Michael Bajek reported that "the sleep of the defendants was restless."[55]

THURSDAY, JUNE 14, 1951

When court reassembled, the Mercer County courthouse resembled a fortress. Almost one hundred policemen and sheriff's deputies surrounded the building, deployed in the lobby, corridors, and inside and outside Judge Smalley's fourth floor courtroom. At 7:40 A.M. the jury announced it had reached a verdict. It took until 8:30 A.M. to collect defendants, court officials, attorneys, and jury into place; the jury looked worn and wan.[56] With every one of the 180 spectator seats filled, utter silence reigned in the jammed room. The clerk, his voice trembling with emotion, asked, "Will the defendants please rise and face your jury?" Then he asked the jury to rise. The clerk inquired, "Ladies and gentlemen of the jury, have you agreed upon your verdict?" The foreman answered, "We have." The clerk: "How do you find?" Mr. Foreman: "We, the members of the jury, find the defendant Ralph Cooper guilty of murder in the first degree with our recommendation of imprisonment for life at hard labor. We find the defendant Collis English guilty of murder in the first degree with our recommendation of imprisonment at hard labor for life. We find defendant McKinley Forrest not guilty. We find defendant John MacKenzie not guilty. We find defendant James H. Thorpe not guilty. We find defendant Horace Wilson not guilty." After the foreman announced the recommendation of mercy for Cooper, an exhalation of breath occurred, as those waiting relaxed slightly and a relieved rustle went through the room. As the verdicts continued to be read out, the audience seemed to lean back in their seats, but it appeared to take time for the results to sink in. Then Thorpe, MacKenzie, Wilson, and Forrest began to smile, while Cooper and English kept tight rein on their emotions, their faces revealing nothing. The court stenographer, asked to repeat the verdicts, read them in a quavering voice.

Prosecutor Volpe stared straight ahead, not moving from his seat, elbows on the prosecutor's table, fingers tightly clenched, throughout the reading of the verdict. Mr. Pellettieri rose to thank the judge and jury for the verdict, "although I might disagree naturally." After all, Pellettieri represented the two found guilty, as well as Thorpe, who had been found not guilty. Mr. Alexander rose to address the court: "I want to express to your Honor and to the members of this jury on behalf of the fifteen million people of colored America whom I represent for your most painstaking care, your deliberations which indicate very clearly that you have given the most cautious and sincere study to this case I think than in any case that has been brought before the Courts of America." Here he broke down sobbing, but recovered himself to add: "It is a remarkable tribute to the State of New Jersey that you members of the jury who have so faithfully served, upheld the great traditions of American justice and justice in New Jersey which will ring throughout the world as an answer to the fact that in America people of difference of race and color could not be given a fair trial in America. . . . And in our effort for the bettering of race relations in America this is the finest answer, the finest, most glorious effort."

At this point in the proceedings, one of the spectators, Leola Page, a friend of the English family, slumped to the floor. As court officials rushed to her side, she revived, screaming: "My God, my God." Another woman jumped to her feet shouting: "Let me out of here, let me out of here" as attendants helped her leave the room. Judge Smalley announced: "I am asking all of you to remain calm, or I will be obliged to clear the court-room." Mr. Katzenbach rose, supported by NAACP attorneys Clifford Moore and J. Mercer Burrell on each side, as tears coursed down his cheeks, "May I just express my heartfelt thanks to the jurors for their belief in my client McKinley Forrest." He could go no further and had to sit down, choked with emotion. Judge Smalley, his voice low, revealing the strain he had been under, then dismissed the jury with these words: "You have the great satisfaction of having given the best that you have and have done a magnificent job. You have done a service to your State. Again I stand in salute. And you are discharged." He then called for a fifteen-minute recess.[57] At this juncture a hearty round of handshaking occurred among defense counsel and the defendants. Alexander then got up, went to Prosecutor Volpe, and brought him over to the defendants. The four freed men looked bewildered and hesitant but took the prosecutor's extended hand. Volpe, shaken and appearing near a breakdown, said, "I have ample faith in the democratic process of our courts and I accept the verdict in that spirit."

Outside in the hallway, Chief Detective Frank Naples, who clearly loathed Pellettieri, having gotten into fierce arguments with him while testifying, said loudly in the presence of half a dozen reporters, "I'll kill that son-of-a-bitch if it's the last thing I do before I die."[58]

The jurors retired to a basement room, where Sheriff Thomas Brennan had arranged reunions with their families, whom they had not seen since early March. Juror John J. Kelly told a reporter, "We wanted to free all of them, but we were afraid of a hung jury." Foreman Edward Kerr told the AP, "We had a terrific wrangle and the ballots we took were too numerous to remember." The jury had gone through each defendant's case individually, then sought to determine guilt or innocence. Kerr recounted, "The jury was split in opinions, but never was as far apart as an even division. When asked if time spent in deciding became a factor, Kerr replied, "We'd have taken a month to decide, if necessary." Other reports had jurors split, four for death for all six, three for life imprisonment, and five to acquit all six. Later, six favored acquittal. Then, after "innumerable ballots," they agreed on a compromise verdict. Another report revealed that Wilson had been the first defendant to be cleared by the jury, and twenty-two ballots were taken before reaching the verdict.[59]

After the recess, before Judge Smalley sentenced Ralph Cooper, George Pellettieri rose to speak, tears in his red-rimmed eyes: "Your Honor, in view of the verdict of the jury which exonerated the person whom the State contended was the assailant and the person who actually did the killing [McKinley Forrest], and the testimony of Mrs. Horner and the other witnesses in the case, particularly the testimony of Mrs. Horner which states that this defendant was not in the store on the day of the murder in question, I feel that there are extenuating circumstances which I respectfully urge upon the Court in not imposing the maximum. I am firmly of the opinion that this verdict in the case of this defendant was a compromise verdict." Judge Smalley answered that the statute provided the penalty and sentenced Ralph Cooper to be imprisoned at hard labor for life. He then repeated the sentence for Collis English, who looked grim but essayed a small smile. Pellettieri, Alexander, and Katzenbach made motions that Thorpe, Wilson, MacKenzie, and Forrest be immediately discharged. Judge Smalley granted these motions and finished by saying, "Well, ladies and gentlemen, I guess that is all. I will not be saying 'I will see you tomorrow.' Good-bye." Thus ended the longest, costliest criminal trial in the history of New Jersey.[60] A banner headline in the *Trenton Evening News* proclaimed to the world "2 Convicted, 4 of Trenton 6 Acquitted," while a smaller one explained "Cooper and English Guilty But

Spared Death Chair." The prosecutor's office declined to make any comment on the trial or its result.[61]

The relatives of the Six had not been permitted in the courtroom for the reading of the verdict. Held under police guard in an adjacent room, they learned the outcome from a newspaperman phoning in his story.[62] At 10:30 A.M. the four exonerated men walked through a jail door with their attorneys and down a flight of stone steps, to freedom and the waiting arms of relatives and friends, all weeping, hugging, kissing, shaking hands. Thorpe put his remaining arm around Pellettieri and kissed him on the cheek. Mrs. Emma English, now recovered somewhat from the verdict, appeared smiling and confident as she greeted Jack MacKenzie and McKinley Forrest. A reporter shouted to her, "Well, you did get two of your menfolk back." She answered: "Yes, and I sure am glad. And we are going to get Collis out soon—I just know it." The press asked the four if they would be fighting for the freedom of English and Cooper. They answered, "You bet we are. We know they are innocent." Asked about their plans for the future, only Horace Wilson had a ready answer; he planned to return to farm work in Robbinsville, which he had been doing when arrested. McKinley Forrest pointed out that he got out just in time for his daughter's fifteenth birthday, four days away.[63] (See figures 12 and 13.)

Lawyer Raymond Pace Alexander told gathered newsmen, "We believe in the complete innocence of Cooper and English. The fight for their ultimate vindication through further appeals to our courts will be continued." Thurgood Marshall told the press that NAACP attorneys would meet with Pellettieri and Hays to determine whether the association would continue in the case. Pellettieri, hired by the Princeton Committee to Free the Trenton Six, along with Arthur Hays of the New York ACLU, announced their intention to fight on, along with James Imbrie, chairman of the committee. Imbrie felt sure that Cooper and English would be acquitted. He told newsmen, "I feel that the situation regarding the 'confessions' is one that reflects on the whole police department and the City of Trenton."[64]

That afternoon a joyous celebration ensued at 247 Church Street, in the heart of Trenton's black neighborhood. The building had become a famous landmark in the previous three years, as home to three of the defendants: English, MacKenzie, and Forrest. Mrs. English had continued to take in laundry to support herself; her granddaughter, Jean had been attending high school in Newark, living with Robert and Sarah Forrest. Mrs. English invited all four freed men to the celebration, but James Thorpe's family swept him away to Allentown, where they currently resided. Thorpe reported no plans for the future as yet. Horace Wilson gladly joined in but remained his usual reserved self. The *Daily Worker* reported, "There was nothing in the bearing or manner of the men to indicate that they had been in jail three years. Dressed in well-fitted suits, one might have thought they were returning from a long trip." When Forrest was asked what he would do next, besides celebrate his daughter's birthday, he responded, "The first thing I'm going to do is go to see Mr. Katzeff. I've got a lot of friends down on Union Street." Forrest planned to return to his life in Trenton. Wilson stated that his former employer, Elmer Hutchinson, who had testified on his behalf in both trials, had invited him to his farm for a short vacation; he planned to accept the invitation and then stay on to work for him. Hutchinson picked him up at the end of the party, and Wilson, now aged forty, resumed his former life. MacKenzie also wished to visit his former employers on Union Street. His uncle, Robert Forrest, then intended to take Jack to his home in Newark "where Volpe couldn't bother him." Jack planned to work for his uncle in his small contracting business. Attorneys Frank Katzenbach, George Pellettieri, Clifford Moore, and J. Mercer Burrell also attended the celebration at the English home. At its end, the attorneys went to New York City, as invited guests of the NAACP, to meet Walter White, head of the organization, and members of its board of directors.

Those taking credit for the four acquittals included the NAACP, the ACLU, the *National Guardian* (especially citing the work of investigative reporter William Reuben), the Civil Rights Congress, and the Progressive Party of New Jersey, chaired by James Imbrie. After a short period of congratulation and celebration, focus soon turned to the Trenton Two.[65]

CHAPTER 7

TWO MEN LEFT

FRIDAY, JUNE 15, 1951

The fight for Collis English and Ralph Cooper commenced immediately. Bessie Mitchell announced, "American justice is still on trial, and until that injustice against my people stops, we have just begun to fight." The Civil Rights Congress demanded that Governor Alfred Driscoll "immediately order the freedom of Collis English and Cooper." It also asked for the indictment of Prosecutor Mario Volpe "and every other official who conspired in this vicious frame-up." The Princeton Committee to Free the Trenton Six, chaired by James Imbrie, announced it would start raising $75,000 immediately to appeal the life sentences given to English and Cooper. George Pellettieri disclosed that he would file an appeal with the New Jersey Supreme Court within thirty days, saying the principal ground of the appeal was the conflict between the verdict and the state's case. Arthur Garfield Hays of the New York chapter of the American Civil Liberties Union (ACLU) added, "There was no question but that they should and can be acquitted and I will give them all the help I can."[1] In trying to understand why the jury chose to declare English and Cooper guilty, it would appear the confessions played an important part. Wilson never signed one, Judge Smalley threw out MacKenzie and Thorpe's, and Dr. Sullivan clearly described Forrest as "dazed" while signing his confession.

SATURDAY, JUNE 16, 1951

Prison officials transferred Collis English and Ralph Cooper from the Mercer County Jail to the Trenton State Prison. An article on their fate in the *Trenton Evening Times* observed that convicted murderers in New Jersey usually received parole after serving fifteen years.[2]

JUNE 20, 1951, AND JUNE 21, 1951

In reporting on the outcome of the second trial, the June 20 issue of the *National Guardian* included a prominent box titled "There's a Job Still to Do." An earnest plea by John T. MacManus pointed out that the Committee to Free the Trenton Six needed $30,000 urgently for the appeal, as it had to be filed within thirty days, and asked for donations to be sent to the treasurer of the committee. In the June 21 *Daily Worker*, writer Abner Berry pointed out the irony of Governor Alfred Driscoll having received an award from the National Association for the Advancement of Colored People (NAACP) for his achievement of pushing civil rights laws through the state legislature, while completely ignoring the plight of the Trenton Six. He called for Driscoll to pardon English and Cooper.

FRIDAY, JUNE 29, 1951

Judge Ralph Smalley heard arguments on a motion by defense attorneys George Pellettieri and Arthur Hays for a new trial for English and Cooper. Pellettieri based his presentation on the fact that the verdict differed from the case the state had offered. According to Mrs. Horner, English was present in the back room of the Horner store when the state contended that Forrest dealt the blow that killed the shopkeeper. Also according to Mrs. Horner, Cooper had not been present in the store on January 27, 1948, the day of the murder. Cigar salesman Frank Eldracher saw two young, light-complexioned men leave the store; both English and Cooper were very dark. Furthermore, the confessions described Forrest as killing Horner, and Wilson as beating Mrs. Horner, yet the jury found both innocent. Thus, "the verdict has no basis in the evidence presented by the State, let alone that presented by the Defense." Pellettieri provided citations as to why the jury verdict was contrary to both New Jersey law and basic justice. Hays then spoke, pointing out that in Cooper's handwritten confession, the one Judge Smalley admitted into evidence, Cooper used words and phrases that would be used only by an educated person, which Cooper certainly was not. Hays remarked pointedly, "In view of the acquittal of the four defendants I should think the District Attorney would feel relieved in his conscience that they never went to the electric chair." Later, he added, "This case will never be at an end so long as the public, men like myself, have doubts whether justice is done in American Courts; will never be at an end until it reaches the highest Court in the land. I am hopeful that your Honor will do the very courageous act, and it would be courageous but I kind of think your Honor has got guts enough to do it, to set this verdict aside."

Prosecutor Volpe then explained why "[t]here had been sufficient corroborating elements in the confessions of both Cooper and English to support a conviction as found by the jury." Judge Smalley agreed: "This jury heard all of the testimony . . . it cannot be said from all of the testimony adduced in the trial that there was not evidence to sustain the verdict as rendered by the jury. Nor can it be said that this is a compromise verdict." He denied the motion.[3]

TUESDAY, JULY 3, 1951

Collis English wrote a letter to his mother, Emma, letting her know that he and Ralph Cooper were holding up as well as could be expected: "Tell Bessie I am still hoping and praying and we know that she will keep on fighting for our freedom and I am very proud of her. I know she will be proud of me because I love her and you with all of my heart and soul. . . . I am hoping you will come down soon. I can have visitors now, so I will be looking for you soon."[4]

SUNDAY, JULY 8, 1951

Horace Wilson, McKinley Forrest, John MacKenzie, and James Thorpe made a joint public appearance at a picnic to raise funds for English and Cooper's appeal, sponsored by the New Brunswick Committee to Free the Trenton Six.[5]

SATURDAY, JULY 28, 1951

Thurgood Marshall of the NAACP, Patrick Malin of the ACLU, and Dr. Edward Corwin, chairman of the Princeton Committee to Free the Trenton Six, announced that an appeal of English and Cooper's case would be carried to the New Jersey Supreme Court and, if necessary, to the U.S. Supreme Court.[6]

TUESDAY, SEPTEMBER 11, 1951

George Pellettieri and Arthur Hays filed a notice of appeal for English and Cooper in the New Jersey Supreme Court.[7]

WEDNESDAY, NOVEMBER 28, 1951

A newly formed organization, the Joint Committee to Free the Trenton Two, placed a fund-raising advertisement in the *New York Times*. Created by the ACLU, the Princeton Committee to Free the Trenton Six, and the NAACP Legal Defense and Educational Fund, the new group listed among its activists the author Pearl Buck for the ACLU, and Mrs. Franklin D. Roosevelt for the NAACP. It began, "Two Americans face life in prison for a crime of which millions of men and women throughout the world believe them innocent." Before providing a synopsis of the case, the article pointed out, "There is a great American tradition that all of our citizens whether rich or poor, Negro or white, shall have equal justice under law. It is the task of each generation to preserve and pass on to posterity that tradition so long as America shall endure." In capital letters, it pointed out that "JUSTICE COSTS MONEY." If Cooper and English had been sentenced to death, New Jersey taxpayers would have borne the costs of appeal, but now $30,000 needed to be raised immediately, just to print the trial record, twenty-four bound volumes of four hundred pages each. The article contained a box to be clipped out and sent in with contributions. Pellettieri and Hays, with J. Mercer Burrell and Clifford Moore assisting, all served without fee on this new defense team.[8]

TUESDAY, MAY 13, 1952

At the request of Prosecutor Mario Volpe, who said he needed more time, the appeal to the New Jersey Supreme Court was postponed until the fall. This proved particularly problematic for Collis English, who was spending most of his time in the prison hospital, having had four heart attacks since the previous June. The most recent proved to be so serious that the warden sent for his family and a minister. Mrs. English appealed to Governor Driscoll to free Collis on bail so she could care for him and he could be seen regularly by a heart specialist. She received no response.[9]

Sanford Bates, commissioner of the New Jersey Department of Institutions and Agencies, still had not granted a request by Emma English that her son be permitted to undergo heart surgery in a New York hospital.[10]

THE SECOND APPEAL

George Pellettieri and Arthur Garfield Hays submitted a one-hundred-page brief on behalf of Cooper and English, making fifteen major points and citing dozens of legal cases. They began by stating, "The Court erred in refusing to direct a judgment of acquittal because (a) there was no legal evidence from which an inference of guilt could properly be drawn; (b) there was neither proof of robbery or attempted robbery or proof of conspiracy."[11] Next they claimed, "The Trial Court's reception in evidence of the alleged admissions and confessions of defendants violated their constitutional rights." Point 3: "The verdict was against the weight of the evidence." Points therein were the same as for the motion for a new trial argued on June 29, 1951. The brief raised a new point: Prosecutor Volpe's attempt to show that Collis English had been previously convicted of a crime, making it something he would have had in common with Cooper, and possibly a reason the two were singled out by the jury as guilty parties. English acknowledged that as a juvenile he had been taken to the police station and questioned regarding a crime he did not commit. Prosecutor Volpe maintained that a record of his conviction existed and referred repeatedly to an FBI file on the case. Directed by Judge Smalley to produce the record, he never did so but nevertheless implied its existence to the jury. Thus, the prosecutor "attempted to prove prior conviction of crime where no conviction of crime existed," causing irreparable harm to English.

Pellettieri and Hays went on to contend, "It was prejudicial error to permit the receipt in evidence of the coat, bottle, and sock found by George English as well as a photograph of the bottle in the cellar." They stated, "No attempt was made to connect the bottle or the sock with either defendant, yet they were received in evidence over objection." Even according to Prosecutor Volpe, the items had been moved several times after originally being found by George English in a shed in his yard. Point 10 of the brief asserted, "The Court [named] below erred in sustaining objections to all questions on cross-examination by the defense of the State's witnesses designed to establish the over-zealousness, motivation, and animus of the police in their investigation which led to the production of the confessions of the various defendants." A later point held that since Forrest had been found not guilty, although according to the state's case, he was the murderer, "the jury could not find Cooper and English guilty without first determining that the perpetrator to whom they were alleged to be accomplices actually committed the crime. . . . The verdict has no basis in reason or fact, is clearly unsupported by the theory or evidence presented by the State and is therefore, an inconsistent verdict which must not be allowed to stand."

In response, Volpe's brief for the state took up each of the appellants' points and explained why it was incorrect, never addressing the case at large. Pellettieri and Hays then submitted a reply brief for the appellants.[12]

Monday, October 20, 1952

The Supreme Court of New Jersey heard the appeal for the men now called the Trenton Two, three and a half years after hearing the appeal of the Trenton Six. Then, the court building had been ringed by police, with others in the hallways and in the overflowing courtroom itself. Now, the half-empty room was quiet. On one side sat two familiar figures, Mrs. Emma English and her daughter Bessie Mitchell. This time a pair of new and relatively young appointees joined their elders on the bench. Arthur Garfield Hays, now seventy years of age, spent forty uninterrupted minutes reviewing the case for the seven justices. He discussed the confessions and emphasized the contrast between the physical descriptions given by witnesses and the appearance of Collis English and Ralph Cooper. He described the obtaining of the confessions and stated that he had "been unable to find any other case, in either state or federal law, where all the evidence was in the confessions," as was the case here.

George Pellettieri then spent ninety minutes articulating the points stated in the brief. Next Prosecutor Volpe rose, nattily dressed, smiling and looking confident. He spoke for ten minutes before being interrupted while discussing the testimony of Mrs. Elizabeth Horner, about whom he said, "The crime had left so deep an imprint on her that she would remember these men to her dying day." Justice Harry Heher, author of the opinion overturning the initial verdict, quietly asked why, if they had made such an impression, she could not identify them at the police station eleven days after the crime. When Volpe responded that her eyes were bothering her, Heher asked why if she were not sure at that time, she could be sure thereafter. Volpe elaborated that she had identified the men at the trial, but another justice asked if she had been shown photographs of all the defendants. Volpe had to agree that as a prosecutor, he needed corroborating evidence and pointed out that Cooper and English had reenacted the crime when taken to the Horner store by the police; he noted as well that a soda-shop proprietress had stated that "two colored men" bought bottles of soda pop the morning of the crime and that evidence showed that the bottles were the murder weapons.

Volpe claimed robbery was the motive, and another judge inquired, "How do you account for so much money being left?" Volpe answered that the robbers had clearly been inept. Volpe then admitted that neither Cooper's nor English's alibis had been investigated. When bringing up the third soda bottle, the one George English insisted he had found in his shed, as evidence linking Ralph Cooper to the crime, Volpe incited the ire of several justices. Upon being asked how the bottle connected Cooper to the crime, Volpe pointed out that Cooper's statement mentioned a bottle in a sock, and here, holding up the evidence, was a bottle in a sock. Justice Heher abruptly asserted that Cooper's statement said Horace Wilson had held the bottle. Volpe, trying to proceed to his next point instead of answering questions, caused one of the new justices, William Brennan, future U.S. Supreme Court justice, to exclaim, "No, Mr. Volpe, answer my question!" Volpe admitted that there was nothing more direct to link Cooper to the crime. The other new justice, Nathan Jacobs, then asked about the bottle in the sock: "Exactly what did it establish?" Volpe: "One of the conspirators used it." Another justice asked: "Which one?" Volpe: "We don't know." Justice Heher broke in: "You can't whittle away presumption of innocence by conjecture, can you?"

Volpe defended his own conduct, described as prejudicial in the defense brief. Justice Oliphant interrupted: "So when you get down to credibility, all the rules of evidence are obliterated, is that your argument?" Volpe went on to attack the testimony of Dr. J. Minor Sullivan III, accusing Sullivan of having "veered from the truth." This caused a justice to ask if anything had been done about a prosecution for perjury. No; Volpe had not wanted to do anything that might prejudice the current hearings. Finally, Volpe asserted that the state never named Forrest and Wilson as the killers: "All we did is produce what evidence we had." Visibly startled, one of the justices asked if the state was now contending that it was conceivable that the jury thought that English and Cooper had done the killing. "That must have been the jury's conclusion," Volpe answered. Justice Wachenfeld asked, "Don't you have to agree that the jury was mistaken?" "No, sir," answered the prosecutor. Well, how could he explain the verdict then, when the only evidence, that contained in the confessions, named Forrest and Wilson as the killers? The answer: "The jury was correct as to two, English and Cooper, and incorrect as to four." The jury's verdict acquitting four of the defendants had been "a miscarriage of justice." The justices hammered Volpe. One informed him, "It is our duty to examine the jury's verdict and find out if it was lawful." A confused Volpe responded, "Undoubtedly, perhaps." Pellettieri had saved forty minutes of his time for a rebuttal, but when the prosecutor finished, Pellettieri told the court he had nothing further to add. The justices had already raised all of Pellettieri's points for him.[13]

Monday, November 24, 1952

The Supreme Court of the State of New Jersey met in session to announce the result of the appeal, with the opinion written and delivered by Associate Justice William A. Wachenfeld. Of the fourteen points brought to their notice by the appellants, the justices agreed with two major ones and one minor one. The minor point was the use in the second trial of notes taken by a patrolman during his questioning of English. These notes, used to refresh the memory of the officer testifying, were marked for identification and eventually admitted into evidence. English never had the opportunity to read these notes or confront them in any way. They were, however, discussed by the prosecutor in his summation, where he referred to them as a "confession," and were available to the jury during its deliberations. The justices found that the notes should not have been allowed into evidence.

Regarding Volpe's hints to the jury about English's criminal record, "A prosecutor has no right to employ such questions if in fact he has knowledge that no such convictions exist. To create a false premise for the consideration of the jury is patently improper practice. . . . The jury may well have conceived the impression that English violated the law, occasioning an investigation by the F.B.I. The prestige enjoyed by this agency and the confidence reposed in it by the American public may have prejudiced the defendant in the eyes of the jury by the repeated reference to the F.B.I. record. It was improperly injected and the disclosure should not have been permitted in the presence of the jury."

The other element the justices focused on was the admission of the two coats and bottle in a sock purportedly found by George English. "The record shows no justification for the admission of these exhibits. They were not found at the home of either of the defendants but at the residence of George English, and the bottle in a sock was in his coat pocket, not the defendant's." They concluded, "The relevancy of these exhibits escapes us completely.

Their admission, we think, was improper, prejudicial and harmful." Because of these errors, "the judgment below is reversed for the reasons herein cited and the cause remanded for a trial *de novo*." All seven justices agreed with this opinion granting a new trial.[14]

Prosecutor Volpe responded to a newspaper inquiry by claiming that "the decision seems to sustain us in almost every respect except one or two technical matters." He stated that the new trial would not start until January 1953 or later. Lewis Moroze, head of the New Jersey branch of the Civil Rights Congress, brought the news of the reversal to Ralph Cooper in prison. Cooper grabbed Lewis's hand and began to cry. "Thank God for the people who stuck by us," he said over and over again. He wondered why a new trial was ordered, declaring, "It is clear that we are both innocent. Why don't they just free us?" Cooper expressed concern for Collis English, declaring he should be transferred to a hospital instead of the Mercer County Jail, where both were scheduled to go. Emma English, reached in Trenton at her job as a domestic worker, said, "I'm glad. I was so scared." She also expressed hope that Collis would be able to receive hospital care. Bessie Mitchell, at work in New York's garment district when the news reached her, responded, "Good, that's real good news. But we still have a way to go." William Patterson, leader of the Civil Rights Congress, while happy with the reversal, pronounced, "Bail should be granted at once."[15]

THURSDAY, DECEMBER 4, 1952

It was becoming increasingly unclear who would carry on any legal fight for the Trenton Two. The ACLU, while "gratified" that a new trial had been granted to Cooper and English, told the *National Guardian* that its "terms of operation precluded it from aiding their defense at a new trial." The NAACP issued a press release saying it would stay in the fight but provided no specifics. James Imbrie of the Princeton Committee to Free the Trenton Six frankly stated that he had no idea how his group would raise funds for a retrial. William Patterson of the CRC called for individuals and organizations to write to Governor Driscoll and Prosecutor Volpe, asking for dismissal of a new trial and bail for both men.[16]

WEDNESDAY, DECEMBER 24, 1952

At the request of Prosecutor Mario Volpe, a Mercer County grand jury handed down an indictment of perjury against Dr. J. Minor Sullivan III.

Volpe accused Sullivan of testifying falsely that Collis English had a heart ailment and that several defendants appeared to have been drugged when he examined them at the time they signed their confessions. Sullivan, now medical inspector of the Mercer County penal institutions, responded that Volpe wished to damage his reputation and practice "out of spite." Free on $1,000 bail, Sullivan called for letters and petitions to Governor Driscoll, urging him to vacate the indictment.[17]

SUNDAY, DECEMBER 28, 1952

Ralph Cooper wrote to a young lady named Lottie on the Civil Rights Congress staff, sending his best wishes to all the staff and hoping that Lottie would both write to and visit him.[18]

TUESDAY, DECEMBER 30, 1952

Collis English received his freedom in death. On the evening of this day, Collis died of a heart attack in the Trenton State Prison Infirmary, attended by prison physicians and a Trenton heart specialist called to the scene.[19]

SATURDAY, JANUARY 3, 1953

Nearly eight hundred people, black and white, friends and defenders, attended the funeral of Collis English. Mourners jammed the largest black church in town, Union Baptist, every seat and every inch of standing room filled, spilling into the basement, choir loft, and street. James Thorpe, John MacKenzie, and McKinley Forrest served as pallbearers. Ralph Cooper, after obtaining permission to attend, was at the last minute not allowed to attend by officials at the Trenton State Prison. Fifteen clergymen spoke at the service, though none had participated in the battles to free the Trenton Six. One of them prayed, "Oh God! Grant us that some good might have come out of this service this morning—and out of the death of this man." Dr. J. Minor Sullivan III, who had testified for the prosecution in both trials but now faced an indictment of perjury by Prosecutor Volpe, spoke briefly, saying he would stand by all of the diagnoses had had made that long-ago day, including the one that Collis English "had to die to prove."

James Imbrie, head of the Committee to Free the Trenton Six, William

Patterson, national secretary of the Civil Rights Congress, lawyer J. Mercer Burrell representing the NAACP, and Lewis Moroze, executive secretary of the New Jersey Civil Rights Congress, all addressed the huge crowd. Patterson, speaking from the pulpit, looking down upon the open coffin, surrounded by floral offerings that extended almost the width of the church, compared Collis English's death with the executions of the Martinsville Seven in Virginia, Paul Washington in Louisiana, and Willie McGee by the state of Mississippi, all black men executed for killing whites, widely regarded as innocent of the crimes. He declared, "Collis English, we who brought you from the death house pledge that those who murdered you will not go unpunished. Mercer County prosecutor Volpe murdered you. Governor Alfred Driscoll let him murder you." The row of clergy sitting behind tried to hush him: "Be careful! Be careful!"

Bessie Mitchell's grief-stricken cries could be heard, raised within the congregation: "Oh, Lord! He was a good boy. He never hurt anyone.... He never even had a girl.... Why did they murder him? Why, Lord, why, why?" Poet Beulah Richardson read messages of condolence from all over the world. The funeral proved lengthy, in spite of the handwritten plea at the bottom of the typewritten list of speakers: "PLEASE confine your remarks to 3 minutes." The funeral procession to the cemetery went on for blocks, with over sixty cars plus buses heading to Greenwood Cemetery. A final irony occurred at the conclusion of the service. Collis English, a World War II veteran dying of an ailment contracted during his service, received all the accolades appropriate for a soldier. As the coffin was lowered into the ground, a Fort Dix military honor guard released a volley of rifle fire. Collis was buried as a hero.[20]

WEDNESDAY, JANUARY 14, 1953

Ralph Cooper wrote to Lottie at the national office of the Civil Rights Congress, whom he regarded as a friend: "The pasing of Collis was such a shock to me, that i have not got over it." He added, "i truely hope that you and your coworkers continue the fight for my freedom." (Letters quoted throughout with original spelling.) Lottie had asked if he needed anything and he told her he could use a shirt, size 16, and a pair of socks, size 11. He had received a letter from William Patterson, for which he expressed his thanks. Authorities had moved him from the Trenton State Prison back to the Mercer County Jail on December 31.[21]

Ralph Cooper wrote to Lottie, thanking her for her letter and the box of socks. He told her, "I was very happy to here from you, and to no that you and others are still fighting for my freedom. I truely hope that it wont be long before I will be a free man again."[22]

SUNDAY, FEBRUARY 15, 1953

Writing again to Lottie, Ralph mentioned that he had received a letter from Mary Griffin, who wanted to come visit him. He explained to Lottie, "i wrote and told her that she could not come to visit me because no friends are permitted to visit me. i hope to here from you real soon. i am still hoping for my freedom some time soon. Give my best regard to Lewis and all of the CRC staff and to your family too."[23]

FRIDAY, FEBRUARY 20, 1953

At a hastily called hearing, Ralph Cooper appeared in court with lawyer George Pellettieri, who had been summoned at short notice. The expectation was that Cooper would plead "innocent" and receive the date for his third trial. Instead he shocked courtroom spectators by pleading "no defense" in the slaying of William Horner before Essex County Judge Joseph E. Conlon. In permitting Cooper to make this plea, Judge Conlon insisted that he answer specific questions: "Were you there?" Cooper admitted to being in the store, and then the judge asked if the others were also, saying each name, to which Cooper had to answer "yes" or "no." Cooper agreed that Collis English, McKinley Forrest, James Thorpe, and Horace Wilson were all in the shop with him, while John MacKenzie stood outside. Strangely, the judge did not ask who actually killed William Horner. Judge Conlon declared, "Your honesty has removed the doubt felt by some persons that the state had prosecuted the proper party. It is to the state's credit that it persisted in spite of certain pressure. I feel that by being honest with the court you have removed a lot of doubts and brought out what actually happened. I am going to be extremely lenient. I could give you anything from a suspended sentence to a 30-year-to-life term. I think you have done a great deal to help yourself. In the turn of events, you have been a very, very lucky person." Conlon sentenced Cooper to six to ten years in Trenton State Prison, beginning with the date of his first arrest on February 7, 1948; with this sentence Cooper could expect to be paroled quite soon.[24]

James Imbrie of the Princeton Committee for the Defense of the Trenton Six charged that Ralph Cooper had been coerced into a second false confession. He and other committee members contended that Cooper was made to believe that unless he confessed, he would have little chance of getting out of prison. Cooper had no relatives to fight for him and had been permitted no visitors in prison for months. Prosecutor Volpe had insisted on a third trial and Cooper was told that there was no defense money for it. In particular, he had been told that his appointed defense counsel would not be George Pellettieri, and Cooper had no faith in anyone else. The committee asserted that Cooper was coerced into naming the other men as guilty, as well as himself, having been told that he could go free soon only if he did so. They observed that Collis English had been informed several years previously that he could get just a short term if he would plead "no defense," but he had refused, insisting that he was innocent.[25]

Lewis Moroze of the New Jersey Civil Rights Congress, described Ralph Cooper's plea as "a frameup to justify a larger frameup." He pointed out that officials pressured Cooper by forcing him to stand trial again, putting him in danger of another life sentence, or even a death sentence. The state's own case against Cooper refuted Cooper's new "confession." Cooper's handwritten confession, admitted by Judge Smalley during the second trial when his oral statement given to police had been thrown out, indicated that Cooper had not been in the store at the time of the murder. William Patterson, executive secretary of the national Civil Rights Congress, commented, "The facts as presented at both trials of the Trenton Six indicate the innocence of Ralph Cooper as well as the other men he is now seeking to implicate." Patterson referred to a national pattern of induced confessions, especially of blacks, as persisting and even expanding in recent years. Clifford Moore of the NAACP, who had defended Horace Wilson, affirmed, "Wilson is innocent of any complicity in the Horner murder, not only by the judgment of the jury but by the facts." J. Mercer Burrell told the *National Guardian*, "All of the defendants were and are actually and legally not guilty of the charge. No statement made by Cooper or any other person at this time can affect the decision of the jury after the second trial when four of the defendants were adjudged not guilty. Since nothing can be changed I see no point in undue recriminations against the unfortunate and naturally desperate Ralph Cooper to whom life and freedom seem sweeter than truth and abstract principle. His decision was a purely personal one not made upon the advice of counsel."[26]

TUESDAY, FEBRUARY 24, 1953

"Three defense lawyers," not named in the *New York Times* story, irate over Cooper's placing of their clients at the crime scene, met with Deputy Attorney General Leon Milmed at the statehouse in Trenton. They issued a statement: "We are going to see the Attorney General and ask him to investigate the circumstances of the plea made by Cooper. We want to know what transpired to make him implicate persons who were acquitted. We also want to know the circumstances surrounding his appearance in court."[27]

TUESDAY, AUGUST 11, 1953

The New Jersey Parole Board announced that it had granted parole to Ralph Cooper, who would be released in November. When he was paroled, Cooper quietly left Trenton, never to be heard from again, as he had promised would occur when released from death row in June 1949.[28]

———

The only other defendant to come to further media notice was James Thorpe, who died at Saint Francis Hospital in Trenton of injuries suffered in an automobile accident on March 25, 1955.[29] After his death, history took no further notice of the Trenton Six. My search for the fate of the other three men, Horace Wilson, McKinley Forrest, and John McKenzie, turned up nothing. They appeared in no obituaries; there were no entries in the Trenton Public Library Trentoniana Collection of Trenton history, and no one in the black community in Trenton, including those familiar with its history, could shed any light on their fate or that of their families. After years of media exposure, presumably they wished to proceed quietly with their lives, out of the spotlight.

———

One individual from the Trenton Six saga did continue in the glare of publicity, quite against his wishes. On January 16, 1956, Dr. J. Minor Sullivan III appeared in Mercer County Court before Judge Charles M.

Morris, accused of perjury at the second trial of the Trenton Six. Assistant Prosecutor Lawton charged that Sullivan radically altered his testimony at the second trial when he claimed two of the men had seemed to be drugged when they signed their confessions. Sullivan claimed he simply answered the questions asked during the cross-examination. The bulk of the state's case produced by Lawton consisted of long quotes from the original trial transcripts, but Judge Morris barred Sullivan from producing his own portions of the transcript, as well as notes he made at the time he originally examined the men. When Lawton summed up, rather than maintaining his focus on Sullivan's possible perjury, he went back to the Horner murder, saying, "William Horner's life was wiped out by a foul and felonious act . . . we cannot have a county where murder and perjury go hand in hand."[30] After a twelve-day trial without a jury, concluding on February 9, 1956, Judge Morris found Sullivan guilty of seven out of eight counts of perjury. Sullivan faced a maximum of seven years in prison. Morris postponed sentencing, and Sullivan remained free on bail. Thorn Lord, Sullivan's attorney, charged that his client was a victim of political persecution by a prosecutor angry at his losses in the second trial of the Trenton Six.[31]

After the perjury trial, politics entered the picture. Dr. Sullivan was a leader in black Democratic Party affairs in Trenton, and his counsel, Thorn Lord, served as Democratic County chairman. Reflecting Sullivan's political prominence, character witnesses on his behalf at the perjury trial included Congressman Frank Thompson; Charles R. Howell, state commissioner of Banking and Insurance; and Trenton Mayor Donal Connolly. Both Prosecutor Volpe and Judge Morris were prominent members of the Republican Party. Sullivan faced the loss of his license to practice, as well as his county and city posts. The all-Democratic Mercer County Board of Freeholders decided on February 10, 1956, to retain Sullivan as deputy Mercer County physician. On April 20 Judge Morris fined Dr. Sullivan $1,500 and placed him on probation for two years.[32]

On April 1, 1957, the New Jersey State Supreme Court, by a vote of four to three, upheld three of the seven perjury counts against Dr. Sullivan. The minority, led by Justice Harry Heher, who had written the opinion overturning the verdict from the initial Trenton Six trial, voted to acquit on all seven counts. Dr. Sullivan now faced disciplinary action by the State Board of Medical Examiners.[33] Raymond Pace Alexander, lawyer for John MacKenzie and Horace Wilson during the second trial, took Sullivan's appeal to the United States Supreme Court, which refused to hear his case on October 14,

1957, leaving his fine and probation in place.[34] He appealed twice more, but the high court never agreed to hear his case.

Dr. Sullivan went on to a prosperous medical practice as Trenton's best-known and most-beloved black physician. He had begun his career in Trenton immediately upon returning from World War II and continued to see patients until 2001. He became bedridden and died in a fire in his home on January 18, 2003. He had served as Mercer County's first African American coroner, provided free medical services to the needy, and maintained his status as a leader in the black community. Five hundred people attended his funeral, which was held at the Union Baptist Church, where Collis English's funeral had been held. His nephew said of him: "He was a lovely, happy person, someone whom everybody in the community knew they could come to for help. He was politically astute, economically astute, socially conscious, and supportive of his people."[35]

———

The fates of others caught up in the drama of the Trenton Six also deserve attention. Journalist William Reuben, whose interviews, articles, capacious notes, and partial book manuscript all provided me with vital information, was unable to find a publisher for his work on the Trenton Six. This was perhaps due to his extreme bias in favor of the Six and against all those in authority. He obviously held very strong beliefs in the importance of justice and felt great frustration when he felt it was being thwarted. After focusing on the Trenton Six, Reuben devoted the rest of his life to the case of Alger Hiss, an accused Soviet spy; Reuben proved to be among Hiss's staunchest defenders and published several books on his trials and travails. In 1974 he filed what may have been the first Freedom of Information Act request for FBI documents, eventually receiving more than 40,000 pages. He died on May 31, 2004 at the age of eighty-eight.[36]

Another major player involved in the Trenton Six from beginning to end was Mercer County Prosecutor Mario Volpe. He continued as county prosecutor until 1957, five years after the Trenton Six trials were over; he left public service to practice corporate law, representing over forty corporations. He married and had one daughter. Volpe was active in organizations such as the American Legion, the Veterans of Foreign Wars, the Elks, and the Trenton Chamber of Commerce. He died in March 1975 at the age of sixty-four. Prominent in his obituary was his service as prosecutor of the Trenton Six. He had been viewed as an up-and-coming star in the Trenton Republican firmament, but the result of the second trial, with only two convictions and no death sentences, slowed his rise.[37]

Frank S. Katzenbach III, lawyer for McKinley Forrest from before the first trial until Forrest's acquittal at the second, also spent a significant portion of his life dealing with the Trenton Six. He continued work in his law firm, Katzenbach and Salvatore, until he died on January 11, 1967, at the age of fifty-six.[38]

We come now to those involved in the first Trenton Six trial, beginning with Judge Charles P. Hutchinson. The Trenton Six followed him to his grave: his obituary in the *New York Times* was headlined: "Ex-Judge Charles P. Hutchinson Dead; Presided at First Trial of Trenton Six." Hutchinson had been an assistant United States attorney, Mercer county clerk for seventeen years, and then sat on the County Court of Common Pleas from 1945 to 1955. When a third appointment as judge was not forthcoming, he established a private law practice in Trenton. He remained active in local legal affairs, veterans' groups, and his church until his death in 1957 at age seventy. His obituary in the *Trenton Evening Times* noted: "[E]ven now, almost 10 years later, references to the Trenton Six case occur from time to time in the news."[39]

James S. Turp, head of the defense team in the first trial, died in 1980 at age eighty-six. Retiring from his own law firm in 1964, he remained active in civic affairs in Hightstown, New Jersey. He served on the board of local banks, the YMCA, and the town board of education. Involved with groups such as the Lions and Masons, he served as elder, trustee, and superintendent of the Sunday school of the First Presbyterian Church of Hightstown. His obituary noted his appointment to head the defense in the Trenton Six case.[40]

The youngest man on the defense team, James A. Waldron, died in Trenton in February 1995, at age seventy-nine. In 1963 he was appointed U.S. commissioner for the federal district court in Trenton, and served as the president of the Mercer County Bar Association. He founded a nonprofit organization, the Kingsbury Corporation, devoted to creating affordable housing in Trenton. Unlike the others, his extensive obituary did not mention the Trenton Six, perhaps because his involvement had occurred early in his long career.[41]

NAACP attorney Robert Queen, the only black attorney in the first trial, merited an obituary in the *New York Times*. It noted that he "gained fame as defense attorney for Clarence Hill in the Duck Island murder case and as one of the court-appointed lawyers in the first 'Trenton Six' murder trial in 1948." He earned repeated court victories striking down school desegregation during his distinguished career. Queen died in Trenton on August 31, 1960, at age seventy-six.[42]

Those in the Civil Rights Congress, which had carried out the first appeal for the Trenton Six, went on to lead lives filled with confrontations against perceived injustice. At the same time that he was working with the Six, William Patterson, executive secretary of the Civil Rights Congress, was working on his book, *We Charge Genocide: The Crime of Government Against the Negro People*. Published in 1951, it listed hundreds of cases in which black Americans had their rights trampled on by the government, local, state, and federal. Patterson presented the work as a petition to the United Nations, showing major violations of the Universal Declaration of Human Rights, and more specifically of the United Nations Convention for the Prevention and Punishment of Genocide.[43] Patterson continued as an active Communist, breaking into national news again when he worked as a lawyer defending the Black Panther Party and Angela Davis in the late 1960s and 1970s. Patterson died in 1980 at age ninety.

O. John Rogge, who argued the first appeal before the New Jersey Supreme Court, went on to have a colorful career. He had been associated with several Communist organizations and once visited the Soviet union as Stalin's personal guest. Rogge went on to serve as counsel for David Greenglass, who eventually testified against his sister and brother-in-law, atomic spies Ethel and Julius Rosenberg, leading him to be called "Rogge the Rat" by previous allies. In 1960 he wrote *The First and the Fifth, with Some Excursions into Others*, and later, *Why Men Confess*. He died on March 22, 1981, at age seventy-seven.[44]

Paul Robeson, whose eloquent, fiery speeches on behalf of the Trenton Six drew much attention and funds to their cause, had an increasingly difficult time in the United States throughout the 1950s' anticommunist hysteria. Although he was known worldwide for his singing and acting, such as his work as the title character in Eugene O'Neill's *Emperor Jones*, Joe in *Show Boat*, and Shakespeare's *Othello* in London and on Broadway, his increasing political activism caused him much trouble at home. From 1950 to 1958 the U.S. State Department revoked his passport, an act the U.S. Supreme Court eventually ruled unconstitutional. When he was again able to travel he spent time in Europe, including Eastern Bloc countries and Russia. The FBI and CIA had him under close surveillance for thirty years. By the end of his life, when he had retired due to ill health, the Cold War was on the wane and his achievements as a political activist for people of color and the economically disadvantaged were beginning to be acknowledged. Worldwide celebrations were held on his seventieth and seventy-fifth birthdays. Robeson died at age seventy-seven on January 23, 1976, in Philadelphia. He continues to be remembered and revered throughout the world.[45]

Judge Ralph Smalley, who presided over the second trial of the Trenton Six, is next to be considered. The Trenton Six also followed him to his grave, as the headline of his *New York Times* obituary illustrates: "Judge of Superior Court in Jersey Presided at Trial of the 'Trenton Six.'" During the trial, he had repeatedly warned feuding attorneys to "settle down" as arguing was "not good for their blood pressure." He died on January 22, 1956, of a heart attack, at just sixty years of age. He had begun his judicial career in 1935 with an appointment as a district court judge in Somerset County. After working his way up, he was appointed by Governor Driscoll as judge on the state Superior Court, a position he held until his death. Four hundred people attended his funeral at which he was lauded as "a man dedicated to justice."[46]

Clifford Moore, who worked as an associate of Raymond Pace Alexander in the second trial, had a promising career tragically cut short. Soon after the end of the second trial, Governor Alfred Driscoll appointed Moore to the New Jersey State Commission on Civil Rights. Then, on September 24, 1952, he was named the first black U.S. commissioner since the days of Reconstruction after the Civil War. The responsibilities of the office involved trying federal petty cases, minor crimes committed on military posts, and arraigning prisoners arrested by FBI agents and U.S. marshals. On July 16, 1956, Moore was found dead of a gunshot wound at the age of forty-two. He had been cleaning a rifle from his extensive gun collection when it apparently accidentally discharged.[47]

George Pellettieri was another key figure in the second trial, having been the defense attorney for Thorpe, English, and Cooper. Pellettieri, who had studied voice and instrumental music before becoming a lawyer, used his voice to expostulate and argue, keeping in mind the larger goal of social justice. His law firm, Pellettieri, Rabstein, and Altman, which still exists, aggressively defended the poor, labor organizations, and employee benefit funds. Several days after his death, a commentary in the *Trenton Times* claimed that "George Pellettieri was the heart of Trenton." Author Larry Kramer described Pellettieri as a man who sang opera "at the drop of a hat" and was devoted to his native city. His clients were often poor, oppressed people who had nowhere else to turn for help. Fortunately for the finances of the law firm, Pellettieri's other clients came from the "top of the social structure." Pellettieri was a power in county and state Democratic politics and a lifelong champion of liberal causes. He died on August 29, 1980, at the age of seventy-seven.[48]

A testimonial dinner to honor Raymond Pace Alexander was held not long after the second Trenton Six trial. Thurgood Marshall, who knew Alexander well, remarked on that occasion, "He lived that case, I mean day in and day out, work, work, work, never giving it up, matching wits with the best of the State of New Jersey, the best they could produce, and licking them every step of the way." In 1951 Alexander began seven years as a Democrat on the Philadelphia City Council. He retired from electoral politics when he was appointed the first African American to serve as a judge on the Philadelphia Court of Common Pleas, retiring in 1970 as presiding judge of that court. In 1963 *Ebony* magazine named him one of the most influential blacks in the United States. Alexander died in his chambers of a heart attack on November 24, 1974, at age seventy-six.[49]

Arthur Garfield Hays, retained by the ACLU for the defense at the second trial, was nearing the end of a storied career when he worked on behalf of Thorpe, English, and Cooper with George Pellettieri. His roster of famous cases included Sacco and Vanzetti, the Scopes "monkey" trial, and the Scottsboro boys. His obituary in the *New York Times* noted that "he grew rich representing corporations and grew famous defending civil liberties without pay." He died of a heart attack at age seventy-three on December 14, 1954.[50]

––––––

The story of the Trenton Six soared to international prominence as a result of the publicity efforts of the Civil Rights Congress in 1949, and stayed there to the end of the second trial, on a level with Sacco and Vanzetti and the Scottsboro Boys. However, soon after Ralph Cooper's plea bargain, their story faded from consciousness, probably for several reasons. After Cooper's deal with Volpe, some who had not been following the case and were unfamiliar with the facts assumed that all six had been guilty all along, notwithstanding that a jury had declared four innocent. The involvement of the Communists played a part too; historical memory of the Six was being formed in the 1950s at the height of the Cold War. Anything associated with Communists became anathema; the magnificent Paul Robeson suffered this fate until the recent resurrection of his reputation. Perhaps most important is that the men did not become martyrs to be remembered, executed by the hand of a careless and unforgiving legal system. The clear exception is the fate suffered by Collis English, who presumably would have lived much longer if properly treated for his heart condition and without the stress of continuous incarceration and court trials. The story of the Trenton Six streaked around the world like a comet, a flash of light that quickly faded and disappeared. As a rare story in which justice more or less triumphed in the end, it deserves to take its rightful place in our national memory.

EPILOGUE

I would love to conclude that the tale of the Trenton Six is merely a manifestation of the nation's evolving justice system in the middle of the twentieth century and could not happen today. However, history has seemingly repeated itself in the Clinton-Bush-Obama era in the case of the Norfolk Four.[1] On July 7, 1997, Michelle Moore-Bosko was raped and murdered in Norfolk, Virginia. She was discovered the next day by her husband, Billy, on his return from a naval cruise. All indications from the crime scene were that one man perpetrated the attack. Police detectives, in particular Robert Ford, focused on neighbor Danial Williams, who soon broke down and confessed. When his DNA did not match, they wrung a confession out of his roommate, Joe Dick. When Joe Dick's DNA did not match, they got the name of Eric Wilson from him and soon Eric Wilson confessed. Then Joe Dick stunned investigators by naming two more men: Derek Tice and Geoffrey Allen Farris. Derek Tice named Richard Dale Pauley Jr. Pauley offered to take a lie detector test, took it, and was told he failed. He later confessed, as did Tice. Each man along the way was told that the others had already explained their parts in the rape and murder and that police knew they were guilty. Most did not ask for lawyers to be present, as they thought legal representation unnecessary, since they knew they had done nothing wrong. By the time they realized they needed attorneys, they had already waived their Miranda rights. When Farris requested an attorney, detectives ignored him and continued their questioning. Each man confessed after being subjected to long hours of interrogation.[2]

However, to the growing consternation and puzzlement of prosecutors, none of the DNA or fingerprints found at the crime scene matched any of the six men. Tice decided to accept a plea bargain, testifying against all the codefendants and identifying a seventh perpetrator, in return for which he would not face a death sentence. He named a friend, John Danser, as the last individual involved in the attack. Detective Ford arrested Danser, gave him a polygraph test, and told him he failed it. Danser demanded a lawyer but then agreed to answer questions without a lawyer being present. Predictably, he ended up confessing. By February 1999, police had seven men in jail, with no DNA match. They now searched for an eighth suspect in a crime in which the apartment had not been visibly disturbed; nothing had been overturned or broken, and Michelle Moore-Bosko's vaginal injuries were consistent with one attacker. The defendants' stories did not mesh with each other. Yet, their confessions led them straight to serious threat of execution, given that Virginia's use of the death penalty is second only to that of Texas. Throughout this entire time, detectives worried that one guilty person was still out there, never considering the obvious: they had seven innocent young men locked up.

On February 22, 1999, Delvie Stover, the mother of Michelle Moore-Bosko's friend Tamika Taylor, handed police a letter to her daughter Karen, in which the writer, Omar Abdul Ballard, wrote about the murdered woman: "Guess who did that. Me, ha, ha. It wasn't the first time. I'm good ain't I. . . . Tell the police, tell the FBI. You thought you knew me. You don't Karen. Trust me. I'm untouchable Karen. And I'm coming." Ballard wrote this frightening letter from the Augusta County Correctional Center in northwestern Virginia, where he was in prison for raping a fourteen-year-old girl ten days after Michelle Moore-Bosko's death. He had been sentenced to forty-one years in prison. Tamika Taylor had asked police to check out Ballard after her friend's murder, but they never did. Detectives told Judge Charles E. Poston at a hearing for John Danser that they now had a lead on an additional suspect.

Ballard's DNA matched that found on the blanket in Moore-Bosko's bedroom. Ballard told detectives that he had committed the crime by himself. Detective Ford repeatedly tried to get Ballard to implicate the other seven defendants, but he refused, saying with some pride that he alone was responsible. With Derek Tice refusing to testify against them, the Commonwealth of Virginia let Pauley, Farris, and Danser go. On June 16, 1999, Eric Wilson's trial proceeded with charges reduced so he no longer faced the death penalty. The jury, going on his confession alone, the only evidence against him, found him guilty of rape and sentenced him to eight and a half years in prison. At his trial, Joe Dick received life in prison without parole. Detective Ford denied threatening Dick with the death penalty or saying he would help him if he confessed. The authors of the book on the Norfolk Four, as Williams,

Dick, Wilson, and Tice came to be called, quote a law professor as writing: "Judges, prosecutors, defense lawyers, and repeat offenders all know that police officers lie under oath. . . . They also know that jurors are more likely to believe them than defendants, and that they can get away with lying in court."[3] A jury sentenced Tice, also with no evidence but his confession, to two consecutive life terms behind bars. On March 22, 1999, Omar Ballard, whose DNA actually did match that found at the murder scene, pleaded guilty to Michelle Moore-Bosko's murder and rape and also received two life sentences without parole.

Derek Tice's father, Larry Tice, convinced that his son was innocent, began a campaign to exonerate him. He wrote to Virginia prison and corrections officials, national news media, members of Congress, the ACLU, and the FBI. The Learning Channel broadcast a television program on the case in June 2001. In May 2002, the Virginia Court of Appeals reversed Tice's conviction. At his retrial in January 2003, he was again found guilty, based on his confession. George Kendall, a leader in finding experienced defense attorneys in capital cases, got involved and recruited other attorneys to assist him. Omar Ballard provided a key affidavit making it clear that he alone committed the rape and murder, saying of the others: "They are all innocent." Eric Wilson was released from prison after serving seven and a half years of his eight-and-a-half-year sentence.

In November 2005, a coordinated campaign began to obtain pardons for Williams, Dick, Wilson, and Tice. The case was featured in *Time* magazine and on *Nightline*. In January 2006, nine of the jurors in Wilson's trial urged Virginia's governor at the time, Mark Warner, to grant clemency to the four men. Former judges, prosecutors, and Virginia attorney generals also got on board. After much legal maneuvering, Warner's successor, Governor Timothy Kaine, announced that he would free the three men still in prison, commuting their sentences to time served. The men, whose lives are circumscribed by the lingering stigma of guilt, are still seeking pardons to clear their names. The case of the Norfolk Four illustrates just how easy it is to find people guilty, and how nearly impossible it is to legally restore their actual innocence.[4]

Since the time of the Trenton Six's harrowing experience, the use of the death penalty has waxed and waned, reflecting cultural mores. One fact has remained constant, however. Since 1976, when the U.S. Supreme Court ruled the use of the death penalty constitutional, with certain safeguards, for approximately every ten executions in the United States, one innocent person on death row has been exonerated, hardly a comforting statistic for an irreversible punishment.[5] The U.S. Congress, disliking the publicity from so many exonerations, ended the program in which federal money had been used to fund attorneys for indigent death row inmates. In addition, Congress passed the Antiterrorism and Effective Death Penalty Act in 1996, which set an almost impossibly high bar for people on death row to obtain a federal hearing. The U.S. Supreme Court had already held, in the 1993 case of *Herrera v. Collins*, that a claim of actual innocence based on new evidence is not grounds for a federal hearing. Justices Blackmun, Stevens, and Souter dissented, with Blackmun saying: "[N]othing could be more contrary to contemporary standards of decency or more shocking to the conscience than to execute a person who is actually innocent."[6]

In response, "innocence projects" have sprung up around the country. Barry Scheck, director of the largest and best known of these, the Innocence Project based in New York City at the Benjamin N. Cardozo School of Law, explained, "Once you are convicted, all odds are stacked against you. To get a conviction vacated is extremely difficult." He cited seven factors found to be the causes of most judicial errors. Of the seven, four appeared to play a part in the Trenton Six case: eyewitness misidentification, false confessions, forensic misconduct, and government misconduct. The Innocence Project takes only cases in which DNA is available for testing. The use of DNA has made it possible to prove without question that innocent people are in prison, thus revealing the systemic flaws in our justice system. But DNA exists in only 15 percent of cases; those accused in the other 85 percent have to find some other way to prove their innocence.[7]

Ironically, the state of New Jersey has played a leading role in these events. One of the earliest groups doing "innocence" work, Centurion Ministries, based in Princeton, was begun in 1980 by James C. McCloskey, working in Trenton State Prison. The primary mission of Centurion Ministries is to vindicate and free innocent individuals from prison. McCloskey named his organization after the Roman centurion who proclaimed, while standing at the foot of Jesus' cross, "Surely this one is innocent." The Centurion Project has freed more than forty inmates.[8]

In a major development in December 2007, New Jersey's state legislature became the first in modern times to abolish the death penalty as a possible punishment for murder. Of the reasons given for this action, four applied to the Trenton Six: eyewitness misidentification, false confessions, forensic misconduct, and government misconduct. Three other factors remain unchanged since 1948: numerous black youths remain functionally illiterate, minorities are imprisoned vastly out of proportion to their number in the population, and virtually all those facing the possibility of execution are too poor to hire attorneys and must take whatever representation is provided for them, typically lawyers with little experience or skill in defending their clients.

Public opinion regarding capital punishment has changed in recent years. The pendulum has swung away from the wholehearted support common during the Reagan "tough on crime" era. Polls show that most Americans now believe that innocent people have been executed and that the death penalty as used in this country is applied in a racially biased manner; in response juries have become more reluctant to mete out death sentences, with the numbers dropping to the lowest in a generation.[9] It seems clear from the Trenton Six case, from the Norfolk Four and others, that the continued use of the death penalty in the American criminal justice system should be questioned. The current system virtually ensures that at some times, in some places, innocent people will take the place of guilty ones, ensuring that some people do, literally, get away with murder, while the innocent pay the ultimate price.

LIST OF PRINCIPALS

THE TRENTON SIX AND THEIR FAMILIES

Ralph Cooper

Cooper was born and raised in Fitzgerald, Georgia, by his grandparents. He left school when he was age ten but could read and write a little. At the time of his arrest at age twenty-three, he was in Robbinsville with Collis English, looking for farm work.

Collis English

English lived with his mother, Emma English, at 247 Church Street. He was twenty-three years old at the time of his arrest and had served in the navy for two and-a half years during World War II, acquiring malaria as well as rheumatic fever, which left him with a damaged heart. Born and raised in Trenton, English attended school partway through tenth grade and could read and write fairly well.

Emma English

Emma Roberts was born in Alabama on September 28, 1888. Her first husband was Henry Williams, with whom she had a daughter, Bessie. She married George English after Henry Williams died. Emma and George English had fourteen children; Collis was the youngest. Collis and Bessie were Emma's only surviving children.

George English

The father of Collis English, George English deserted his son and wife when Collis was an infant. At the time of the Horner murder he lived at 12 Behm Street with his second wife, Rubie English, and his stepdaughter Myrtis Fields.

McKinley Forrest

Forrest was born in Richland, Georgia, on December 21, 1918, son of "Boss" and Ida Forrest. He attended a country school and never went beyond first grade; he could not read or write and had a noticeable stutter. He came north when he was fifteen, bringing with him his nephew John MacKenzie. In 1935 he married Delia English, Collis English's sister, who died in 1947. They had one child, Jean Ida, thirteen years old, who lived with her father in the English household. Character witnesses at the trial described Forrest as "decent, hardworking, and sober."

Robert Forrest

Brother of McKinley Forrest, he lived with his wife, Sarah, in Newark, where he owned a small construction company. He and Sarah visited McKinley regularly throughout his time in jail and prison.

John MacKenzie

John MacKenzie, called Jack by his family, was McKinley Forrest's nephew, the oldest son of one of McKinley's Forrest's two sisters. He was born in Americus, Georgia, on February 14, 1923. When his parents died, he went north with his uncle. He attended school in Trenton until eighth grade and could read and write fairly well. He served in the army during World War II. After receiving an honorable discharge on January 1, 1946, he began work at Community Slaughterhouse on Union Street, adjacent to McKinley Forrest's employer, Katzeff and Wieners.

Bessie Mitchell

Daughter of Emma English and sister of Collis English, Bessie Mitchell was the first person to believe that all of the Six were innocent and to try to find them legal assistance.

James Thorpe

Aged twenty-four at the time of his arrest, he lived with his grandparents at 24 Grant Street. In 1947 his right arm had been badly smashed in a car accident, and on January 7, 1948, doctors amputated. Born in Warren, North Carolina in August 1923, Thorpe attended a country school to second grade and could not read or write. He was quite light-complexioned compared to the other five defendants and had a serious speech impediment that made him difficult to understand.

Horace Wilson

Wilson was born in Heineman, South Carolina. He had eleven brothers and sisters. He married and had a child in South Carolina, then came north in July 1939, without his family. He had attended school for only two months, could not read at all, and could write only his name, but he carried himself with great dignity and composure. He worked as a field laborer, harvesting grain, potatoes, and corn. He was thirty-seven years old at the time of his arrest.

The Victim and His Associates

Garrett "Jerry" Griswold

Griswold was a thirty-eight-year-old single white man who periodically worked for William Horner. Griswold claimed he had left Trenton two days before the murder to go to Baltimore and returned on the afternoon of January 27. Locals suspected that he was present at Horner's murder.

Ellen Horner

The legal wife of William Horner and mother of his six children lived in Bordentown. In 1916 William abandoned his legal family in Bordentown and moved to Trenton.

William Horner

After he left his wife and six children in Bordentown in 1916 and moved to Trenton, he established a small secondhand store with Elizabeth McGuire. He was murdered in his store on January 27, 1948, by being struck in the back of his head, probably with a glass bottle.

Elizabeth McGuire [Horner]

Living as William Horner's wife, she had moved in with him in 1916, when she was twenty-seven and he was forty. On January 27, 1948, she sustained injuries during an attack in William Horner's secondhand store.

DEFENSE TEAM

Raymond Pace Alexander

Brought into the Trenton Six case at the request of Thurgood Marshall, black lawyer Raymond Pace Alexander represented John MacKenzie and Horace Wilson in their second trial. He worked for desegregation in schools and public accommodation in Philadelphia and throughout Pennsylvania and served as counsel to the NAACP Legal Defense and Educational Fund.

J. Mercer Burrell

Burrell, the local attorney for the NAACP, assisted Raymond Pace Alexander in the second trial. representing John MacKenzie and Horace Wilson

Arthur Garfield Hays

A highly regarded civil liberties attorney, Hays represented Ralph Cooper, Collis English, and James Thorpe in their second trial.

Frank S. Katzenbach III

Katzenbach had been a Mercer County judge from 1940 to 1945, served three sessions in the state assembly, and attended the Democratic National Convention as a delegate in 1940. After clerking for his uncle Nicholas Katzenbach, he formed the law firm Katzenbach and Salvatore. He represented McKinley Forrest at both trials.

Clifford H. Moore

A Trenton attorney, Moore, who was black, assisted Alexander in representing John MacKenzie and Horace Wilson in their second trial.

William Patterson

Patterson, the executive director of the Civil Rights Congress, which was sponsored by the Communist Party USA, received a law degree from the University of California. He was black and headed the Communist Party USA's efforts to recruit black members.

George Pellettieri

Pellettieri represented Ralph Cooper, Collis English, and James Thorpe in their second trial. A champion of liberal causes, Pellettieri was regarded as one of Trenton's foremost criminal and labor lawyers.

Robert Queen

One of the few black attorneys in Trenton and executive director of the New Jersey NAACP, Queen assisted with John MacKenzie's defense and represented Ralph Cooper in the first trial.

O. John Rogge

Hired by William Patterson of the Civil Rights Congress to lead the appeal of the death sentences of the Trenton Six to the New Jersey Supreme Court, Rogge was a prominent champion of radical causes. He routinely defended organizations deemed subversive by the Department of Justice that he had previously served as an assistant attorney general.

William Reuben

Reuben, a freelance journalist and author, was hired by the *National Guardian* to do a series on civil rights. Beginning on October 25, 1948, he focused on the case of the Trenton Six. Through him, the *Guardian*'s coverage brought the case of the Six to the attention of the outside world.

Paul Robeson

A world-famous actor, singer, and political activist, Robeson headed the Committee to Free the Trenton Six.

James S. Turp

Head of the defense team in the first trial, Turp received his law degree from George Washington University in 1920.

James Waldron

Son of one of Trenton's five city commissioners, Waldron represented Collis English in the first trial. He was the youngest member of the defense team.

PROSECUTION AND POLICE

Andrew Delate

At the time of the Horner murder, Delate was an acting captain in the Trenton Police Department. He was placed in charge of the investigation instead of someone from the Detective Bureau, which would have been usual procedure. Delate was closely involved with the questioning and subsequent confessions of the Trenton Six.

Andrew J. Duch

Duch, Trenton's director of public safety at the time of the Horner murder, was a Trenton native. He had served as a lieutenant in World War I and after the war entered local Republican politics; he was subsequently appointed clerk of the police court, police court judge, and, in 1937, Mercer County prosecutor.

Frank Lawton

Lawton was the Mercer County assistant prosecutor who worked with Prosecutor Mario Volpe throughout all trials and appeals of the Trenton Six.

Frank A. Naples

Naples served as Trenton's chief of detectives for five years and was with the detective bureau for twenty-five years. He was closely involved in the formulation of the confessions of the Trenton Six.

James Minor Sullivan III

One of Trenton's few black physicians, Sullivan was called by police to examine the Trenton Six during their middle-of-the-night confession session.

Mario Volpe

As Mercer County prosecutor, Volpe headed the prosecution throughout all trials and appeals of the Trenton Six. He had grown up in Trenton and attended Rutgers University on a scholarship from the *Trenton Evening Times*; he remained one of the newspapers' favorite subjects.

JUDGES

Charles P. Hutchinson

The Mercer County judge who presided at the first trial of the Trenton Six, Judge Hutchinson had been appointed to the County Court of Common Pleas in 1945.

Ralph J. Smalley

An administrative judge for several New Jersey counties, Smalley presided over the second trial of the Trenton Six.

NOTES

A note about names and titles: The transcripts and contemporary material use a variety of spellings for the names of the many participants in this series of events. Police and civilian titles also vary depending upon date and source. I have used the spellings and titles that seemed to have been used most frequently in the sources.

SHORT TITLES USED IN NOTES

Reuben Papers: William Reuben Papers, Special Collections Library, Harlan Hatcher Graduate Library, University of Michigan, Ann Arbor.

Reuben typescript: William Reuben, Trenton Six typescript, Tamiment 289, Box 14, Robert F. Wagner Labor Archives, Tamiment Library, New York University, New York City.

SCNJ : *Supreme Court of New Jersey*, State Law Library, State Library, 185 W. State Street, Trenton. These are original copies, in bound volumes, of the proceedings of the New Jersey Supreme Court, kept in the basement of the State Law Library. (The actual decisions are separate and are in the regular library upstairs.) The volumes are numbered, titled *Supreme Court of New Jersey*, and inside give the case name and then the particulars of the case. They are not court trial transcripts. Trenton Six transcripts are included because they were added as an appendix. The courts only keep transcripts a certain number of years; the rules have changed over time, but it is not very long, so the only reason the transcripts existed at all for these sixty-year-old trials is because they were appendices for the two appeals and thus entered a permanent record. Without the transcripts, I would have lost my most important primary source.

CHAPTER 1 — THE CRIME AND THE TRENTON SIX

1. "Elderly Couple Beaten in Holdup By 3 Thugs At Second-Hand Store," *Trenton Evening Times*, January 27, 1948; "Victim Dies of Beating, Four Sought," *Trenton Evening Times*, January 28, 1948.
2. Reuben typescript, 3; *SCNJ*, 196:364a.
3. Reuben typescript, 4–6.
4. *SCNJ* 32:3173a; Reuben typescript, 8.
5. Reuben typescript, 9 and 10.

6. Editorial, "The Idle Death Chair," *Trenton Evening Times*, January 29, 1948.

7. Jon Blackwell, *Notorious New Jersey* (New Brunswick, NJ: Rivergate Books, Rutgers University Press, 2007), 295.

8. Stuart Banner, *The Death Penalty: An American History* (Cambridge, MA: Harvard University Press, 2002), 179–183.

9. Frederick Drimmer, *Until You Are Dead: The Book of Executions in America* (New York: Windsor Publishing, 1992), 61–63.

10. Harry Camisa and Jim Franklin, *Inside Out: Fifty Years Behind the Walls of New Jersey's Trenton State Prison* (Adelphia, NJ: Windsor Press and Publishing, 2003), 53.

11. Ibid., 55.

12. Ibid., 54.

13. Ibid., 56.

14. The Espy File, Executions in the U.S. 1608–2002, Executions by State, New Jersey, found on the Web site of the Death Penalty Information Center, deathpenaltyinfo.org (accessed May 5, 2006).

15. Editorial, "The Idle Death Chair."

16. Reuben typescript, 1d.

17. "Crime Squad Starts Patrol," *Trenton Evening Times*, February 3, 1948.

18. Elwood Dean, *The Story of the Trenton Six* (New York: New Century, 1949), 4–5; *Trentonian*, February 5, 1948.

19. Reuben typescript, 1c.

20. Ibid., 21.

21. John T. Cumbler, *A Social History of Economic Decline: Business, Politics, and Work in Trenton* (New Brunswick, NJ: Rutgers University Press, 1989), 149.

22. Reuben typescript, 1c; Cumbler, *Social History*, 154–155.

23. William Dwyer, "This Is the Task: Findings of the Trenton, New Jersey, Human Relations Self-Survey" (community project aided by the Race Relations Department of Fisk University, Nashville, TN, 1953), 4–5.

24. Reuben typescript, 3c; Cumbler, *Social History*, 156.

25. Gerald Horne, *Communist Front? The Civil Rights Congress, 1946–1956* (Rutherford, NJ: Associated University Presses, 1988), 131.

26. "Slain Man's Wife Clears First Suspect," *Trenton Evening Times*, January 29, 1948.

27. Research Notes: Personalities 2, Box 1, Reuben Papers.

28. "Bordentown Woman Claims She Was Wife of Murdered Storeman Here, Seeks Estate," *Trenton Evening Times*, February 4, 1948.

29. Reuben typescript, 1c–8c.

30. *SCNJ* 31:1220a–1223a.

31. Trenton Profile, Reuben typescript, 5.

32. All material about the six defendants comes from trial testimony and their interviews with journalist William Reuben.

33. Reuben typescript, 9e–11e.

34. Box 2, Folder 1, Reuben Papers.

35. Reuben typescript, 105–106.

36. Ibid., 15.

37. Ibid., 23–24.

38. Ibid., 25–26.

39. Ibid., 15–17.

40. Ibid., 17–18.

41. Ibid., 19–21.

42. Ibid., 27–28.

43. Editorial, *Trenton Evening Times*, February 11, 1948.

44. Ibid., 183.

45. Ibid., 204–206.

46. Ibid., 204–206.

47. *SCNJ*, 30:8a.

48. Reuben typescript, 183–185.

49. Ibid., 27–28.

50. Ibid., 28 and 31.

51. Ibid., 514–515.

52. Jack Washington, *Quest for Equality: Trenton's Black Community: 1890–1965* (Trenton, NJ: Africa World Press, 1993), 79.

53. "Frank Katzenbach, Former Judge, Dies," *Trentonian*, January 13, 1967; "Katzenbach Rites Slated Wednesday," *Sunday Times Advertiser*, January 12, 1967.

54. http://politicalgraveyard.com/bio/karol-kauffman;.answers.com/topic/nicholas katzenbach (accessed May 7, 2006).

55. Obituary, "James S. Turp, 86, Former Judge, Mayor," *Trenton Times*, July 31, 1980.

56. Obituary, "James A. Waldron, Partner in Historic Trenton Law Firm," *Trenton Evening Times*, February 5, 1995.

57. Washington, *The Quest for Equality*, 26–30.

58. Ibid., 101–102.

59. Ibid., 87–88.

60. Ibid., 105–106.

61. Jon Blackwell, "1943: School Spirit," *Trentonian*, http:www.capitalcentury.com /1943 (accessed June 9, 2006).

62. "Four Lawyers To Defend Six In Death Case," *Trenton Evening Times*, March 16, 1948; *SCNJ* 30:14b.

63. Reuben typescript, 6b.

64. Ibid., 10b.

65. Material on Donal Connolly from Research Notes: Personalities 2, Box 1, Reuben Papers, and Reuben typescript, 3b–10b.

66. Blackwell, *Notorious*, 313–316.

67. Research Notes: Personalities 2, Box 1, Reuben Papers,.

68. Reuben typescript, 11b–14b; *Trenton Evening Times*, September 13, 1946.

69. Reuben typescript, 3d–12d.

70. Dean, *Trenton Six*, 10.

71. Research Notes: Personalities 2, Box 1, Reuben Papers.

72. CRC Research Notes, Civil Rights Congress 1, Box 1, Reuben Papers.

CHAPTER 2 — THE TRIAL, PROSECUTION

1. Jury Outline in Research Notes: Personalities 2, Box 1, Reuben Papers.

2. Research Notes: Personalities 2, Box 1, Reuben Papers.

3. Reuben typescript, 15b–22b.

4. Article clipping about Charles P. Hutchinson from the *Sunday Times Advertiser*, found in Vertical File: Biography, Trentoniana Collection, Trenton Public Library; obituary, Charles P. Hutchinson, *New York Times*, December 15, 1957.

5. *SCNJ*, 30:82a–90a.

6. Ibid., 30:89a.

7. Ibid., 30:93a.

8. Ibid., 30:98a.

9. Ibid., 30:99a and 30:105a.

10. Ibid., 30:110a–162a.

11. Ibid., 30:163a–178a.

12. Ibid., 30:182a–191a.

13. "Widow Puts 3 at Scene of Murder," *Trenton Evening Times*, June 17, 1948.

14. *SCNJ*,, 30:270a–271a, 30:277a, and 30:281a.

15. Ibid., 30:290a–291a and 30:297a–299a.

16. Ibid., 30:301a–302a, 30:304a–306a, and 30:313a–314a; complete testimony of Elizabeth Horner, ibid., 30:224a–318a.

17. *SCNJ*, 30:351a–356a; Abner Berry, "The Trenton Story," *Masses and Mainstream* 4 (June 1951): 71, 75.

18. *SCNJ*, 30:358a–367a.

18. Ibid., 30:3756a–380a.

20. Ibid., 30:384a–390a.

21. Ibid., 30:404a–421a.

22. Ibid., 30:427a–428a; entire testimony 30:421a–428a.

23. Ibid., 30:449a–454a.

24. Ibid., 30:458a–459a.

25. Ibid., 30:464a–465a.

26. Ibid., 30:468a–469a.

27. Ibid., 30:469a and 30:470a.

28. Miranda v. Arizona 384 U.S. 476 (1966).

29. *SCNJ*, 30:471a–472a.

30. Ibid., 30:485a.

31. "Wrote Own Statement in Slaying," *Trenton Evening Times*, June 28, 1948; "Murder Trial Is Financial Headache for Freeholders," *Trenton Evening Times*, June 30, 1948.

32. *SCNJ*, 30:463–525a.

33. Henry Steele Commager, *Documents of American History*, 5th ed. (New York: Appleton-Century-Crofts, 1949), 2:51.

34. *SCNJ*, 30:626a–627a.

35. Ibid., 30:996a–998a.

36. Ibid., 30:1017–1019a.

37. "Defense Hits Police Photos in Death Trial," *Trenton Evening Times*, June 23, 1948.

38. *SCNJ*, 31:1391a.

39. Ibid., 31:1495a–1501a.

40. "State Rests In Trial of Death Case," *Trenton Evening Times*, July 14, 1948.

41. Entire discussion found in *SCNJ*, 31:1874a–1983a.

42. Ibid., 31:1878a; ibid., 31:1891a.

43. Ibid., 31:1891A.

44. Ibid., 31:1903a and 31:1906a.

45. Ibid., 31:1914a and 31:1920a.

46. Ibid., 31:1932a and 31:1940a.

47. "Murder Trial Is Financial Headache For Freeholders."

48. "Confessions Are Upheld as Evidence," *Trenton Evening Times*, July 6, 1948, and *SCNJ*, 31:1952a–1983a.

49. *SCNJ*, 31:1994a–1995a.

50. Ibid., 31:2002a–2003a.

51. Ibid., 31:2017a–2020a.

56. Ibid., 31:2197a–2204a.

57. "Murder Case Confessions Read to Jury," *Trenton Evening Times*, July 8, 1948.

58. Reuben typescript, 80.

59. *SCNJ*, 31:2238a.

60. Quotation, *SCNJ*, 31:2247a; entire statement, *SCNJ*, 31:2235a–2247a.

61. Ibid., 31:2259a.

62. Ibid., 31:2259a–2260a.
63. Ibid., 31:2278a.
64. Ibid., 31:2283a–2298a.
65. Ibid., 31:2330a.
66. Ibid., 31:2333a.
67. Ibid., 31:2336a.
68. Ibid., 31:2351a.
69. Ibid., 32:2403a.
70. Ibid., 32:2446a.
71. Ibid., 32:2524a–2525a.
72. Ibid., 32:2538a–2539a.
73. Ibid., 32:2545a–2546a.
74. Ibid., 32:2557a–2558a.
75. Ibid., 32:2565a–2566a.
76. Ibid., 32:2567a; 2577a.
77. Ibid., 32:2578a, 32:2580a, and 32:2584a.
78. Ibid., 32:2664a–2665a.
79. Reuben typescript, 260.
80. *SCNJ*, 32:2662a–2679a.
81. Ibid., 32:2684a.
82. Ibid., 32:2690–2704a.
83. Ibid., 32:2704a–2706a.
84. Ibid., 32:2719a–2720a.
85. Ibid., 32:2724a.
86. Ibid., 32:2738a.
87. Berry, "The Trenton Story," 70.
88. *SCNJ*, 32:2768a.
89. Ibid., 32:2790a, 32:2791a, 32:2793a, 32:2795a–2796a, and 32:2804a–2808a.
90. Ibid., 32:2809a.
91. Ibid., 32:2812a–2813a.
92. Ibid., 32:2826a.
93. Ibid., 32:2830a.
94. *SCNJ*, 32:2851a–2889a for all of the following cross-examination.
95. Ibid., 32:2852a, 2857a, 2883a, 32:2854a, 32:2871a, and 32:2879a–2880a.
96. Ibid., 32:2859a.
97. Ibid., 32:2929a.
98. Ibid., 32:2920a–2930a.

CHAPTER 3 — THE TRIAL, DEFENSE

1. *SCNJ*, 32:2934a–2974a; quotation, *SCNJ*, 32:2973a–2975a.
2. Ibid., 32:2983a.
3. Ibid., 32:2984a.
4. Ibid., 32:3054a–3057a.
5. "Volpe Reviled Him, Wilson Cries at Trial," *Trenton Evening Times*, July 15, 1948.
6. *SCNJ*, 32:3063a.
7. Ibid., 32:3117a.
8. Ibid., 32:3158a–3159a.
9. Ibid., 32:3196a–3223a.
10. Ibid., 32:3244a–3253a.
11. Ibid., 32:3282a–3283a.

12. Ibid., 32:3287a–3309a.

13. Entire testimony, *SCNJ*, 32:3322a–3639a.

14. *SCNJ*, 32:3351a.

15. Ibid., 32:3363a.

16. Ibid., 32:3366a.

17. Ibid., 32:3370a.

18. Ibid., 32:3377a.

19. Ibid., 32:3382.

20. Ibid., 32:3337a–3338a.

21. Ibid., 32:3391a–3403a.

22. Reuben typescript, 176.

23. *SCNJ*, 32:3440a.

24. Ibid., 32:3545a.

25. Ibid., 33:3639a–3681a.

26. Ibid., 33:3774a.

27. Reuben typescript, 192, 170.

28. *SCNJ*, 33:3846a.

29. Ibid., 33:3847a, 33:3848a, 33:3849a, and 33:3856a.

30. Ibid., 33:3905a–3914a.

31. Ibid., 33:3915a–3916a.

32. Ibid., 33:3917a–3920a.

33. Ibid., 33:3921a–3943a.

34. "Murder Jury Hears Forest [sic] Make Denial," *Trenton Evening Times*, July 22, 1948.

35. *SCNJ*, 33:4014a.

36. "2 Witnesses Called to Aid Forest's [sic] Alibi," *Trenton Evening Times*, July 23, 1948.

37. *SCNJ*, 33:4160a–4167a.

38. Ibid., 33:4264.

39. Ibid., 33:4281a and 33:4283.

40. Ibid., 33:4290.

41. "Call Cooper to Stand in Slaying Trial," *Trenton Evening Times*, July 26, 1948.

42. *SCNJ*, 33:4295.

43. Ibid., 33:4304a–4311a.

44. Ibid., 33:4328a–4334a.

45. Ibid., 33:4336a–4343a.

46. Ibid., 33:4356a–4447a.

47. "Cooper Steadfastly Claims Innocence in Horner Slaying," *Trenton Evening Times*, July 27, 1948.

48. *SCNJ*, 33:4477a.

49. Ibid., 33:4512a.

50. "Cooper Steadfastly Claims Innocence in Horner Slaying."

51. *SCNJ*, 33:4593a–4613a.

52. Ibid., 33:4614a.

53. Ibid., 33:4615a.

54. Ibid., 33:4617a–4631a.

55. Ibid., 33:4702a–4743a.

56. Ibid., 34:4756a–4779a.

57. Ibid., 34:4791a–4792a.

58. Ibid., 34:4799a–4802a; quotation, ibid., 4802a.

59. *SCNJ*, 34:4806a–4807a.

60. Ibid., 34:4807a–4814a and 34:4815a–4819a.
61. Ibid., 34:4889a–4891a.
62. Ibid., 34:4982a–4999a.
63. Ibid., 34:5013a.
64. Ibid., 34:5146a–5158a.
65. Ibid., 34:5258a, 34:5261a, and 34:5271a.
66. Ibid., 34:5304a–5321a.
67. Ibid., 34:5371a–5407a.
68. Ibid., 34:5462a–5467a.
69. Ibid., 34:5483a–5494a.
70. Ibid., 34:5497a–5532a.
71. Ibid., 34:5498a and 34:5503a–5504a.
72. Ibid., 34:5512a.
73. Ibid., 34:5532a.
74. Ibid., 34:5535a.
75. Ibid., 34:5537a.
76. Ibid., 34:5547a and 34:5548a.
77. Ibid., 34:5556a.
78. Research Notes: Second Trial, Box 1, Reuben Papers.
79. *SCNJ*, 34:5571a–5572a.
80. Ibid., 34:5594a and 34:5599a–5600a.
81. Ibid., 34:5604a, 34:5605a, and 34:5607a.
82. Ibid., 34:5609a.
83. Ibid., 34:5629a.
84. Ibid., 34:5631.
85. Ibid., 34:5634a.
86. Ibid., 34:5645a and 34:5647a.
87. Ibid., 34:5651a–5657a.
88. Ibid., 34:5657a and 34:5666a.
89. Ibid., 34:5668a and 34:5669a.
90. Ibid., 34: 5674a, 34:5759a, 34:5681a–5682a, and 34:5688a.
91. Ibid., 34:5692a and 34:5689a–5710a.
92. Ibid., 34:5710–5735a.
93. Ibid., 34:5741a and 34:5748a.
94. Ibid., 34:5757a.
95. Ibid., 34:5753a–5767a.
96. Ibid., 34:5763a.
97. Ibid., 34:5770a–5771a.
98. Ibid., 34:5772a–5827a.
99. Reuben typescript, 487.
100. *SCNJ*, 34:5428a–5862a.
101. "Six Sentenced to Die For Slaying of Horner," *Trenton Evening Times*, August 6, 1948.
102. Reuben typescript, 513a.
103. *SCNJ*, 34:5846a–5873a.
104. Associated Press story, August 6, 1948, Other Writings, Radio Reports, and Wire Service Reports, Box 1, Reuben Papers.
105. "Six Sentenced to Die For Slaying of Horner."
106. Biblical quote from Amos 5:24; account of day in Other Writings, Radio Reports, and Wire Service Reports, Box 1, Reuben Papers.
107. Quoted in Reuben typescript, 13a insert.

108. Reuben typescript, 502–503.

109. Harry Camisa and Jim Franklin, *Inside Out: Fifty Years Behind the Walls of New Jersey's Trenton State Prison* (Adelphia, NJ: Windsor Press and Publishing, 2009), 359.

110. Ibid., 319.

CHAPTER 4 — BESSIE MITCHELL FINDS HELP

1. Emma English to Mac [McKinley Forrest], April 25, 1949, Family Letters, Box 1, Reuben Papers.

2. Alphonso Strauss to McKinley Forrest, June 16, 1949, Family Letters.

3. John MacKenzie to Bessie Mitchell, March 4, 1949, Family Letters.

4. Sarah Forrest to John MacKenzie August 18, 1948, Family Letters.

5. Sarah Forrest to John MacKenzie, December 3, 1948, Family Letters.

6. Sarah Forrest to John MacKenzie, February 6, 1949, Family Letters.

7. Sarah Forrest to John MacKenzie, June 3, 1949, Family Letters.

8. Sarah Forrest to John Mackenzie, September 8, 1948, and December 6, 1948, Family Letters.

9. Robert Queen to John MacKenzie, October 3, 1948, Family Letters.

10. Sarah Forrest to John Mackenzie, August 28, 1948, Family Letters.

11. Research Notes: Progressive Party, Box 1, Reuben Papers.

12. Research Notes: Communist Party, Box 1, Reuben Papers.

13. Reuben typescript, 514–516.

14. Ibid., 516–517.

15. Ibid., 518–520.

16. Ibid., 521–522.

17. Ibid., 523–524.

18. Ibid., 525–527.

19. Elwood Dean, *The Story of the Trenton Six* (New York: New Century Publishers, 1949), 15.

20. William L. Patterson, "The Scottsboro Case," *The Man Who Cried Genocide* (New York: International Publishers, 1979), 81–82.

21. Reuben typescript, 504.

22. Ibid., 557–559.

23. Ibid., 527–529.

24. William Reuben, "The Day the Trenton Six Waited to Die," *National Guardian*, July 25, 1949; "Trenton Victim's Death House Story," *Daily Worker*, July 18, 1949; Abner W. Berry, "Map Action Now to Free Collis English and Cooper," *Daily Worker*, June 15, 1951.

25. Peter Salwen, "Remembering the Trenton Six Case," August 6, 1998, http://salwen.com/ trenton6 (accessed June 17, 2006).

26. Research Notes 2, Box 1, Reuben Papers.

27. Salwen, "Remembering the Trenton Six Case," 4.

28. Reuben typescript, 547.

29. Ibid., 543–544.

30. Ibid., 543–548.

31. Ibid., 551.

32. Ibid., 551–552.

33. Ibid., 553–555.

34. Ibid., 555–556 and 560–561.

35. Ibid., 562–563.

36. General Correspondence 2, Box 1, Reuben Papers.

37. Earl Ofari Hutchinson, *Blacks and Reds: Race and Class in Conflict, 1919–1990* (East Lansing: Michigan State University Press, 1995), 200; http://www.hometoharlem. com/HARLEM/hthcult.nsf/4475d09ab4 (accessed October 11, 2007).

38. Reuben typescript, 532–538.

39. Ibid., 521–539.

40. Civil Rights Congress 3, Box 1, Reuben Papers; Memo to Patterson, April 23, 1949, Civil Rights Congress 1, Box 1, Reuben Papers.

41. Civil Rights Congress 3, Box 1, Reuben Papers.

42. Reuben manuscript, 227–228, Box 2, Reuben Papers. .

43. Reuben typescript, 564–565.

44. Ibid., 567–569.

45. Fact Sheet 1, Correspondence, Box 38, Records of Governor Alfred E. Driscoll, New Jersey State Archive.

46. Reuben typescript, 538–539; "New Client," *Time*, June 12, 1950.

47. Phillip Deery, "A Divided Soul? The Cold War Odyssey of O. John Rogge," *Cold War History* (May 2006): 6, no. 2; Research Notes, Box 1, Reuben Papers.

48. *[Newark] Telegram*, March 6, 1949; "Patterson Appeals to NAACP to Help Free 6 Trenton Negroes," unknown newspaper clipping dated March 9, 1949, Schomburg Center for the Study of Black Culture, New York Public Library.

49. Research Notes, Box 1, Reuben Papers; O. John Rogge, "Trenton Case Is a Northern Scottsboro," *National Guardian*, January 31, 1949; Vera Strauss to John MacKenzie, January 27, 1949, Family Correspondence, Box 1, Reuben Papers.

50. "Protest Vaux Hall Burning of Cross, Pastor Leads Group Asking Investigation," *New York Age*, March 5, 1949; "Patterson Appeals to NAACP"; Fact Sheet 1, Correspondence, Box 38, Records of Governor Alfred E. Driscoll.

51. Gerald Horner, *Communist Front? The Civil Rights Congress, 1946–1956* (Rutherford, NJ: Fairleigh Dickinson University Press, 1988), 150.

52. O. John Rogge and Thomas I. Emerson, *Our Vanishing Civil Liberties* (New York: Gaer Associates, 1949), 253–270.

53. Research Notes, Box 1, Reuben Papers.

54. Research Notes, Box 1, Reuben Papers; Correspondence, Box 38, Contents: Treas-Trenton, Records of Governor Alfred E. Driscoll.

55. "Paul Robeson," Miscellaneous Drafts 4, Box 2, Reuben Papers.

56. Obituary, Irving Feiner, *New York Times*, February 3, 2009.

57. Research Notes, Box 1, Reuben Papers.

58. Postcard from Bessie Mitchell to John MacKenzie, Family Correspondence, Box 1, Reuben Papers.

59. Civil Rights Congress 2, Box 1, Reuben Papers.

60. Fred Jerome, *The Einstein File: J. Edgar Hoover's Secret War Against the World's Most Famous Scientist* (New York: St. Martin's Griffin, 2003), 130.

61. Entire series of correspondence from the Eleanor Roosevelt Papers, Franklin D. Roosevelt Presidential Library, Hyde Park, New York.

62. Civil Rights Congress 2, Box 1, Reuben Papers; CRC Newsletters and Releases, Reuben Papers; Miscellaneous Drafts 4, Box 2, Reuben Papers.

63. Box 38, Contents: Treas-Trenton, Records of Governor Alfred E. Driscoll.

64. CRC Newsletters and Releases, Box 1, Reuben Papers.

65. Research Notes, Box 1, Reuben Papers; http://www.bayarearobeson.org.

66. CRC Newsletters and Releases, Box 1, Reuben Papers.

67. Federal Bureau of Investigation File of Eleanor Roosevelt, Section 11 d.

68. CRC Newsletters and Releases, Box 1, Reuben Papers.

69. *SCNJ*, 29: 59–62, Appendix to Brief, Order Amending Return to Writ of Error.

70. *SCNJ*, 29: CRC Brief, 20.

71. Ibid., 29:21–59.

72. Ibid., 29:81.

73. *SCNJ*, 29: Brief for MacKenzie and Wilson, 17.

74. *SCNJ*, 29: Katzenbach brief for Forrest, 23–24.

75. Ibid., 29:25.

76. *SCNJ*, 29: NAACP amicus brief, 1.

77. Ibid., 29:9–11.

78. Ibid., 29:15–16.

79. Ibid., 29:19.

80. *SCNJ*, 29: State Brief, 13.

81. Ibid., 29:43–44.

82. Ibid., 29:46.

83. *SCNJ*, 29: CRC Reply Brief, 1.

84. Reuben manuscript, 598, Box 2, Reuben Papers.

85. Ibid., 603.

86. Ibid., 606.

87. Ibid., 607.

88. Profile of Trenton, N.J., Box 2, Reuben Papers.

89. John Henrik Clarke, "Paul Robeson, the Artist as Activist and Social Thinker," http://www.nbufront.org/ html/MastersMuseums/JHClarke/Contem. .. (accessed June 17, 2006).

90. Reuben manuscript, 608–610, Box 2, Reuben Papers,,.

91. 2 N.J. 540; 67 A. 2d 298; 1949 N.J. LEXIS 287, 2.

92. Ibid., 4.

93. Ibid., 5.

94. Ibid., 6.

95. Ibid., 7.

96. "Victory for the Trenton Six! New Jersey Supreme Court Orders a New Trial," *National Guardian*, July 4, 1949.

97. "Trenton '6' Verdict Upset," *Daily Worker*, July 1, 1949.

98. Ibid.

99. Ibid.

100. Victory for the Trenton Six! New Jersey Supreme Court Orders a New Trial," *National Guardian*, July 4, 1949.

101. Ibid.

102. *New York Times*, July 1, 1949, and *Chicago Sun-Times*, July 1, 1949, cited in Reuben manuscript, 623–624, Box 2, Reuben Papers.

103. William Reuben, "A Brief Moment of Freedom for the Trenton Six," *National Guardian*, July 18, 1949.

104. Collis English to William Reuben, Letters, Box 1, Reuben Papers.

105. Edgar Holt [of New York City] to John MacKenzie, undated, CRC letters, Box 1, Reuben Papers.

106. Philip S. Foner, *Paul Robeson Speaks* (New York: Carol Publishing Group, 1978), 221, speech originally published in the *Philadelphia Tribune*, July 24, 1949.

107. *SCNJ*, 203:8434a; Reuben Manuscript, Box 2, Reuben Papers; "Court Hears Horner Case Bond Appeal," *Trenton Evening Times*, July 22, 1949.

108. *SCNJ*, 203:1a–13a.

109. John F. Norman, "Find New Data on Trenton Frameup," *Daily Worker*, December 22, 1949.

110. *SCNJ*, 203:8432a–8437a.

111. *SCNJ*, 203:38a–95a; Civil Rights Congress, Box 1, Reuben Papers.

112. "Lawyers to Fight Trenton Removal," *New York Times*, December 18, 1949.

113. "Juror Names Being Drawn," *Trenton Evening Times*, December 19, 1949.

114. Research Notes: Personality 2, Box 1, Reuben Papers,.

115. "Trenton 6 Witness Murdered," *Daily Worker*, January 25, 1950.

116. "3 Appeal to Halt Trial in Murder," *New York Times*, December 23, 1949; "Rogge Pleads Reinstatement in 'Six' Case," *Trenton Evening Times*, January 16, 1949.

117. "It's Worse Around Xmas . . . ," *Daily Worker*, December 25, 1949.

118. "Decision Reserved on 'Alien' Lawyers," *New York Times*, May 25, 1950.

119. William Patterson to Ralph Cooper, June 19, 1950, CRC Correspondence, Box 1, Reuben Papers.

120. "Framed Trenton Six Are Denied Letters as Trial Approaches," *Daily Worker*, July 10, 1950.

121. "Judge Held Wrong in Ban on Lawyers," *New York Times*, July 22, 1950.

122. "10,000 Ask Judge for the Trenton Six," *Daily Worker*, September 20, 1950.

123. "Ralph J. Smalley, Jurist, 60, Dead," *New York Times*, January 22, 1956.

124. *SCNJ*, 203:8442a–8453a; *Daily Worker*, December 21, 1949.

125. Cedric Belfrage and James Aronson, *Something to Guard: The Stormy Life of the National Guardian, 1948–1967* (New York: Columbia University Press, 1978), 133.

CHAPTER 5 — SECOND TRIAL, PROSECUTION

1. "Arthur Garfield Hays Dies at 73; Counsel to Civil Liberties Union," *New York Times*, December 15, 1954.

2. Joseph William Carlevale, *Americans of Italian Descent in New Jersey* (Clifton, NJ: North Jersey Press, 1950), 512; "Pellettieri Dies at 77," *Trenton Times*, August 29, 1980; Larry Kramer, "George Pellettieri Was the Heart of Trenton," *Trenton Times*, September 3, 1980.

3. "Judge Alexander, Aided 'Trenton 6,'" *Trenton Evening Times*, November 24, 1974.

4. Clifford R. Moore, Vertical File: Biography, Trentoniana Collection, Trenton Public Library, Trenton.

5. *SCNJ*, 203:8454a–8463a; Moore File, Trentoniana Collection.

6. "Clashes Mark Opening of Trenton Six Re-Trial," *Trenton Evening Times*, February 5, 1951.

7. "1 Horner Juror Chosen; Trial Opens with Legal Tiff," *Trentonian*, February 6, 1951; "Mistrial In Trenton Six Case as Appendicitis Fells Volpe," *Trenton Evening Times*, February 6, 1951; "State Demands Death for Framed '6' as Trenton Trial Opens," *Daily Worker*, February 6, 1951.

8. *SCNJ*, 203:8467a–8473a; "Trenton 6 Trial Opens Tomorrow," *New York Times*, February 4, 1951.

9. *SCNJ*, 196:130a–133a.

10. *SCNJ*, 196:142a–183a; Abner W. Berry, "Trial of Trenton Six Postponed for Month," *Daily Worker*, February 7, 1951; "Want Trenton 6 Case Shifted from Mercer," *Trenton Evening Times*, February 7, 1951.

11. *SCNJ*, 196:195a–253a.

12. *SCNJ*, 196:343a–382a; Abner W. Berry, "53 Witnesses—But None Had Ever Seen Trenton 6," *Daily Worker*, February 21, 1951.

13. "Records Confirm Defense Theories," *National Guardian*, February 28, 1951.

14. "Trenton 6 Lawyers Hit Bid to Stir Race Hate," *Trenton Evening Times*, March 6, 1951; "Jury Selection Slow In Trenton Six Case," *Trenton Evening Times*, March 7, 1951.

15. *SCNJ*, 203:8485a–8489a; "State Asks Death of All 'Trenton 6' Defendants," *Trenton Evening Times*, March 5, 1951; "2 Jurors Chosen in Trenton Trial," *New York Times*, March 6, 1951

16. "Leftists Scored in Trenton Trial," *New York Times*, March 7, 1951; *SCNJ*, 203:8490a–8493a.

17. Abner W. Berry, "Redbaiting Marks Trial of Trenton Six," *Daily Worker*, March 7, 1951.

18. "Seek to Speed Selection of Trenton Six Jurors," *Trenton Evening Times*, March 8, 1951; "Defendant's Illness May Delay Trial," *Trenton Evening Times*, March 9, 1951.

19. *SCNJ*, 203:8506a–8510a; "Defendant's Illness May Delay Trial"; Ralph Jones, "Try 'Red' Smear During First Day," *Philadelphia Afro-American*, March 10, 1951.

20. *SCNJ*, 203:8511a–8518a; "Horner Case Juror Panel Is Now At 7," *Trenton Evening Times*, March 12, 1951.

21. *SCNJ*, 203:8519a–8525a; Ten Jurors For Horner Case, Four More Needed," *Trenton Evening Times*, March 13, 1951; "Trenton Six Jury Nears Completion," *Trenton Evening Times*, March 14, 1951; Abner W. Berry, "Examine 235 to Pick 12 for Trenton 6 Jury," *Daily Worker*, March 14, 1951.

22. Abner W. Berry, "Jury Completed; Trenton 6 Trial Starts Saturday," *Daily Worker*, March 15, 1951; "Jury Completed For Trenton Six," *New York Times*, March 15, 1951; "Jury Drawn, Horner Case Start Waits," *Trenton Evening Times*, March 15, 1951.

23. *SCNJ*, 196:1a–18a.

24. Ibid., 196:19a–36a.

25. Ibid., 196:40a–46a.

26. *SCNJ*, 196:55a–58a; Abner W. Berry, "Trenton 6 Attorneys Tell Jury 'Jersey Justice Is on Trial,'" *Daily Worker*, March 19, 1951.

27. *SCNJ* 196:108a and 196:78a–100a.

28. Ibid., 196:112a–152a; quotation, 132a.

29. Ibid., 196:172a.

30. Abner W. Berry, "Horror Photos Flashed Before Trenton 6 Jury," *Daily Worker*, March 20, 1951.

31. *SCNJ*, 196:221a and 196:222a.

32. Ibid., 196:240a.

33. Ibid., 196:242a, 196:245a, and 196:248a–249a.

34. Ibid., 196:259a–264a.

35. Abner W. Berry, "Witness Admits Not Identifying Trenton 6 10 Days After Slaying," *Daily Worker*, March 21, 1951; *SCNJ*, 196:266a–267a and 196:273a.

36. Ibid., 196:287a and 196:290a–291a; entire testimony, 196:209a–303a.

37. Ibid., 196:336a–367a.

38. Ibid., 197:436a–448a.

39. Ibid., 197:436a–469a.

40. Ibid., 197:473a.

41. Ibid., 197:493a–510a.

42. Ibid., 197:535a.

43. Ibid., 197:558a.

44. "Murder Jurors Exempted from Attending Mass," *Trenton Evening Times*, March 23, 1951.

45. *SCNJ*, 197:644a.

46. Ibid., 197:692a.

47. Ibid., 197:714a.

48. Ibid., 197:660a.

49. Ibid., 197:736a–814a.

50. *SCNJ*, 197:823a–826a; "'Terrorism' Charged In Horner Case," *Trenton Evening Times*, March 27, 1951.

51. *SCNJ*, 197:867a.

52. *SCNJ*, 197:888a–889a; Abner W. Berry, "Woman in Trenton Court Cries Out: 'They're Not Guilty,'" *Daily Worker*, March 28, 1951.

53. *SCNJ*, 197:920a.

54. Ibid., 197:990a.

55. Ibid., 203:8543a–8544a.

56. Ibid., 197:1119a.

57. Ibid., 197:1291a.

58. Ibid., 197:1303a and 197:1307a–1309a.

59. Ibid., 197:1378a.

60. "Did Racketeers Commit Crime for Which Trenton 6 Were Framed?" *Daily Worker*, March 30, 1951.

61. *SCNJ*, 197:1487a–1494a.

62. Ibid., 198:1655a.

63. *SCNJ*, 198:1838a; "Trenton Trial Recessed; One of Six Accused of Murder Suffers Heart Ailment," *New York Times*, April 6, 1951; "Doctor Says Trenton 6 Not Abused: Dr. Sullivan Describes Scene at Time of Confessions," *Trenton Evening Times*, April 5, 1951.

64. William Reuben, "Defendants Acted Drugged at 'Confession,' Doctor Says," *National Guardian*, April 4, 1951.

65. *SCNJ*, 203:8550a; Abner W. Berry, "Trenton Trial Recessed as Defendant Has Heart Attack," *Daily Worker*, April 6, 1951.

66. Associated Press, April 6, 1951; *SCNJ*, 203:8551a.

67. *SCNJ*, 198:1878a–1950a; Reuben, "Defendants Acted Drugged at 'Confession,' Doctor Says."

68. "Horner Case On, Dr. Corio Takes Stand," *Trenton Evening Times*, April 9, 1951.

69. Abner W. Berry, "End Argument on Trenton 'Statement,'" *Daily Worker*, April 10, 1951.

70. *SCNJ*, 198:2182a.

71. Ibid., 198:2189a.

72. Ibid., 2140a–2208a.

73. Ibid., 198:2209–2210.

74. Ibid., 198:2234a–2235a.

75. Ibid., 198:2234a.

76. Ibid., 198:2247a.

77. Ibid., 198: 2294a and 198:2256a.

78. Ibid., 198:2259a and 198:2262a–2263a.

79. Ibid., 198:2290a–2305a.

80. Ibid., 198:2306a–2319a.

81. Ibid., 198:2394a–2423a.

82. Ibid., 198:2447a.

83. *SCNJ*, 198:2486a–2534a; "Surprise Testimony Hits Horner Defendant's Story," *Trenton Evening Times*, April 13, 1951.

84. *SCNJ*, 198:2569a–2572a; William Reuben, "Judge Rules out Three of Trenton Six 'Confessions,'" *National Guardian*, April 11, 1951; "3 of 6 'Confessions' Barred in Trenton," *New York Times*, April 14, 1951.

85. *SCNJ*, 198:2576a.

86. Abner W. Berry, "Cop at Trenton Trial Bares 18-Hour Grilling," *Daily Worker*, April 17, 1951.

87. Abner W. Berry, "Prosecutor Gags His Own Witness at Trenton Trial," *Daily Worker*, April 18, 1951.

88. *SCNJ*, 199:3086a and 199:3098a–3115a.

89. Ibid., 199:3121a–3125a and 199:3146a.

90. Ibid., 199:3197a; "Trenton 6 Win Point, Police Officer Admits Lack of Evidence Against 3 Men," *New York Times*, April 20, 1951.

91. *SCNJ*, 199:3202a and 199:3239a.

92. Ibid., 199:3275a–3276a.

93. Ibid., 199:3360a.

94. Ibid., 199:3428a–3429a and 199:3479a–3490a.

95. *SCNJ*, 199:3499a–3507a; Abner W. Berry, "Volpe's Witness in Trenton Puts New Holes in His Case," *Daily Worker*, April 25, 1951; "Doctor Cites Nervousness Of Defendant," *Trenton Evening Times*, April 25, 1951.

96. *SCNJ*, 199:3436a–3616a.

97. Ibid., 199:3655a–3656a.

98. Ibid., 199:3695a–3705a; "Naples Says Forrest Got No Sedative," *Trenton Evening Times*, April 27, 1951.

99. *SCNJ*, 199:3759a.

100. Ibid., 199:3792a–3801a.

101. Ibid., 199:3869a.

102. "Chief Naples Under Quiz By Defense," *Trenton Evening Times*, April 30, 1951.

103. *SCNJ*, 199:3880a–3971a.

104. "Chief Naples Says Lawyer 'Makes Face,'" *Trenton Evening Times*, May 1, 1951.

105. *SCNJ*, 200:4047a–4059a.

106. *SCNJ*, 200:4060a–4078a; Box 2, Miscellaneous Drafts 4, Reuben Papers.

107. *SCNJ*, 200:4079a–4110a.

108. "May Day Marchers Booed and Pelted," *New York Times*, May 2, 1951; Howard Fast, "May Day—1951," *Socialistic Publishing Society*, 1951, found in Box 2, Miscellaneous Papers, Reuben Papers.

109. *SCNJ*, 200:4127a–4177a.

110. *SCNJ*, 200:4216a; "Defendant's Kin Assailed By Attorneys," *Trenton Evening Times*, May 2, 1951.

111. *SCNJ*, 200:4221a–4233a.

112. *SCNJ*, 200:4243a–4251a; "Court Admits Bottle, Sock in 'Six' Case," *Trenton Evening Times*, May 3, 1951.

113. *SCNJ*, 200:4261a–4308a.

114. Ibid., 200:4309a–4316a.

115. Ibid., 200:4334a–4348a,

116. Ibid., 200:4400a–4405a.

117. Ibid., 200:4463a–4481a.

118. "A Counsel Asks Acquittal for 'Trenton Six,'" *Trenton Evening Times*, May 8, 1951.

119. *SCNJ*, 200:4703a–4706a.

CHAPTER 6 — SECOND TRIAL, DEFENSE

1. *SCNJ*, 200: 4706–4767a.

2. Ibid., 200:4781a–4983a.

3. Ibid., 200:5000a–5020a.

4. *SCNJ*, 200:5021a–5044a.

5. *SCNJ*, 200:5054a–5114a.

6. "Collis English Describes 4-Day Terror in Trenton Police Station," *Daily Worker*, May 16, 1951.

7. "State Starts Cross-Quiz of English," *Trenton Evening Times*, May 16, 1951; *SCNJ*, 201:5203a–5206a; "Alibi Again Given Court by English," *Trenton Evening Times*, May 15, 1951.

8. *SCNJ*, 201:5223a–5246a.

9. Ibid., 201: 5247a–5252a.

10. *SCNJ*, 203:8591a

11. "Collis English Describes 4-Day Terror in Trenton Police Station."

12. *SCNJ*, 201:5412a.

13. "State Attacks Cooper Tale of Black-Out," *Daily Worker*, May 18, 1951; *SCNJ*, 201:5484a–5500a.

14. *SCNJ*, 201:5558a–5593a.

15. Ibid., 201:5650a–5664a.

16. "2 of Trenton 6 Tell How Volpe Tried to Get 'Confessions,'" *Daily Worker*, May 22, 1951; *SCNJ*, 201:5751a–5788a.

17. "2 of Trenton 6 Tell How Volpe Tried to Get 'Confessions'"; "Last of Six Testifies He Blanked Out," *Trenton Evening Times*, May 22, 1951; *SCNJ*, 201:5812a–5831a.

18. *SCNJ*, 201:5876a–5967a.

19. "Son's Alibi Backed by Mrs. English," *Trenton Evening Times*, May 23, 1951; *SCNJ*, 201:6176a; "Volpe Fails to Shake McKenzie Story," *Daily Worker*, May 23, 1951.

20. *SCNJ*, 201:6251a–6252a.

21. Ibid., 201:6248a–6298a.

22. Ibid., 202:6432a.

23. Associated Press report, Box 1, Reuben Papers.

24. *SCNJ*, 202:6545a–6567a.

25. "'6' Defendant in Hospital; Defer Trial," *Trenton Evening Times*, May 28, 1951; *SCNJ*, 203:8604a.

26. "Script Expert Backs Trenton Defendant," *New York Times*, May 30, 1951.

27. "Expert Testifies Trenton 'Confessions' Are Phony," *Daily Worker*, June 1, 1951; *SCNJ*, 202:6841a–6905a.

28. *SCNJ*, 202:6923a–7021a.

29. Ibid., 202:7024a–7059a.

30. Ibid., 202:7096a–7128a.

31. "Says 3 Men Drove from Death Scene," *Trenton Evening Times*, June 1, 1951; *SCNJ*, 202:7170a.

32. *SCNJ*, 202:7186–7215

33. *SCNJ*, 202:7352a–7361a.

34. *SCNJ*, 202:7475a–7519a; "Trenton 6 Defense Strikes at Testimony of Farmer," *Trenton Evening Times*, June 6, 1951.

35. *SCNJ*, 202:7554a–203:7603a.

36. Ibid., 203:7604a–7651a.

37. Ibid., 203:7657a.

38. Ibid., 203:7742a–7747a.

39. Ibid., 203:7778a–7811a.

40. Ibid., 203:7824a.

41. Ibid., 203:7825a–7889a.

42. *SCNJ*, 203:7905a–7965a; "Trenton 6 Counsel Start Summations," *Trenton Evening Times*, June 11, 1951.

43. *SCNJ*, 203:7966a–8071a.

44. Ibid., 203:8075a–8119a.

45. "Volpe Launches Summation," *Trenton Evening Times*, June 12, 1951, and "Fate of Trenton 6 Nears Jury's Hands," *Trenton Evening Times*, June 13, 1951.

46. *SCNJ*, 203:8141a–8148a.

47. *SCNJ*: MacKenzie 203:8149–8160; Forrest 203:8160a–8178a; Wilson 203:8178a–8198a; Cooper 203:8199a–8213a; English should be 203:8214a–8228a; Volpe's summation 203:8229a–8271a.

48. Miscellaneous Drafts 4, Box 2, Reuben Papers.

49. "Judge Will Charge Jury Today in Case of Trenton Six," *Daily Worker*, June 13, 1951.

50. SCNJ, 203:8272a–8295a.

51. Ibid., 203:8296a–8303a.

52. 203:8303a–8312a.

53. *SCNJ*, 203:8312a–8318a.

54. Ibid., 203:8319a–8338a.

55. "2 Convicted, 4 of Trenton Six Acquitted," *Trenton Evening Times*, June 14, 1951.

56. Associated Press wire story, June 14, 1951, found in Box 2, "Other Writings," Reuben Papers.

57. SCNJ, 203:8339a–8346a.

58. William Reuben, "Trenton 6 Free, 2 Get Life," *The Compass*, June 14, 1951.

59. "2 of 'Trenton Six' Get Life, 4 Freed," *New York Times*, June 15, 1951; "New Life Begun by Four Cleared in Horner Murder," *Trenton Evening Times*, June 15, 1951.

60. *SCNJ*, 203:8339a–8346a.

61. "Of Trenton 6, V for Victory in Their Fight for Freedom," *Trenton Evening Times*, June 14, 1951.

62. Reuben, "Trenton 6 Free, 2 Get Life."

63. Associated Press wire story, June 14, 1951, found in Box 2, "Other Writings," Reuben Papers; "Protest Saves 4 in Trenton; Continues to Free 2 Given Life," *Daily Worker*, June 14, 1951.

64. Reuben, "Trenton 6 Free, 2 Get Life."

65. "Protest Saves 4 in Trenton; Continues to Free 2 Given Life," *Daily Worker*, June 14, 1951; "Map Actions Now to Free Collis English and Cooper," *Daily Worker*, June 15, 1951; Reuben, "Trenton 6 Free, 2 Get Life"; "New Life Begun by Four Cleared in Horner Murder."

CHAPTER 7 — TWO MEN LEFT

1. "Map Actions Now to Free Collis English and Cooper," *Daily Worker*, June 15, 1951; "2 of 'Trenton Six' Get Life, 4 Freed," *New York Times*, June 15, 1951; "Trenton 2 and 4," *New York Times*, June 17, 1951.

2. "New Life Begun by Four Cleared in Horner Murder" and "Acquitted Men Will Aid Convicted Pair," both in *Trenton Evening Times*, June 15, 1951.

3. *SCNJ*, 203:8384a–8426a.

4. Collis English to Emma English, July 3, 1951, Family Correspondence 1, Box 1, Reuben Papers.

5. "Trenton 2 Appeal Proceeds on 'Faith,'" *National Guardian*, July 11, 1951.

6. "Appeal for Trenton Pair," *New York Times*, July 29, 1951.

7. *SCNJ*, 203:8427a.

8. "Last 2 Win Retrial in 'Trenton 6' Case," *New York Times*, November 25, 1952.

9. "Appeal of Trenton Victims Is Postponed Until Fall," *Daily Worker*, May 14, 1952.

10. "Trenton 2 Appeal Near," *National Guardian*, October 2, 1952.

11. *SCNJ*, 196: Brief for Appellants, 1–100.

12. *SCNJ*, 196: Brief for the State, Brief for the Appellants.

13. Writings Miscellaneous and Unidentified 1, Box 2, Reuben Papers; "Trenton Two Ask Court to Reverse Their Conviction," *National Guardian*, October 30, 1952.

14. *New Jersey Reports*, v. 10, 1952, *State v. Cooper*, 532–569

15. "Last 2 Win Retrial in 'Trenton 6' Case, " *New York Times*, November 25, 1952; "New Trial Is Ordered for Trenton 6," *Daily Worker*, November 25, 1952; "Win New Trial for Trenton 2," *The Worker*, November 30, 1952.

16. "Freedom Hope Still Dim for Trenton 2," *National Guardian*, December 4, 1952; NAACP Papers and Notes, Box 1, Reuben Papers.

17. Elihu S. Hicks, "Prosecutor of Trenton 6 Has Negro MD Indicted," *Daily Worker*, January 6, 1953.

18. Ralph Cooper to Lottie [?], Civil Rights Congress, Box 1, Reuben Papers.

19. "Dies Awaiting 3rd Trial, Trenton Six Case Defendant Has Heart Attack in Prison," *New York Times*, December 31, 1952.

20. "Collis English: He Got His Freedom in Death," *National Guardian*, January 8, 1953; Miscellaneous Organizations Announcements, Box 1, Reuben Papers; "800, Negro and White, at Rites for Collis English," *Daily Worker*, January 5, 1953; "Prosecutor of Trenton 6 Has Negro MD Indicted," *Daily Worker*, January 6, 1953.

21. Cooper to Lottie [?], January 14, 1953, Prison Correspondence, Box 1, Reuben Papers.

22. Cooper to Lottie, February 5, 1953, Prison Correspondence, Box 1, Reuben Papers.

23. Cooper to Lottie, February 15, 1953, Prison Correspondence, Box 1, Reuben Papers.

24. "Cooper Drops Fight, Links All in Murder," *Trenton Evening Times*, February 20, 1953; "Last of 'Trenton 6' Draws 6–10 Years," *New York Times*, February 21, 1953; "Surprise Plea Claims Trenton Six Did Slay," *Daily Worker*, February 21; "Ralph Cooper's 2d 'Confession' Held Obtained by Pressure," *Daily Worker*, February 23, 1953; "Judge's Statement to Ralph Cooper Highlights Deal," *Daily Worker*, February 24, 1953.

25. "Say Last of Trenton 6 Confessed to Get Out," *New York Post*, February 21, 1953.

26. "Ralph Cooper's 2d 'Confession' Held Obtained by Pressure"; "Last of Trenton Six 'Confesses'; Pressure Is Charged," *National Guardian*, February 26, 1953.

27. "Inquiry Is Sought in 'Trenton Six' Case," *New York Times*, February 25, 1953.

28. "Cooper, Last 6 Defendant, Given Parole," *Trenton Evening Times*, August 11, 1953.

29. "'Trenton Six' Man Dies, Auto Accident Injuries Fatal to Acquitted Defendant," *New York Times*, March 27, 1955.

30. "Doctor on Trial as Perjurer on Trenton Six," *New York Post*, January 16, 1956; "Convict Dr. Sullivan, 'Trenton 6' Figure," *Daily Worker*, February 10, 1956.

31. "State Closes Case Against Dr. Sullivan," *Trenton Evening Times*, January 26, 1956, and "Physician Guilty On 7 Counts," *Trenton Evening Times*, February 9, 1956; "Trenton 6 MD Convicted of Perjury," *New York Post*, February 9, 1956.

32. "Sullivan Appeal Likely; Doctor Career Periled," *Trenton Evening Times*, February 10, 1956; "Physician Guilty in Trenton 6 Case," *New York Times*, February 10, 1956.

33. "Dr. Sullivan Guilty Verdict Is Upheld," *Trenton Evening Times*, April 1, 1957.

34. "New Appeal Planned by Dr. Sullivan," *Trenton Evening Times*, October 15, 1957.

35. "Dr. Sullivan, a City Legend, Dies in Fire," *Trentonian*, January 20, 2003; obituary, Dr. J. Minor Sullivan, *Trenton Evening Times*, January 19, 2003.

36. http://homepages.nyu.edu/~th15/newsx.html (accessed June 16, 2006).

37. Obituary, Mario Volpe, *Trentonian*, March 8, 1975; Joseph William Carlevale, *Americans of Italian Descent in New Jersey* (Clifton, NJ: North Jersey Press, 1950), 714–715.

38. "Frank Katzenbach, Former Judge, Dies," *Trentonian*, January 13, 1967; "Katzenbach Rites Slated Wednesday," *Sunday Times Advertiser*, January 12, 1967.

39. Obituary, Charles P. Hutchinson, *New York Times*, December 14, 1957; obituary, Charles P. Hutchinson, *Trenton Evening Times*, December 15, 1957.

40. Obituary, James S. Turp, *Trenton Times*, July 31, 1980.

41. Obituary, James A. Waldron, *Trenton Times*, February 5, 1995.

42. Obituary, Robert Queen, *New York Times*, September 3, 1960; obituary, Robert Queen, *Trenton Evening Times*, September 1, 1960.

43. William Patterson, *We Charge Genocide: The Crime of Government Against the Negro People* (New York: International Publishers, 1970), reprint of original edition; http://www.hometoharlem.com.

44. "New Client," *Time*, June 12, 1950; O. John Rogge, *The First and the Fifth, with Some Excursions into Others* (Edinburgh: Thomas Nelson and Sons, 1960); Phillip Deery, "A Divided Soul? The Cold War Odyssey of O. John Rogge," *Cold War History* 6 (2006):177–204; obituary, O. John Rogge, *New York Times*, March 23, 1981.

45. Philip S. Foner, *Paul Robeson Speaks* (New York: Carol Publishing Group, 1978).

46. "Ralph J. Smalley, Jurist, 60, Dead," *New York Times*, January 22, 1956; "Judge Smalley's Rites," *New York Times*, January 25, 1956.

47. Clifford R. Moore Vertical File, Trentoniana Collection; "'Trenton 6' Counsel Is Found Shot Dead," *New York Times*, July 16, 1956.

48. "Pellettieri Dies t 77," *Trenton Times*, August 29, 1980: Larry Kramer, George Pellettieri Was the Heart of Trenton, *Trenton Times*, September 3, 1980; Pellettieri, Rabstein and Altman, www.pralaw.com.

49. Mark V. Tushnet, ed., *Thurgood Marshall: His Speeches, Writings, Arguments, Opinions, and Reminiscences* (Chicago: Lawrence Hill Books, 2001), 141; "Judge Alexander, Aided 'Trenton 6,'" *Trenton Evening Times*, November 25, 1977.

50. Obituary, Arthur Garfield Hays, *New York Times*, December 15, 1954.

EPILOGUE

1. Tom Wells and Richard A. Leo, *The Wrong Guys: Murder, False Confessions, and the Norfolk Four* (New York: New Press, 2008).

2. Ibid.; "Freed, Not Cleared," *Washington Post*, August 8, 2009.

3. Wells and Leo, *The Wrong Guys*, 224.

4. "Freed, Not Cleared."

5. Death Penalty Information Center, http://www.deathpenaltyinfo.org/innocence-and-death-penalty.

6. Supreme Court of the United States, argued October 7, 1992, decided January 25, 1993: *Leonel Torres Herrera, Petitioner v. James A. Collins, Director, Texas Department of Criminal Justice, Institutional Division*, 506 U.S. 390.

7. Innocence Project, http://www.innocenceproject.org.

8. "Working to Save Innocent Souls," *Washington Post*, October 25, 2008; Centurion Ministries, http://www. centurionministries.org.

9. Death Penalty Information Center, http://www.deathpenaltyinfo.org/public-opinion-about-death-penalty.

INDEX

ABOUT THE AUTHOR

Cathy D. Knepper is the author of *Dear Mrs. Roosevelt: Letters to Eleanor Roosevelt Through Depression and War,* and *Greenbelt, Maryland: A Living Legacy of the New Deal.* She has a doctorate in American Studies from the University of Maryland at College Park, specializing in twentieth-century history and culture. She lives in Kensington, Maryland.